CISCO
and
IP Addressing

CISCO
and
IP Addressing

Louis D. Rossi

Louis R. Rossi

Thomas Rossi

McGraw-Hill

New York   San Francisco   Washington, D.C.
Auckland   Bogotá   Caracas   Lisbon   London
Madrid   Mexico City   Milan   Montreal   New Delhi
San Juan   Singapore   Sydney   Tokyo   Toronto

McGraw-Hill

A Division of The McGraw-Hill Companies

The views expressed in this book are solely those of the author, and do not represent the views of any other party or parties.

1 2 3 4 5 6 7 8 9 0   DOC/DOC   9 0 4 3 2 1 0 9

ISBN 0-07-134925-1

The sponsoring editor for this book was Steven Elliot and the production supervisor was Clare Stanley. It was set in Cochin by Patricia Wallenburg.

Printed and bound by R. R. Donnelley & Sons.

McGraw-Hill books are available at special quantity discounts to use as premiums and sales promotions, or for use in corporate training programs. For more information, please write to the Director of Special Sales, McGraw-Hill, 11 West 19th Street, New York, NY 10011. Or contact your local bookstore.

 This book is printed on recycled, acid-free paper containing a minimum of 50% recycled, de-inked fiber.

Acknowledgment

I would like to express my gratitude to the thousands of students I have had the pleasure to meet over the years.

Teaching is about the best learning process one can have.

In gratitude to all the students who have helped me in the past I would like to help all future students by setting up a scholarship fund for all graduates of the Cisco Network Academy Program.

This fund will initially be funded with 10% of the proceeds from this book.

For more information concerning this scholarship please send email to **scholarship@CCprep.com**.

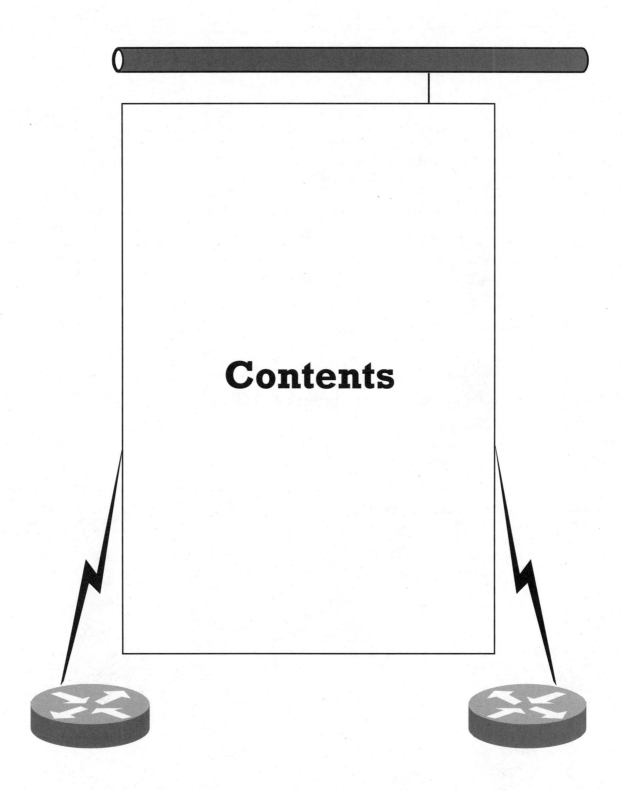

Contents

Chapter 6   Classful Routing Protocols
and Network Topology   67

Chapter 7   Variable Length Subnet Masking (VLSM)   77

Chapter 8   Classless Routing Protocols   85

Chapter 9   Wild Card Masks   91

Contents

Chapter 10   Route Summarization and Classless Interdomain Routing (CIDR)   97

Chapter 11   Hello Cisco!   107

Chapter 12   Configuring IP RIP   117

Chapter 13   Configuring IGRP   131

Chapter 14   Configuring OSPF   143

Chapter 15   Configuring EIGRP   161

Contents

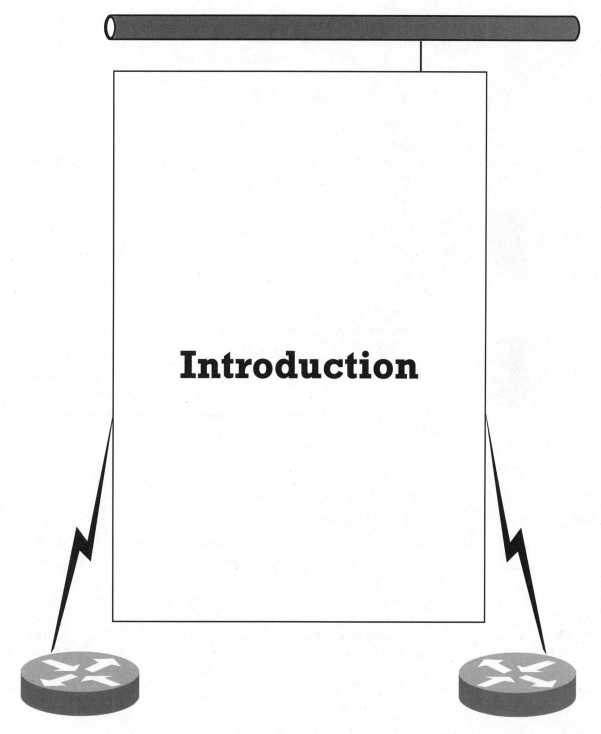

Introduction

The book is intended mainly for administrators and engineers that are being introduced to IP addressing for the first time. Or for those that may have experience but never understood how an IP address is constructed.

The following are objectives of this book:

1. To describe the concept of IP addressing
2. To describe how to configure IP addresses on a Cisco Router
3. To describe how to configure IP routing protocols on a Cisco router
4. Provide IP practice questions and answers for the Cisco Certification exams.

The following are NOT objectives of this book.

1. To provide OSI layer model information
2. To provide RFC content (we have provided a list of RFCs in Appendix F)
3. To provide complex Cisco router configuration information
4. To provide details of how specific routing protocols operate

The intent is to provide a complete explanation of IP addressing while at the same time provide basic information relating to IP routing protocols.

We do assume you know how to login to a Cisco router and get into the privilege mode.

This book has is divided into three parts:

- Part 1 Concepts
- Part 2 Configuring a Cisco Router.
- Part 3 Practice Questions

I have found very few books that explain IP addressing from the ground up, it always seems books assume some level of knowledge that the reader may or may not have.

We assume no IP knowledge we begin explaining IP addressing from the beginning not the middle!

I am sure that many of you have been in this field for years and still do not really understand IP addressing, I know that that was the case for me. I would address from a pattern without the understanding why I was doing what I was doing.

More experienced readers will benefit from this logical presentation of IP addressing since we have found, after teaching thousands of students, that this topic can be very difficult to understand.

This book is NOT intended to explain the inner workings of routing protocols or HSRP and NAT.

We show basic example configurations that will help the beginner to understand the concepts and the basic configurations.

This book will NOT refer to RFCs, if you would like to refer to an RFC we have provided a list in the Appendix F.

There are literally dozens of books available that will provide all the gory details of specific routing protocols and some are very good. The intention of this book is be very specific about IP addressing and then show how to configure IP addressing on a Cisco router.

We will begin with the IP address which include VLSM and CIDR, then move on to routing protocols and provide examples of how to configure IP RIP, IGRP, OSPF and EIGRP. The final two chapters of Part 2 are basic configurations of HSRP and NAT.

Part 3 provides the reader with practice questions, answers and explanations that simulate Cisco's certification exams.

One final thought regarding McGraw Hill's Cisco Technical Expert series. To achieve the ultimate goal of CCIE certification there are a multitude of skills required. This book addresses several of those skills on the beginner level, but one must begin somewhere and as an instructor for over 30 years I believe the beginning is a very good place.

Thank you very much.
Lou Rossi Sr.

CHAPTER 1

IP Addresses

Objectives

- Define and describe the function of a MAC address.
- Describe data-link addresses and network addresses and identify the key differences between them.
- Describe the different classes of IP addresses.
- Describe the two parts of network addressing, then identify the parts in specific protocol address examples.
- Describe the purpose of the network mask.
- Describe the logical AND process.

What Is a MAC Address?

A Media Access Control address (MAC) is unique for each computing device. This address defines the network connection of the computing device.

The purpose of the MAC address is to locate a unique computing device. This address is most often burned into the circuitry of the Network Interface Card (NIC) hence sometimes this address is called the burned-in address or BIA.

The MAC address is 48 bits in length expressed as 12 hexadecimal digits (0-F). One hex digit represents 4 binary bits.

24 bits are used to describe the vendor who manufactured the card. This number is also called a vendor code or an Organizational Unit Identifier (OUI). Examples are shown in Table 1-1.

TABLE 1-1

Organizational
Units Identifiers

OUI Numbers	
CISCO	00 00 0c xx xx xx
Novell	00 00 1b xx xx xx
3COM	02 60 8c xx xx xx
DECNET	AA 00 04 xx xx xx

The remaining 24 bits are used to describe the card uniquely (serial number).

The following is the MAC address of the E0 interface of Router_C:
00.00.0c.03.df.60
The vendor code is 00.00.0c.
The serial number is 03.df.60.
The MAC address and the BIA address are the same in most network environments (see Figure 1.1). There are exceptions, but these will be left for a later discussion.

FIGURE 1.1 The MAC Address

```
routerC>sh interface e0
Ethernet0 is administratively down, line protocol is down
```

Hardware is Lance, address is 0060.09c3.df60 (bia 0060.09c3.df60)
MTU 1500 bytes, BW 10000 Kbit, DLY 1000 usec, rely 255/255,
　　load 1/255
Encapsulation ARPA, loopback not set, keepalive set (10 sec)
ARP type: ARPA, ARP Timeout 04:00:00
Last input never, output never, output hang never
Last clearing of "show interface" counters never
Queueing strategy: fifo
Output queue 0/40, 0 drops; input queue 0/75, 0 drops
5 minute input rate 0 bits/sec, 0 packets/sec
5 minute output rate 0 bits/sec, 0 packets/sec
　　0 packets input, 0 bytes, 0 no buffer
　　Received 0 broadcasts, 0 runts, 0 giants, 0 throttles
　　0 input errors, 0 CRC, 0 frame, 0 overrun, 0 ignored, 0 abort
　　0 input packets with dribble condition detected
　　0 packets output, 0 bytes, 0 underruns
　　0 output errors, 0 collisions, 1 interface resets
　　0 babbles, 0 late collision, 0 deferred
　　0 lost carrier, 0 no carrier
　　0 output buffer failures, 0 output buffers swapped out

Other names for the MAC address include: BIA (Burned in Address), link-layer address, physical address, and hardware address.

To change the BIA address of a device a new NIC must be installed.

As the name implies the MAC address controls access to the media. For a device to gain access to the wire, that device must have a MAC address. For a frame to arrive at a destination it must have the MAC address of the destination.

An analogy might be, if we think of our postal service address, how would we get mail if we did not have an address?

A MAC address that is set to all binary 1, or in hex ff.ff.ff.ff.ff.ff, defines all computing devices on a wire. This address is called a broadcast address. Think of a broadcast address as the mail you get that is addressed to "occupant". The sender did not use your name but you got it any way.

If all the computing devices are on the same wire we can use the MAC address to locate which NIC is the destination. For instance, if everyone lived on the same street, we would not need a street address, just a house number. There would be no need for an additional part of an address.

A valid question is: how does a sending device know what the MAC address is of the destination? The simple answer is ARP, but we will leave that for a later discussion.

How does a frame arrive at a destination device that is not located on the same wire as the source?

In other words, everyone does not live on the same street so we will have to add another part of the address to identify the street. That part we will add is called a network address.

What Is a Network Address?

I like to think of it as a wire address. The reason I prefer the term wire address is because we use the term network in so many different ways and it gets to be confusing to the beginner. Think about the "wire" to which the computing devices are connected. This wire will have an address.

Sometimes a network address is called a logical address because the administrator will assign this address based upon some logic.

This address is hierarchical in nature because it will define which wire the host is connected to, just as a snail mail address (U.S. Postal Service address) will define which street the recipient lives on.

For that very reason, often a network address has two parts: a network portion and a host portion.

There are many different vendors who use their own unique way to describe network addresses.

A few examples are:

Novell (IPX)	DAD. 0060.09c3.df60
Banyan Vines	30011722:8001
Apple	110.192
DECnet	5.6

In each of the examples above, the address has two parts. The IPX host for example is located on wire DAD and the host address is 0060.09c3.df60.

I did not include an IP address in the list above because there is no vendor who owns the right to an IP address. The American public owns this addressing scheme, due to the fact that the Department of Defense paid for it several years ago.

Because this is the address used on the Internet, it is the most popular addressing used today.

APPLE, Novell and other vendors are replacing their addressing scheme with that of IP.

What Is an IP Address?

Before we begin to talk about IP addresses, let's discuss two other addresses I am sure you understand and use every day, your snail mail address and your voice address (phone number).

For the sake of this discussion, we will assume your snail mail address has three parts.

Snail Mail

Part 1 Name
Part 2 Street
Part 3 City, State, ZIP Code

Now think about who or what looks at each of these parts.

Part 1 is looked at by the addressee (the resident of Part 2).
Part 2 is looked at by the mail carrier
Part 3 is looked at by the Post Office

When a letter is dropped in a local mailbox it will be brought to the local post office where they will look at Part 3. The letter will be forwarded until it eventually arrives at the remote post office that services the area described in Part 3. At this point, it will be given to the mail carrier who services Part 2. The mail carrier will then drop it in the mailbox defined by Part 2. When you go to the mailbox, you will look at Part 1 to determine who gets the letter.

Keep in mind that the post office does not care about Part 1. You have gotten mail delivered to your house with someone else's name on Part 1. The mail carrier doesn't care about the information in Part 3, assuming that the post office has done their job correctly. And finally you don't care about Parts 2 and 3 because you assume that the post office and the mail carrier have done their job correctly.

For a letter to get to the destination we need to have a mailing address of the destination.

TIP

Voice Address

We will assume that a voice address has 3 parts: 800-555-1212

Part 1 Area Code (800)
Part 2 Prefix or Exchange Code(555)
Part 3 Local Identifier(1212)

Part 1 is looked at by the local switch on the caller's side
Part 2 is looked at by a remote switch
Part 3 is looked at by a local switch on the receiver's side

When you call a friend you may or may not use Part 1. A phone switch doesn't like you to use Part 1 if it's a local call, because your phone switch does not need Part 1. The switch looks at Part 2 and forwards it to the appropriate port of the switch. If your friend is "long distance" your local switch would look at Part 1 and continue forwarding the call until it gets to the switch that services Part 2. Finally the call would be forwarded to the appropriate port.

For a voice call to get to its destination we need to have a voice address of the destination.

TIP

Notice how easy it is for us to distinguish the different parts of both of the addresses used above.

For a snail mail address each part is on a different line. For a voice address each part is separated by a dash.

Network Address

If we want to send data through a network to a destination we need some type of address that uniquely identifies the destination.

For the purpose of this discussion let's define a network as a group of computing devices that are connected to several different networks or wires.

We could have a group of computing devices all connected to the same wire. In this case we do not need a network address; we could use Windows 95 and NetBEUI addresses. If everybody lived on the same street would we need a street address to get mail to the destination?

TIP

For data to get to the destination we need to have a network address to the destination.

The IP Address

For the sake of this discussion we will describe the IP address as having two parts.

Part 1 describes the network or the wire address
Part 2 describes the host address

The IP address contains 32 bits: these 32 bits have been divided into 4 octets (8 bits) (see Table 1.2).

Each of these octets is represented in decimal form. The *entire address* represents the address of the *wire* and the *address* of the *host*. The host can be a workstation attached to the wire or an interface of a router that is attached to the wire.

TABLE 1.2
The IP address 192.20.30.1 represented in binary.

128	64	32	16	8	4	2	1	128	64	32	16	8	4	2	1	128	64	32	16	8	4	2	1	128	64	32	16	8	4	2	1
1	1	0	0	0	0	0	0	0	0	0	1	0	1	0	0	0	0	0	1	1	1	1	0	0	0	0	0	0	0	0	1

Each bit value is calculated as shown below:

$2^7 = 128$
$2^6 = 64$
$2^5 = 32$
$2^4 = 16$

$2^3 = 8$
$2^2 = 4$
$2^1 = 2$
$2^0 = 1$

First Octet value is 128+64
Second Octet value is 16+4
Third Octet value is 16+8+4+2
Fourth Octet value is just 1

When all the bits of an octet are turned on (a binary 1 in each position) the octet would have a value of 255:

$128+64+32+16+8+4+2+1 = 255$

At the end of this section are more examples for you to try on your own.

There are 5 different classes of an IP address; for this discussion we will only be concerned with Class A, B, & C addresses.

The classes are determined by the first three bits of the first octet. The address 102.116.96.103 is a Class A address because the first bit of the first octet is 0. The rules are as follows:

First bit of 0 is a Class A
First two bits of 10 is a Class B
First three bits of 110 is a Class C

Some addresses have been reserved and other addresses are illegal; we will discuss some of these restrictions later.

NOTE

First Octet Rules
If the first bit is 0 it is a Class A address.
If the first two bits are 10 it is a Class B address.
If the first three bits are 110 it is a class C address.
No address can have a value of zero (0) in the first octet.
The address of 127 will be reserved for loopback addresses.

The above rules provide us with the following ranges:

Class A   1–126
Class B   128–191
Class C   192–223

KNOW these ranges!

I have included Class D and Class E for your information.

Class D   224–239 Multicast addresses (refer to Appendix A)
Class E   240–255 Experimental Addresses

Along with each class of address there is also a default mask that will be assigned.

TIP

Default mask for Class A is 255.0.0.0
Default mask for Class B is 255.255.0.0
Default mask for Class C is 255.255.255.0

What Is the Purpose of the Network Mask?

Earlier we said it was very easy to distinguish the different parts of a snail mail or a voice address.

It is not so easy to determine the different parts of an IP address because we do not use separate lines or dashes. We use what is called a mask.

The mask is also 32 bits in length and it is used to differentiate the network and the host address. Keep in mind that there are two parts to an IP address. We need the mask to know where part 1 ends and part 2 begins. The mask defines the number of bits used for the network address. The remaining bits are host bits.

Another point to remember is you cannot change the bits to which the mask refers. In other words, in a Class C address the first 24 bits (the first 3 octets) *cannot be changed*. The bits of the 4th octet can be manipulated. These are the bits we will use for subnetting.

Example

Address   172.20.100.16
Mask   255.255.0.0
Wire portion   172.20 Network ID
Host portion   100.16 Host ID

In this example the first 16 bits (172.16) describe the network. The remaining 16 bits (100.16) describe the host.

Think of the network address as being the address of the wire!

A router is a network device that "routes" a packet of information from one wire to another. To perform this task successfully the router needs to have a wire or network address.

The router uses wire or network addresses to determine the path packets will take on their way to the destination

Take a look at the routing table below:

FIGURE 1.2   Router_A Routing Table

```
Router_A#sh ip route
Codes: C - connected, S - static, I - IGRP, R - RIP, M - mobile, B - BGP
    D - EIGRP, EX - EIGRP external, O - OSPF, IA - OSPF inter area
    N1 - OSPF NSSA external type 1, N2 - OSPF NSSA external type 2
    E1 - OSPF external type 1, E2 - OSPF external type 2, E - EGP
    i - IS-IS, L1 - IS-IS level-1, L2 - IS-IS level-2, * - candidate default
    U - per-user static route, o - ODR
Gateway of last resort is not set
C  20.0.0.0/8 is directly connected, Serial0/0
I  175.20.0.0/16 [100/90956] via 20.0.0.2, 00:00:48, Serial0/0
C  10.0.0.0/8 is directly connected, Ethernet0/0
I  150.20.0.0/16 [100/10476] via 20.0.0.2, 00:00:48, Serial0/0
```

The router is concerned only with the address of the network (wire address). In this case, if the router receives a packet with the destination address of 150.20.0.2, the packet will be sent to interface S0/0. If the packet is addressed to 10.0.0.14 it will be sent to E0/0.

When the router is configured, the router uses two pieces of information to calculate the wire address:

1. The interface IP address (all 32 bits)
2. The network mask

The mask can also be presented by what is called the "slash" format.

/16 represents 255.255.0.0
/8 represents 255.0.0.0
/24 represents 255.255.255.0
/28 represents 255.255.255.240

I like the "slash" format; it is not only short but it tells us how many bits are used to describe the wire address. For instance, if the mask is /24 we know that 24 bits are used for the wire address and 8 bits are used for the host (32-24=8). Remember there are only 32 bits in the address so if 24 are used for wire that only leaves 8 for host.

The routing table of Figure 1.2 shows that Router_A is using the default mask for each of its directly connected networks and the networks it learns about are represented with the default mask.

How Is the Wire or Network Address Calculated?

The logical AND method

Let us assume you give a router the address of 150.20.0.2 and we are using the default mask 255.255.0.0 or /16. The router performs what is called the *logical AND* process to calculate the wire address. Table 1.3 represents the 32 bit address, the default mask and the resulting wire address.

TABLE 1.3

Logical AND

Binary:

	128	64	32	16	8	4	2	1	128	64	32	16	8	4	2	1	128	64	32	16	8	4	2	1	128	64	32	16	8	4	2	1
Address	1	0	0	1	0	1	1	0	0	0	0	1	0	1	0	0	0	0	0	0	0	0	0	0	0	0	0	0	0	0	1	0
Mask	1	1	1	1	1	1	1	1	1	1	1	1	1	1	1	1	0	0	0	0	0	0	0	0	0	0	0	0	0	0	0	0
Wire	1	0	0	1	0	1	1	0	0	0	0	1	0	1	0	0	0	0	0	0	0	0	0	0	0	0	0	0	0	0	0	0

Decimal:

Address	150.20.0.2
Mask	255.255.0.0
Wire	150.20.0.0

The logical AND can be explained using truth tables where:

True **AND** True = True
True **AND** False = False
False **AND** False = False

As an example, consider the statement "Lou Rossi Sr. is fifty years old and needs to gain 30 pounds." I am fifty but I need to loose 30 pounds. These facts make our statement false.

Consider the True part as a 1 and the False part as a 0.

1 "AND" 1 = 1
1 "AND" 0 = 0
0 "AND" 0 = 0

Therefore the IP address of the wire is **150.20.0.0** and this is verified by referring to Routing Table 1.1.

The host portion of the address is the last two octets or 150.20.**0.2**.

When an octet has a value of 255 that means that all bits of the octet are set to 1. Therefore when the logical AND process is calculated, the result will always be the initial value of the octet.

134 "AND" 255 is 134
156 "AND" 255 is 156

Would you not agree that if I do not give you the first part of a statement and I tell you the second part is true, the complete statement will always have the same value as the first part?

Or in truth table format:

T "AND" T is T
F "AND" T is F

Summary

- MAC addresses are used for network communication.
- Network addresses are logical addresses to determine location of network devices.
- IP addresses are organized into 5 different classes.
- The network address has two parts: the network (wire) part and the host part.
- The network mask is used to distinguish the network part from the host part.
- The logical "AND" process is used to calculate the network or wire address.

Exercises

1.1: Complete the chart below:

Octet Value	128	64	32	16	8	4	2	1
202	1	1	0	0	1	0	1	0
	1	0	0	0	1	1	0	1
	1	0	1	0	1	0	1	0
	1	1	1	1	0	0	0	1
	0	0	0	1	1	1	1	1
	1	1	1	1	1	1	1	0

1.2: How many bits in an octet?

1.3: How many bits in an IP address?

1.4: How many octets in an IP address?

1.5: What is the highest value an octet can have?

1.6: What octet is used to determine the class of an address?

1.7: How many bits are used to determine a Class B address?

1.8: Assume the default mask and complete the chart below:

Address	Default Mask	Class	Wire Address	Host Address
123.34.56.7	255.0.0.0	A	123.0.0.0	0.34.56.7
12.43.98.3				
191.76.5.34				
212.45.6.5				
192.34.5.67				

1.9: With a Class C address and the default mask how many bits can be changed?

1.10: With a Class B address and the default mask how many bits can be changed?

1.11: With a Class A address and the default mask how many bits can be changed?

Answers

1.1

Octet Value	128	64	32	16	8	4	2	1
202	1	1	0	0	1	0	1	0
141	1	0	0	0	1	1	0	1
170	1	0	1	0	1	0	1	0
241	1	1	1	1	0	0	0	1
31	0	0	0	1	1	1	1	1
254	1	1	1	1	1	1	1	0

1.2: 8 bits in an octet.

1.3: 32 bits in an IP address.

1.4: 4 octets in an IP address.

1.5: The highest value an octet can have is 255.

1.6: The 1st octet is used to determine the class of an address.

1.7: 2 bits are used to determine a Class B address.

1.8: The completed chart:

Address	Default Mask	Class	Wire Address	Host Address
123.34.56.7	255.0.0.0	A	123.0.0.0	0.34.56.7
12.43.98.3	255.0.0.0	A	12.0.0.0	0.43.98.3
191.76.5.34	255.255.0.0	B	191.76.0.0	0.0.5.34
212.45.6.5	255.255.255.0	C	212.45.6.0	0.0.0.5
192.34.5.67	255.255.255.0	C	192.34.5.0	0.0.0.67

1.9: With a Class C address and the default mask, 8 bits can be changed.

1.10: With a Class B address and the default mask, 16 bits can be changed.

1.11: With a Class A address and the default mask, 24 bits can be changed.

CHAPTER **2**

The Mystery of Subnetting

Objectives

- Describe the reason for subnetting.
- Describe calculation of combinations.
- Describe the process of determining what subnet should be used.
- Apply an IP addressing scheme to a fictional organization.
- Describe broadcast addresses.

Why Do We Subnet?

The IP addressing scheme was developed in the late 60s. It was never conceived at that point that so many organizations would want to access what is now called the Internet. The limited addressing space of 32 bits leaves us in a pickle for available bits.

Many people have experienced the same type of problem with voice addresses recently.

For instance, my area code changed from 904 to 850 because the phone company was running out of 904 addressing space. So in effect what the phone company created a sub-area with a different area code. Now the 850 area code is geographically inside what once was the 904 area code.

In the world of IP addressing the same idea was used as a solution to lack of addressing space. We will place one network inside another net-work. This is called *subnetting*.

Assume for a moment that an organization has been assigned a single Class B address of 132.10.0.0. We learned from Chapter 1 that the net-work portion of this address is 132.10.0.0. This address describes a sin-gle wire only.

This organization will most likely have hundreds of wires.

How will this company address all of its wires?

TIP

Subnetting is a solution.

Before we begin our discussion of subnetting let's briefly discuss combi-nations.

Combinations

In our example of 132.10.0.0, if we look at the host bits only, there are 65,536 unique combinations. This number is calculated by using the formula 2n, where n is the total number of bits 216=65,536.

Suppose we want the number of combinations of just 4 bits, 2^4 yields 16 combinations.

TABLE 2.1

4-bit Combinations

	Bit 1	Bit 2	Bit 3	Bit 4
Combo 1	0	0	0	0
Combo 2	0	0	0	1
Combo 3	0	0	1	0
Combo 4	0	0	1	1
Combo 5	0	1	0	0
Combo 6	0	1	0	1
Combo 7	0	1	1	0
Combo 8	0	1	1	1
Combo 9	1	0	0	0
Combo 10	1	0	0	1
Combo 11	1	0	1	0
Combo 12	1	0	1	1
Combo 13	1	1	0	0
Combo 14	1	1	0	1
Combo 15	1	1	1	0
Combo 16	1	1	1	1

Notice the all-zero and the all-one combinations (1, 2, 15, and 16). We will discuss these combinations later.

TABLE 2.2

Total Combinations

Bits	Combinations
0	–
1	2
2	4
3	8
4	16
5	32
6	64

continued on next page

Bits	Combinations
7	128
8	256
9	512
10	1024
11	2048
12	4096
13	8192
14	16384
15	32768
16	65536

Combinations and Subnets

Why are we talking about combinations when we want to learn about subnets?

Subnetting is the process of taking bits from the host portion of the address and using them to describe networks. Before we can subnet we need to determine how many bits we should take from the host portion. The number of bits we take is dependent upon the total number of combinations.

For instance, suppose we needed to have at least 10 subnets; Table 2.2 indicates that if we take 4 bits from the host portion we can get 16 combinations.

Adjusting the Formula for Network Bit Combinations

If we include the combinations of all 1s and all 0s this could cause some problems with some internetworking devices. We will adjust our formula by deducting two from the total number of combinations.

As a result, the formula for calculating the total number of network combinations is:

$2^N - 2$ where N is the number of network bits.

Adjusting the Formula for Host Bit Combinations

We will deduct 2 from our host combinations as well, but for different reasons.

- When all host bits are 0, the resulting address describes a network.
- When all host bits are 1, the resulting address describes a broadcast address.

As a result, the formula for calculating the total number of host combinations is:

$2^N - 2$ where N is the number of host bits.

TABLE 2.3

Total Combinations Adjusted by Subtracting 2

Bits	Combinations
0	–
1	0
2	2
3	6
4	14
5	30
6	62
7	126
8	254
9	510
10	1022
11	2046
12	4094
13	8190
14	16382
15	32766
16	65534

If we have 10 bits to describe networks and 6 bits to describe hosts we have address space for:

Networks $2^{10}-2 = 1022$
Hosts $2^6-2 = 62$

Total host addressing space is: $1022 \times 62 = 63,364$

What determines how many combinations I need?

To answer this question we need to answer a few other questions first.

■ How many unique networks or wires does my organization need?
■ What is the maximum number of hosts required on any one of these unique wires?

Assume that an organization called ARI has received a Class C IP address (Figure 2.1). For the sake of this example, we will use the address of 192.16.12.0/24.

FIGURE 2.1

ARI Topology

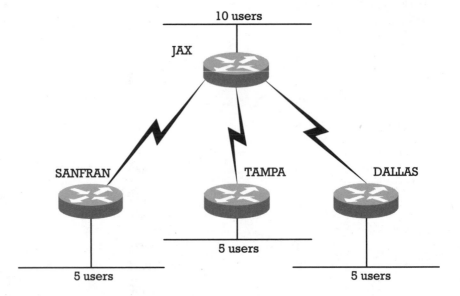

The total number of network combinations needed by ARI is 7.

3 Serial wires
4 Ethernet wires

The total number of host combinations needed by ARI is 11.
    The Ethernet interface of the JAX router will require an IP host address, hence 11 host addresses will be required.

There are 11 hosts in JAX; the other locations only require host addressing space for 6.

Based on the above answers, how many bits should we take from the fourth octet to describe wires or networks?

Referring to Table 2.3, we would have to have at least 4 bits to provide us with 7 combinations:

$$2^4-2=14$$

If we took 3 bits we would only have 6 combinations:

$$2^3-2=6$$

If we took 4 bits, we would have 14 unique combinations, which would provide us an additional 7 combinations. We might be able to use these additional combinations to describe future networks if ARI expands.

Before we begin implementing our address scheme, we need to make sure we have enough host addressing space. We need to provide addresses for the 11 hosts in JAX.

Again referring to Table 2.3, if we take 4 bits to describe networks, that would leave us 4 bits to describe hosts.

Keep in mind we only have 8 bits (4th octet) to manipulate.

Four host bits would provide 14 unique combinations.

This provides enough host addressing space to meet ARI's requirements.

How many host addresses will be required for the serial links between JAX and the other three sites?

We have a serial interface on each end that we will address. Only two host addresses will be required. We will see that there is a waste of precious addressing space on these serial links. We do have solutions and will investigate those solutions in later chapters.

What Is the Value of the Mask If We Have Four Subnet Bits?

The value of the mask is the value of the 32 bits when all network bits are 1 and the hosts bits are 0.

In the case of ARI they will use a mask of 255.255.255.240 (Table 2.4).

TABLE 2.4

Mask of
255.255.255.240
Represented in
Binary

DEFAULT MASK OF 255.255.255 OR /24

First Octet	Second Octet	Third Octet
128 64 32 16 8 4 2 1	128 64 32 16 8 4 2 1	128 64 32 16 8 4 2 1
1 1 1 1 1 1 1 1	1 1 1 1 1 1 1 1	1 1 1 1 1 1 1 1

SUBNET MASK OF 240 (4 BITS)

128 64 32 16 8 4 2 1

1 1 1 1 1 1 1 1

128+64+32+16 =240

What Addresses Will Identify the Networks of ARI?

As we begin to take a look at the available addresses, let us agree that we can put the first three octets aside. These bits cannot be changed. They are registered to ARI and every frame that goes out on the Internet must have a source address that identifies ARI. The first 24 bits of 192.16.12.0 must never be changed.

Now we can concentrate our efforts on the 4th octet.

TABLE 2.5

Fourth Octet
Network
Combinations
with a 240 Mask

	128	64	32	16	8	4	2	1	Network Address
Combo 1	0	0	0	0	0	0	0	0	0
Combo 2	0	0	0	1	0	0	0	0	16
Combo 3	0	0	1	0	0	0	0	0	32
Combo 4	0	0	1	1	0	0	0	0	48
Combo 5	0	1	0	0	0	0	0	0	64
Combo 6	0	1	0	1	0	0	0	0	80
Combo 7	0	1	1	0	0	0	0	0	96
Combo 8	0	1	1	1	0	0	0	0	112
Combo 9	1	0	0	0	0	0	0	0	128
Combo 10	1	0	0	1	0	0	0	0	144
Combo 11	1	0	1	0	0	0	0	0	160
Combo 12	1	0	1	1	0	0	0	0	176

continued on next page

	128	64	32	16	8	4	2	1	Network Address
Combo 13	1	1	0	0	0	0	0	0	192
Combo 14	1	1	0	1	0	0	0	0	208
Combo 15	1	1	1	0	0	0	0	0	224
Combo 16	1	1	1	1	0	0	0	0	240

Notice that the 4th octet value of the network address are all multiples of 16.

Notice also that 16 is the value of the least significant subnet bit.

Network addresses are always multiples of the least significant subnet bit.

I have highlighted the all 0 and the all 1 combinations as a reminder that we cannot use these as networks.

What Addresses Will Identify the Hosts of ARI?

To answer this question we will pick one of the ARI networks at random and examine all the possible addresses that would be available on that particular wire.

192.16.12.144 represents one of the available wire addresses for ARI.

To determine the host addresses, we look at all the combinations of the host bits.

TABLE 2.4

Fourth Octet Host Combinations of the 192.16.12.144 Network

	128	64	32	16	8	4	2	1		
Combo 10	1	0	0	1	0	0	0	0	144	Wire Address
	1	0	0	1	0	0	0	1	145	Host Address
	1	0	0	1	0	0	1	0	146	Host Address
	1	0	0	1	0	0	1	1	147	Host Address
	1	0	0	1	0	1	0	0	148	Host Address
	1	0	0	1	0	1	0	1	149	Host Address
Wire	1	0	0	1	0	1	1	0	150	Host Address
Address	1	0	0	1	0	1	1	1	151	Host Address
is	1	0	0	1	1	0	0	0	152	Host Address
144	1	0	0	1	1	0	0	1	153	Host Address

continued on next page

128	64	32	16	8	4	2	1		
1	0	0	1	1	0	1	0	154	Host Address
1	0	0	1	1	0	1	1	155	Host Address
1	0	0	1	1	1	0	0	156	Host Address
1	0	0	1	1	1	0	1	157	Host Address
1	0	0	1	1	1	1	0	158	Host Address
1	0	0	1	1	1	1	1	159	Broadcast Addres

Remember, we have to deduct the all 1 (one) and the all 0 (zero) combinations.

■ The all 0 combination describes the 192.16.12.144 wire.
■ The all 1 combination describes the broadcast address for wire 192.16.12.144.

The address range of 145 through 158 can be used to describe hosts.

Each of the 14 networks can have a maximum of 14 hosts ($2^4-2=14$).

As a result, the total number of hosts that ARI can address with this single CLASS C address is 14×14=196.

At present, JAX requires 11 hosts addresses. If that office should grow, we would then have 3 addresses available.

The other sites require 6 addresses at this time. So we have 8 addresses that will not be used, but would be available in case of growth.

The serial connections are a different story. They require two addresses now, two addresses tomorrow, and two addresses forever. We will never be able to use the 12 "extra" addresses for each of those serial links, so they are wasted.

In later chapters we will look at classless routing protocols and VLSM as a solution to these wasted addresses.

What Addresses Will Be Identified as Broadcast Addresses?

A broadcast address is an address that addresses all hosts.

During a class several years ago, a student described the broadcast address as the address at the end of the wire. I think that is a wonderful description. If we use the example above, the address of 160 represents the next wire. The address of 159 is the last address on wire 144. 159 is the broadcast address for the 144 wire.

When all host bits are set to 1 the result is a broadcast address as shown in Table 2.5

Assume we have a Class C address and are using the 5 bit mask. If we examine the first available network (8) we know that there are 6 legal host addresses (2^N-2). These addresses range from 9 to 14 and the next address of 15 is the broadcast address. The next address of 16 is the second available wire address. Hence the broadcast address for a given network is one less than the next available network.

TABLE 2.5

Broadcast Address of 15

	128	64	32	16	8	4	2	1	Value
Network	0	0	0	0	1	0	0	0	8
Last Host	0	0	0	0	1	1	1	0	14
Broadcast	0	0	0	0	1	1	1	1	15
Next Wire	0	0	0	1	0	0	0	0	16

Applying the Address Scheme to ARI

Here is one possible addressing solution. Other solutions are possible.

192.16.12.128 wire address to describe the serial segment between JAX and SANFRAN.
192.16.12.144 wire address to describe the serial segment between JAX and TAMPA.
192.16.12.160 wire address to describe the serial segment between JAX and DALLAS.

192.16.12.176 wire address to describe the Ethernet segment of JAX.
192.16.12.192 wire address to describe the Ethernet segment of SAN-FRAN.
192.16.12.208 wire address to describe the Ethernet segment of TAMPA.
192.16.12.224 wire address to describe the Ethernet segment of DAL-LAS.

Summary

- Subnetting allows for additional network addressing.
- Combinations are used to determine how many bits should be used for subnetting.
- The number of networks and the number of hosts on each network determines how many bits are used for subnetting.
- A broadcast address is the result of all host bits being set to 1.

Exercises

2.1: What are the host addresses for each of the following networks of ARI with a 255.255.255.240 mask?

a) network 16
b) network 32
c) network 48
d) network 64
e) network 80
f) network 96
g) network 112
h) network 128
i) network 160
j) network 176
k) network 192
l) network 208
m) network 224

2.2: What is the broadcast address for each of the following networks of ARI?

a) network 16
b) network 32
c) network 48
d) network 64
e) network 80
f) network 96
g) network 112
h) network 128

        i) network 160
        j) network 176
        k) network 192
        l) network 208
        m) network 224

2.3: All the networks of ARI are multiples of:
    a) 32
    b) 16
    c) 64
    d) 128

2.4: A broadcast address can be used as a host address. (T/F)

2.5: A broadcast address addresses all hosts on a given network. (T/F)

2.6: A broadcast address is identified as "all host bits have a value of 0". (T/F)

2.7: The address immediately preceding a wire address is a broadcast address. (T/F)

Answers

2.1:
    a) 192.16.12.17 through 192.16.12.30
    b) 192.16.12.33 through 192.16.12.46
    c) 192.16.12.49 through 192.16.12.62
    d) 192.16.12.65 through 192.16.12.78
    e) 192.16.12.81 through 192.16.12.94
    f) 192.16.12.97 through 192.16.12.110
    g) 192.16.12.113 through 192.16.12.126
    h) 192.16.12.129 through 192.16.12.142
    i) 192.16.12.161 through 192.16.12.174
    j) 192.16.12.177 through 192.16.12.190
    k) 192.16.12.193 through 192.16.12.206
    l) 192.16.12.209 through 192.16.12.222
    m) 192.16.12.225 through 192.16.12.238

2.2:

    a) 192.16.12.31
    b) 192.16.12.47
    c) 192.16.12.63
    d) 192.16.12.79
    e) 192.16.12.95
    f) 192.16.12.111
    g) 192.16.12.127
    h) 192.16.12.143
    i) 192.16.12.175
    j) 192.16.12.191
    k) 192.16.12.207
    l) 192.16.12.223
    m) 192.16.12.239

2.3: b) 16

2.4: False

2.5: True

2.6: False

2.7: True

CHAPTER **3**

Subnetting and Class C Addresses

Objectives

- Describe the process of subnetting a Class C address.
- Describe the multiple process.

All examples in this chapter assume a Class C address.

The best way to understand subnetting is to look at the bit pattern.

How many network addresses would be available with a 1-bit mask?

TABLE 3.1

All Combinations of a 1-bit Mask

	128	64	32	16	8	4	2	1	Network
1-bit Mask	1	0	0	0	0	0	0	0	
Combo 1	0	0	0	0	0	0	0	0	0
Combo 2	1	0	0	0	0	0	0	0	128

$2^1 - 2 = 0$

Combo 1 and combo 2 are illegal.

As a result networks 0 and 128 cannot be used and we have *NO* network addresses available.

Remember that we cannot use the all-zero or the all-one combination.

In later chapters we will continue our discussion of these two combinations and investigate times when we could use these addresses. These two combinations are called the zero and the broadcast subnet respectively.

How many network addresses would be available with a 2-bit mask?

TABLE 3.2

All Combinations of a 2-bit Mask

	128	64	32	16	8	4	2	1	Network
2-bit Mask	1	1	0	0	0	0	0	0	
Combo 1	0	0	0	0	0	0	0	0	0
Combo 2	0	1	0	0	0	0	0	0	64
Combo 3	1	0	0	0	0	0	0	0	128
Combo 4	1	1	0	0	0	0	0	0	192

$2^2 - 2 = 2$

Combo 1 and combo 4 are illegal.

Networks that can be used are 64 and 128; as a result we have 2 available networks.

How many network addresses would be available with a 3-bit mask?

	128	64	32	16	8	4	2	1	Network
3-bit Mask	1	1	1	0	0	0	0	0	
Combo 1	0	0	0	0	0	0	0	0	0
Combo 2	0	0	1	0	0	0	0	0	32
Combo 3	0	1	0	0	0	0	0	0	64
Combo 4	0	1	1	0	0	0	0	0	96
Combo 5	1	0	0	0	0	0	0	0	128
Combo 6	1	0	1	0	0	0	0	0	160
Combo 7	1	1	0	0	0	0	0	0	192
Combo 8	1	1	1	0	0	0	0	0	224

TABLE 3.3

All Combinations of a 3-bit Mask

$2^3 - 2 = 6$

Combo 1 and combo 8 are illegal.

Networks that can be used are 32, 64, 96, 128, 160, and 192. What do all these networks have in common, other than the fact that they are all even numbers?

How many network addresses would be available with a 4-bit mask?

TABLE 3.4

All Combinations of a 4-bit Mask

	128	64	32	16	8	4	2	1	Network
Combo 1	0	0	0	0	0	0	0	0	0
Combo 2	0	0	0	1	0	0	0	0	16
Combo 3	0	0	1	0	0	0	0	0	32
Combo 4	0	0	1	1	0	0	0	0	48
Combo 5	0	1	0	0	0	0	0	0	64
Combo 6	0	1	0	1	0	0	0	0	80
Combo 7	0	1	1	0	0	0	0	0	96
Combo 8	0	1	1	1	0	0	0	0	112
Combo 9	1	0	0	0	0	0	0	0	128
Combo 10	1	0	0	1	0	0	0	0	144
Combo 11	1	0	1	0	0	0	0	0	160
Combo 12	1	0	1	1	0	0	0	0	176
Combo 13	1	1	0	0	0	0	0	0	192
Combo 14	1	1	0	1	0	0	0	0	208
Combo 15	1	1	1	0	0	0	0	0	224
Combo 16	1	1	1	1	0	0	0	0	240

$2^4 - 2 = 14$

Combo 1 and combo 16 are illegal.

Networks that can be used are 32, 64, 96, 128, 160, and 192. What do all these networks have in common, other than the fact that they are all even numbers? Do you see a pattern developing?

The Multiple Process

In Chapter 1 we discussed the logical AND process to calculate network addresses. I would now like to introduce the *multiple process*.

With the multiple process instead of the logical AND process, it is easier to calculate the wire and broadcast address.

TIP

Network addresses are always multiples of the least significant subnet bit.

In the 3-bit mask example above, all the network address are multiples of 32.

Example 1

If we had an address of 192.16.12.52 with a mask of 255.255.255.240, we could easily calculate the wire address.

The 240 mask is a 4-bit mask, therefore all wire addresses are multiples of 16 (refer to Table 3.4).

To determine the wire address, answer the following question.

What is the highest multiple of 16 that is less than 52?

Since 48 is the highest multiple of 16 that is less than 52:
    The network address is 192.16.12.48.

To determine the broadcast address, answer the following question.

What address is one less than the next wire address?

The next wire address is 64 (the next multiple of 16), so the broadcast address is 192.16.12.63.

Example 2

What is the wire and broadcast address of 192.30.20.17 with a mask of 255.255.255.252?

What is the highest multiple of 4 that is less than 17?

The network address is 192.30.20.16.

To determine the broadcast address, answer the following question.

What address is one less than the next wire address?

The next wire address is 20 (the next multiple of 4), so the broadcast address is 192.30.20.19.

NOTE

Just as a review of the logical AND process, examine examples 3.1 and 3.2.

Example 3.1

	128 64 32 16 8 4 2 1	128 64 32 16 8 4 2 1	128 64 32 16 8 4 2 1	128 64 32 16	Host Bits 8 4 2 1
192.16.12.52	1 1 0 0 0 0 0 0	0 0 0 1 0 0 0 0	0 0 0 0 1 1 0 0	0 0 1 1	0 1 0 0
255.255.255.240	1 1 1 1 1 1 1 1	1 1 1 1 1 1 1 1	1 1 1 1 1 1 1 1	1 1 1 1	0 0 0 0
192.16.12.48	1 1 0 0 0 0 0 0	0 0 0 1 0 0 0 0	0 0 0 0 1 1 0 0	0 0 1 1	0 0 0 0
192.16.12.63	1 1 0 0 0 0 0 0	0 0 0 1 0 0 0 0	0 0 0 0 1 1 0 0	0 0 1 1	1 1 1 1

TIP

Keep in mind that the definition of a broadcast address is when all the host bits have a value of 1.

Example 3.2

	128 64 32 16 8 4 2 1	128 64 32 16 8 4 2 1	128 64 32 16 8 4 2 1	128 64 32 16 8 4	H H 2 1
192.20.30.17	1 1 0 0 0 0 0 0	0 0 0 1 0 1 0 0	0 0 0 1 1 1 1 0	0 0 0 1 0 0	0 1
255.255.255.252	1 1 1 1 1 1 1 1	1 1 1 1 1 1 1 1	1 1 1 1 1 1 1 1	1 1 1 1 1 1	0 0
192.20.30.16	1 1 0 0 0 0 0 0	0 0 0 1 0 1 0 0	0 0 0 1 1 1 1 0	0 0 0 1 0 0	0 0
192.20.30.19	1 1 0 0 0 0 0 0	0 0 0 1 0 1 0 0	0 0 0 1 1 1 1 0	0 0 0 1 0 0	1 1

Summary

- With a Class C address there are only 8 bits (4th octet) that can be manipulated or changed.
- 2^N-2 is the formula to use to calculate the available number of hosts and networks.
- A broadcast address for a network is when all host bits have a value of 1.
- A broadcast address is always the last address on a wire.
- A broadcast address identifies all hosts on a network.

■ Wire addresses are always multiples of the least significant subnet bit.

■ To calculate a wire address you must have an IP address and a mask.

■ The multiple process is a quick and easy way to determine wire and broadcast addresses.

Exercises

3.1: How many network addresses would be available with a 5-bit mask?

3.2: How many network addresses would be available with a 6-bit mask?

3.3: Why would a 7- or 8-bit mask not be used with a Class C address?

3.4: Given a Class C address, what is the mask value for:
a) 2-bit mask 255.255.255.192
b) 3-bit mask
c) 4-bit mask
d) 5-bit mask
e) 6-bit mask

3.5: Complete the chart below:

Host Address	Class	Mask	Wire Address	Broadcast Address
194.24.64.78		255.255.255.248		
201.10.56.34		255.255.255.224		
192.34.23.5		255.255.255.252		
210.10.10.134		255.255.255.240		
223.12.4.34		255.255.255.248		

3.6: Using the combination form 2^2–2 complete the chart below:

Host Address	Mask	Number of Subnet Bits	Number of Subnets	Number of Host Bits	Number of Hosts	Total Host Addressing
194.24.64.78	255.255.255.248	5	30	3	6	180
201.10.56.34	255.255.255.224					
192.34.23.5	255.255.255.252					
210.10.10.134	255.255.255.240					
223.12.4.34	255.255.255.248					

Answers

3.1: 2^5–2 = 30

3.2: 2^6–2 = 62

3.3: There would be no addressing space left for hosts.

3.4: Given a Class C address, the mask value for:
   a) 2-bit mask: 255.255.255.192
   b) 3-bit mask: 255.255.255.224
   c) 4-bit mask: 255.255.255.240
   d) 5-bit mask: 255.255.255.248
   e) 6-bit mask: 255.255.255.252

3.5:

Host Address	Class	Mask	Wire Address	Broadcast Address
194.24.64.78	C	255.255.255.248	194.24.64.72	194.24.64.79
201.10.56.34	C	255.255.255.224	201.10.56.32	201.10.56.63
192.34.23.5	C	255.255.255.252	192.34.23.4	192.34.23.7
210.10.10.134	C	255.255.255.240	210.10.10.128	210.10.10.143
223.12.4.34	C	255.255.255.248	223.12.4.32	223.12.4.39

3.6:

Host Address	Mask	Number of Subnet Bits	Number of Subnets	Number of Host Bits	Number of Hosts	Total Host Addressing
194.24.64.78	255.255.255.248	5	30	3	6	180
201.10.56.34	255.255.255.224	3	6	5	30	180
192.34.23.5	255.255.255.252	6	62	2	2	124
210.10.10.134	255.255.255.240	4	14	4	14	196
223.12.4.34	255.255.255.248	5	30	3	6	180

CHAPTER **4**

Class B
Addresses

Objectives

- Describe the process of subnetting a Class B address.
- Describe the multiple process as it pertains to Class B addresses.

All examples used in this Chapter refer to Class B addresses.

Everything we have learned so far also extends to Class B addresses. There are no new rules or any unique nuances about Class B addresses.

The reason I have created a separate discussion for Class B addresses is because students tend to have more difficulty dealing with Class B addresses, because there are more bits that can be manipulated.

Just keep in mind that everything you have learned so far also applies to Class B addresses; the only difference is we have more bits to manipulate.

The Class B Address

A Class B address contains a first octet value of 128-191.

The Class B default mask is 255.255.0.0

The first 3 octets of a Class C address are not to be changed, meaning we have only the 4th octet to manipulate.

TIP

The first 2 octets of a Class B address are not to be changed, meaning we have two octets that we can change.

Because there are 16 bits that can be manipulated, we have a great deal more addressing space to work with.

Assume we have a Class B address of 172.16.0.0 and we take a 4-bit mask. As we discussed in the previous chapter, a 4-bit mask allows us to have 14 unique networks.

What does change is the number of host bits. We now have 12 host bits.

4 from the 3rd octet
8 from the 4th octet

How many hosts can be addressed on this network?

The formula is the same:

$2^{12}-2 = 4096$ hosts

When working with a Class C address it made no sense to discuss a 7-bit mask, because we would only have 1 host bit available for addressing and in the case of an 8-bit mask we would have 0 bits available for host addressing.

This is not the case for Class B addresses.

A 7-bit mask used with a Class B address still leaves 9 bits to be used for hosts.

An 8-bit mask used with a Class B address still leaves 8 bits to be used for hosts.

Class B Example 4.1

We are given an address of 148.15.0.0. We have determined we need to have addressing space to identify at most 500 locations with at most 100 hosts at each location.

By referring to Table 2.3 and using the combination formula of 2^n-2, n must be 9 to give us at least 500 combinations:

$2^9-2 = 510$

If we use 9 bits to describe our networks or wires we have 7 remaining bits to describe hosts:

$2^7-2 = 126$. This provides sufficient host addressing space per wire.

Therefore the mask we shall use is: 255.255.255.128 or /25.

Network Addresses

A mask of 255.255.255.128 means that the 3rd octet can have values between 1 and 255 while the 4th octet will have the most significant bit set as 1 or 0. Refer to Table 4.1.

TABLE 4.1

Networks with a /25 Mask

148	15	0	0	Zero Subnet
148	15	0	128	**First Available Subnet**
148	15	1	0	
148	15	1	128	
148	15	2	0	
148	15	2	128	
148	15	3	0	
148	15	3	128	

This pattern continues...

continued on next page

148	15	253	0	
148	15	253	128	
148	15	254	0	
148	15	254	128	
148	15	255	0	**Last available Subnet**
148	15	255	128	Broadcast Subnet

Notice that the multiple rule still applies.

The 4th octet value of all the subnets is a multiple of the least significant subnet bit, in this case either a 0 or 128. Don't let the zero cause confusion. Zero (0) is a multiple of 128.

Host Addresses

The remaining 7 bits of the 4th octet are host bits, the host addresses for the 148.15.0.128 network shown in Table 4.2.

TABLE 4.2

Hosts Addresses on the 148.15.0.128 Wire

148	15	0	128	Network
148	15	0	129	**First Host**
148	15	0	130	
148	15	0	131	
148	15	0	132	
148	15	0	133	
			This pattern continues...	
148	15	0	251	
148	15	0	252	
148	15	0	253	
148	15	0	254	**Last Host**
148	15	0	255	Broadcast
148	15	1	0	Next Wire

Class B Example 4.2

We are given an address of 148.15.0.0. We have determined we need to have addressing space to identify at most 200 locations with at most 200 hosts at each location.

By referring to Table 2.3 and using the combination formula of 2^n-2, n must be 8 to give us at least 200 combinations:

$2^8=254$

If we use 8 bits to describe our networks or wires, we have 8 remaining bits (4th octet) to describe hosts:

$2^8-2=254$. This provides sufficient host addressing space per wire.

Therefore the mask we shall use is: 255.255.255.0 or /24.

The above case is a very common mask for a Class B address.

Network addresses will range from 148.15.1.0 through 148.15.254.0.

Host addresses for each wire will range from 1 through 254 and if a value of 255 is in the 4th octet, this will identify the broadcast address.

Class A Addresses

A Class A address works in the same way, the difference being that a Class A address provides us with 24 bits that can be manipulated.

Table 4.3 facilitates looking up information for different masks, BUT you should be able to derive every number in this table!

TABLE 4.3
Subnet and
Mask Table

Mask	Binary Mask	Prefix Hosts	Class A Subnets	Class A Subnets	Class A Subnets
255.255.255.252	11111111.11111111.11111111.11111100	/30	2	4,194,302.00	16,382.00	62
255.255.255.248	11111111.11111111.11111111.11111000	/29	6	2,097,150.00	8,190.00	30
255.255.255.240	11111111.11111111.11111111.11110000	/28	14	1,048,574.00	4,094.00	14
255.255.255.224	11111111.11111111.11111111.11100000	/27	30	524,286.00	2,046.00	6
255.255.255.192	11111111.11111111.11111111.11000000	/26	62	262,142.00	1,022.00	2
255.255.255.128	11111111.11111111.11111111.10000000	/25	126	131,070.00	510.00	0 Subnet
255.255.255.0	11111111.11111111.11111111.00000000	/24	254	65,534.00	254.00	0
255.255.254.0	11111111.11111111.11111110.00000000	/23	510	32,766.00	126.00	0
255.255.252.0	11111111.11111111.11111100.00000000	/22	1,022	16,382.00	62.00	
255.255.248.0	11111111.11111111.11111000.00000000	/21	2,046	8,190.00	30.00	
255.255.240.0	11111111.11111111.11110000.00000000	/20	4,094	4,094.00	14.00	
255.255.224.0	11111111.11111111.11100000.00000000	/19	8,190	2,046.00	6.00	
255.255.192.0	11111111.11111111.11000000.00000000	/18	16,382	1,022.00	2.00	
255.255.128.0	11111111.11111111.10000000.00000000	/17	32,766	510	0 Subnet	
255.255.0.0	11111111.11111111.00000000.00000000	/16	65,534	254	0	
255.254.0.0	11111111.11111110.00000000.00000000	/15	131,070	126		
255.252.0.0	11111111.11111100.00000000.00000000	/14	262,142	62		
255.248.0.0	11111111.11111000.00000000.00000000	/13	524,286	30		
255.240.0.0	11111111.11110000.00000000.00000000	/12	1,048,574	14		
255.224.0.0	11111111.11100000.00000000.00000000	/11	2,097,150	6		
255.192.0.0	11111111.11000000.00000000.00000000	/10	4,194,302	2		
255.128.0.0	11111111.10000000.00000000.00000000	/9	8,388,606	0 Subnet		
255.0.0.0	11111111.00000000.00000000.00000000	/8	1,677,214	0		

Summary

- Class B addresses provide us with a great deal more addressing space, because there are 16 bits that we can use for addressing as opposed to a Class C address, where there are only 8 bits that we can use for addressing.
- The multiple process can be used with Class B addresses as well as Class C addresses

Exercises

NOTE

Assume a Class B address for all exercises.

4.1: How many networks could be addressed per wire with a 4-bit mask?

4.2: How many networks could be addressed per wire with a 5-bit mask?

4.3: How many networks could be addressed per wire with a 6-bit mask?

4.4: How many networks could be addressed per wire with a 7-bit mask?

4.5: How many networks could be addressed per wire with a 8-bit mask?

4.6: How many networks could be addressed per wire with a 9-bit mask?

4.7: How many hosts could be addressed with a 10-bit mask?

4.8: Why can a 7- or 8-bit mask be used with a Class B address?

4.9: Would a 1-bit mask be logical?

4.10: Given a Class B address what is the mask value for:
   a) 2-bit mask 255.255.192.0
   b) 3-bit mask
   c) 4-bit mask
   d) 5-bit mask
   e) 6-bit mask
   f) 7-bit mask
   g) 8-bit mask
   h) 9-bit mask
   i) 10-bit mask
   j) 11-bit mask
   k) 12-bit mask

4.11: Complete the chart below:

Host Address	Class	Mask	Wire Address	Broadcast Address
132.24.64.78		255.255.255.248		
167.10.56.34		255.255.224.0		
143.34.23.200		255.255.255.128		
130.10.69.134		255.255.248.0		
191.12.29.3		255.255.252.0		

4.12: Using the combination form 2^2-2 complete the chart below:

Host Address	Mask	Number of Subnet Bits	Number of Subnets	Number of Host Bits	Number of Hosts	Total Host Addressing
174.24.64.78	255.255.255.248	13	8190	3	6	49140
167.10.56.34	255.255.255.224					0
143.34.23.5	255.255.252.0					0
139.10.10.134	255.255.248.0					0
182.12.4.34	255.255.224.0					0

Answers

4.1: $2^4-2 = 14$

4.2: $2^5-2 = 30$

4.3: $2^6-2 = 62$

4.4: $2^7-2 = 126$

4.5: $2^8-2 = 254$

4.6: $2^9-2 = 510$

4.7: $2^6 - 2 = 62$

4.8: A 7- or 8-bit mask still leaves 9 or 8 bits respectively for host addressing.

4.9: In most cases no, because there is no addressing space with a single-bit mask. The zero subnet can be used in certain circumstances.

4.10:

a) 2-bit mask	255.255.192.0
b) 3-bit mask	255.255.224.0
c) 4-bit mask	255.255.240.0
d) 5-bit mask	255.255.248.0
e) 6-bit mask	255.255.252.0
f) 7-bit mask	255.255.254.0
g) 8-bit mask	255.255.255.0
h) 9-bit mask	255.255.255.128
i) 10-bit mask	255.255.255.192
g) 11-bit mask	255.255.255.224
k) 12-bit mask	255.255.255.240

4.11:

Host Address	Class	Mask	Wire Address	Broadcast Address
132.24.64.78	B	255.255.255.248	132.24.64.72	132.24.64.79
167.10.56.34	B	255.255.224.0	167.10.32.0	167.10.63.255
143.34.23.200	B	255.255.255.128	143.34.23.128	143.34.23.255
139.10.69.134	B	255.255.248.0	139.10.64.0	139.10.71.255
191.12.29.3	B	255.255.252.0	191.12.28.0	191.12.31.255

4.12:

Host Address	Mask	Number of Subnet Bits	Number of Subnets	Number of Host Bits	Number of Hosts	Total Host Addressing
174.24.64.78	255.255.255.248	13	8190	3	6	49140
167.10.56.34	255.255.255.224	11	2046	5	30	61380
143.34.23.5	255.255.252.0	6	62	10	1022	63364
139.10.10.134	255.255.248.0	5	30	11	2046	61380
182.12.4.34	255.255.224.0	3	6	13	8190	49140

CHAPTER 5

Introduction to IP Routing Protocols

Objectives

- Describe the basic function of a router.
- Define a routing protocol.
- Describe the basic differences between distance-vector and link-state routing protocols.
- Define a hybrid routing protocol.
- Define metric.
- Define administrative distance;
- Define convergence.
- Define load balancing and load sharing.

■ Describe interior routing protocols.
■ Describe exterior routing protocols.
■ Define a static route.
■ Define a default route.

A router has two main functions:

■ Path determination
■ Switching packets to the appropriate interface.

Path determination is a process in which the router "learns" of the different paths to each possible destination in the topology, picks the best path, based upon some criteria, and then places that information in a table.

Once this table is complete the router is able to take data packets from the incoming interface, examine the destination address and, based on the information contained in the table, "switch" the packet to the appropriate outgoing interface.

What Is a Routing Protocol?

This is the language that routers use to talk to each other. The purpose of this communication is to allow routers to "see" the network topology so that a best path can be selected. We might use the analogy: if cities could talk to each other to inform neighboring cities what roads they are connected to, a map could be created.

When routers communicate to each other a "map" is being created that will allow each router to discover the best path to each destination network.

There are two basic types of routing protocols, Distance Vector (DV) and Link State.

Why is a distance-vector protocol called a distance-vector protocol?

When routers communicate using a DV protocol, this communication includes information concerning distance and direction (vector).

Distance can be measured in a variety of ways; IP RIP uses hops to measure distance and IPX RIP uses tick ([1/18]th of a second) and hop count.

Refer to Figure 5.1. Assuming Router_A was running a DV protocol, Router_A would communicate information about its Ethernet link to Router_B. Router_B would receive this information and know that Router_A's Ethernet network is 1 hop away (distance) and it should use its Serial 0 interface (vector) to get there.

Why is a link-state protocol called a link-state protocol?

When routers talk to other routers they communicate the status (state) of their links to their neighbors.

If a link-state protocol were running in Figure 5.1, Router_A would test the directly connected Ethernet link and then communicate that information to the other routers if, and only if, the state had changed from the previous test. The only exception to this would be if the router had just been powered on; it would then "flood" information about its links to all other routers. The main point here is: if no change has taken place in the state of the link from the previous test, no communication will take place.

OSPF is an example of a link-state protocol. We will discuss this more in a later chapter.

A link-state protocol does not communicate distances, but there is a cost associated with each link. For example, when OSPF is running on a Cisco router, each link would have a default cost of 10^8 divided by the bandwidth of the link.

For example, a 10 Mbps Ethernet link would have a default cost of 10 ($10^8/10^7$). The total cost to get to a network would be the sum cost of each individual network.

What Are the Basic Differences Between Distance-Vector and Link-State Routing Protocols?

To help understand the difference between DV and link state, I ask students to answer the following three questions:

- What does the routing protocol communicate?
- When does the routing protocol communicate?
- To whom does the routing protocol communicate?

Distance Vector

A distance-vector protocol communicates the entire routing table (with some exceptions that we do not have to worry about in this discussion).

A distance-vector protocol communicates periodically. For example IP RIP communicates every 30 seconds, while IPX RIP communicates every 60 seconds.

A distance-vector protocol communicates to directly connected neighbors.

FIGURE 5.1

4 Router Topology

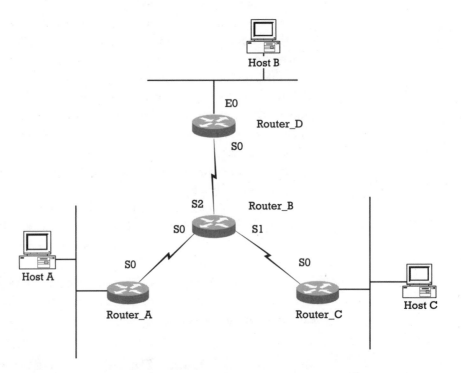

If in Figure 5.1 the DV protocol of IP RIP were running on all routers, the following would be true:

- Router_A would send its routing table to Router_B every 30 seconds. Router_A would not communicate to any other router.
- Router_C would send its routing table to Router_B every 30 seconds. Router_C would not communicate to any other router.
- In fact all routers other than Router_B would only communicate to Router_B. They would never send IP RIP packets to each other.

■ Router_B would send its routing table to all other routers periodically (every 30 seconds).

Because routers running a DV protocol only communicate to directly connected routers the process has sometimes been referred to as *rumor routing*.

In our topology Router_A has no direct communication with Router_D. Router_A only knows through "rumor" that there is an Ethernet network out there someplace that is 2 hops away.

Router_A does not know that there is a router named Router_D, Router_A knows only of hops.

Distance-vector protocols have some habits that cause additional processing and traffic. Consider, if you will, that all networks are up and running and everything is fine in Camelot.

All routers would still send their routing tables periodically, in this case every 30 seconds, to their directly connected neighbors.

Why is it necessary for these routers to burn up bandwidth and processing time to look at information that has not changed?

This is like your mother calling you up every night and going through your entire family tree to tell you everyone is alive and no one died since yesterday.

Let's make a policy, a protocol we might say; Mom will call only when someone dies. If we don't hear from Mom we will assume everyone is still alive and well.

If Mom agrees to our proposal, we are using a link-state protocol.

Link State

Link state communicates just the state of the link to all neighbors when the state of the link changes; this makes it a much more efficient protocol.

Referring to Figure 5.1, Router_A can communicate with all other routers. Router_A will know the identification (ID) of all other routers. There are no more rumors, because Router_A received communication from Router_D about Router_D's directly connected links.

Further more Router_A will know the exact path taken to get to Router_D. Router_A knows that a packet must go through Router_B to get to Router_D.

There is one problem with the mother analogy: if we tell Mom to call only when someone dies what happens if Mom dies?

As a result a link-state protocol will use a "hello protocol" periodically to let neighbors know that it is still alive.

In other words, we will tell Mom to call us every night just to say "hello" and hang up; as a result we will know that no one in our family has died and Mom is alive.

What Is a Hybrid Routing Protocol?

EIGRP is an example of a hybrid routing protocol because it shares attributes of both distance-vector and link-state routing protocols.

EIGRP communicates the routing table with directly connected neighbors, but only when a change occurs.

What Is Metric?

Metric is the criteria used by a routing protocol to determine which is the best path to a destination.

Earlier in this chapter we stated that IP RIP uses hop count to measure distances. Put in another way, IP RIP uses hop count as its metric.

As an analogy, my friend Rudy was in Tampa last year and wanted to come to Tallahassee to visit me. He asked the best route to take. Since he was also a Cisco instructor I asked him what his metric was.

In other words, was Rudy interested in how fast he could get to Tallahassee or was he more interested in taking his time and enjoying the scenery?

His metric might influence his route choices.

It works much the same way for routers, depending on the metric used by the routing protocol. Since IP RIP uses hop count as its metric, a router has no way to distinguish between a T1 link and a 56K link. As a result, if there are multiple ways to get to a destination network with the same hop count, a router may choose the 56K link, not exactly the way you would like your packets to travel.

To illustrate this point let us change our topology slightly.

Notice we have an additional Ethernet link between Router_A and Router_C and the serial links to Router_A and Router_C have been identified as T1 and 56K links respectively.

If Router_B receives a packet destined for Host E, Router_B has two ways to send the packet. It could use the Serial 0 or the Serial 1 interface.

FIGURE 5.2
Router Topology
with Multiple Ways
to the Destination

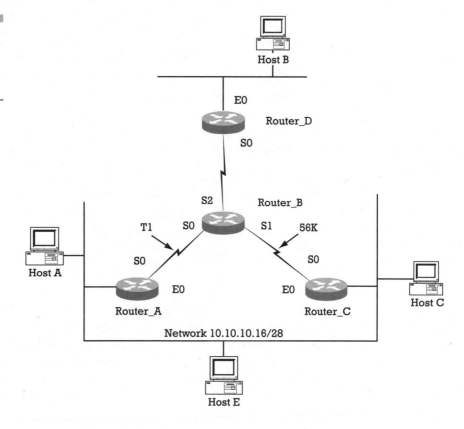

Which one will it use? Or will it use both?

That depends upon the metric being used. If we assume RIP is running, the hop count is the same for either of the two ways. IP RIP has no way to distinguish the difference in bandwidth of the two links. RIP will pick one of those ways. If these routers are Cisco routers Router_B will load balance and use both ways to get to network 10.10.10.16.

What is a routing table?

As routes or paths are learned, the "best paths" will be placed in a routing table. The routing table will contain a list of networks associated with an interface that represents the best path to each of the networks.

What is the best path?

Each router, based on the metric for a particular routing protocol, discovers the best path to a destination network. The best path to a destination is the one with the lowest metric. These routes are then placed in the routing table. Routers also receive information concerning paths that are not the best; these routes are not entered into the routing table.

I have set the Figure 5.2 topology up in the LAB so I can show you the routing table of Router_B. Refer to Figure 5.3.

FIGURE 5.3   IP RIP Routing Table of Router_B

```
Router_B#sh ip route
Codes: C - connected, S - static, I - IGRP, R - RIP, M - mobile, B - BGP
    D - EIGRP, EX - EIGRP external, O - OSPF, IA - OSPF inter area
    N1 - OSPF NSSA external type 1, N2 - OSPF NSSA external type 2
    E1 - OSPF external type 1, E2 - OSPF external type 2, E - EGP
    i - IS-IS, L1 - IS-IS level-1, L2 - IS-IS level-2, * - candidate default
    U - per-user static route, o - ODR
Gateway of last resort is not set
    10.0.0.0/28 is subnetted, 4 subnets
R      10.10.10.16 [120/1] via 10.10.10.34, 00:00:22, Serial0
       [120/1] via 10.10.10.66, 00:00:15, Serial1
C      10.10.10.32 is directly connected, Serial0
C      10.10.10.64 is directly connected, Serial1
C      10.10.10.96 is directly connected, Serial2
```

The bolded lines show that Router_B has two ways to get to network 10.10.10.16. Router_B will use both Serial 0 and Serial 1. The metric in each case is 1 hop.

Now we will throw a new wrinkle into the mix. Suppose we used IGRP as the routing protocol? (We will discuss IGRP in more detail later.)

How does IGRP differ from IP RIP?

IGRP uses a composite metric of bandwidth, delay, load, reliability and MTU.

It has the ability to "realize" that the Serial 0 connection is the better path to network 10.10.16.0.

Assuming all Cisco defaults, Router_B will always take the Serial 0 link as the routing table shows in Figure 5.4.

FIGURE 5.4   IGRP Routing Table of Router_B

```
Router_B#sh ip route
Codes: C - connected, S - static, I - IGRP, R - RIP, M - mobile, B - BGP
    D - EIGRP, EX - EIGRP external, O - OSPF, IA - OSPF inter area
    N1 - OSPF NSSA external type 1, N2 - OSPF NSSA external type 2
    E1 - OSPF external type 1, E2 - OSPF external type 2, E - EGP
    i - IS-IS, L1 - IS-IS level-1, L2 - IS-IS level-2, * - candidate default
    U - per-user static route, o - ODR
Gateway of last resort is not set
    10.0.0.0/28 is subnetted, 4 subnets
I     10.10.10.16 [100/8576] via 10.10.10.34, 00:00:04, Serial0
C     10.10.10.32 is directly connected, Serial0
C     10.10.10.64 is directly connected, Serial1
C     10.10.10.96 is directly connected, Serial2
```

Clearly the bolded line shows only one path will be used by Router_B to get to network 10.10.10.16. The path using the Serial 1 interface has a higher metric and therefore is not used.

What Is the Meaning of Administrative Distance?

This is a Cisco term which deals with the reliability of the information that routers receive.

If a router receives two updates concerning a specific network and each of these updates comes from two different routing protocols, which routing update should the router use to determine the best path?

Cisco uses administrative distance to solve this dilemma. Each routing protocol carries an administrative distance value. The lower the value, the higher the reliability of the protocol.

TABLE 5.1

IP Protocols and Administrative Distances (AD)

Protocol	AD
EIGRP	90
IGRP	100
OSPF	110
RIP	120
BGP	180

Table 5.1 indicates that the EIGRP routing protocol is considered the most reliable.

If IGRP and RIP were running on all routers in Figure 5.1, the routing table would indicate that IGRP information would be used to get to all destinations.

What Does Convergence Mean?

Keep in mind that a routing protocol is the communication among routers for the purpose of discovering the network topology and determining the best path.

When all routers agree on what the network topology is, convergence has been achieved. When there is no convergence, data packets will be unable to reach their destination. The time it takes to converge is an important element of a routing protocol. Link-state routing protocols typically converge faster than distance-vector protocols.

What Is Load Sharing?

Load sharing is when equal or unequal cost routes exist to a single destination network, and the traffic to that network is proportionally distributed across the multiple routes.

Cisco's IGRP is an example of a routing protocol that can perform load sharing. Assume that two routes exist to Network A; one of these routes goes over a 512K link and the other route goes over a T1 link. IGRP can be configured with a variance of 2 so that for every packet that goes the 512K route two packets will travel the T1 route.

Figure 5.5 illustrates a load-sharing scenario. Notice that the metric is not the same but both routes are placed in the routing table.

FIGURE 5.5   IGRP Configured with Variance

```
Gateway of last resort is not set
    10.0.0.0/28 is subnetted, 4 subnets
I     10.10.10.16 [100/8576] via 10.10.10.34, 00:00:07, Serial0
      [100/180671] via 10.10.10.66, 00:00:07, Serial1
C     10.10.10.32 is directly connected, Serial0
C     10.10.10.64 is directly connected, Serial1
C     10.10.10.96 is directly connected, Serial2
```

The metric for the Serial 0 route is 8576 while the metric for the Serial 1 route is 180671. Do not worry about where these numbers come from; at this point it is not important. Just remember the lower the number the better the route.

What Is the Difference Between an Interior Gateway Protocol and an Exterior Gateway Protocol?

An IGP communicates within a defined region referred to as an Autonomous System (AS).

An EGP communicates between different autonomous systems.

An AS is defined as a group of routers under common administration. We will cover that topic in a later chapter.

In this book we will configure only the IGP routing protocols of IP RIP, IGRP, EIGRP, and OSPF.

What Is a Static Route?

A dynamic route is a route discovered by the router using a routing protocol. Assume there is only one way to a destination or you want the router to send data packets in a certain direction. You may not want a router to spend all the processing time and bandwidth required just to discover that there is only way to that destination. You may just want to point the router to the appropriate interface for certain destinations; this is called a *static route*.

For years I would travel to strange cities doing Novell and Cisco classes. If I wanted to visit some point of interest I could use a map and spend my time finding my current location and finding my destination, then mapping out a route to that destination. Or if I was lucky a student in the class might know exactly the best way to get to that destination and give me specific directions (static route).

Using a static route does present the administrator with the additional task of keeping all of the static routes current.

Also we may have an additional problem. Go back to my analogy for a minute; suppose I write out the directions to my destination and I start on my trip only to discover that a road is blocked. Since I only have the directions and not the map I do not have the ability to "discover" an alternate route.

This will also be true of the router. Since the router has a static route configured it will not have the ability to discover another path. If there is only one way to the destination it does not make any difference, but static routes can be used any time, not only for one-way destinations.

Suppose a router discovers a route to the same destination for which there is a static route configured?

Static routes will carry an administrative distance of 0 or 1. As we learned earlier the lower the administrative distance the more the reliable the route. The router will always put the static route in its routing table. It is possible to raise the administrative distance of a static route. In such a case we would be using the static route as a backup route or a "floating static route" because if the original path should be lost the static route will float to the top.

What Is a Default Route?

In this scenario assume a packet arrives at the router, the router reads the destination IP address, then goes to the routing table to determine the interface to which the packet should be sent, but the destination is not listed in the routing table.

If no destination exists in the routing table the router will drop the packet, unless a default route is configured.

In this case we are telling the router that if we do not know where to send a packet, always send it to a particular interface.

Think of your organization using the Internet. Do you want your router to have all the different networks of the Internet in the routing table? You do not; so we configure a default route which points to our ISP.

Figure 5.6 is a summary outline of several routing protocols.

FIGURE 5.6 Routing Protocol Outline

I Interior Gateway Routing Protocols (IGP)

A. Distance Vector

1. IP RIP
2. Cisco's IGRP
3. IPX RIP (Novell)

4. Applecommunicate RTMP

B. Link State

1. OSPF
2. NLSP (Novell)

C. Hybrid

1. Cisco's EIGRP
2. IS_IS

II Exterior Gateway Routing Protocols (EGP)

1. BGP4

Summary

- An interior routing protocol communicates within an autonomous system.
- An exterior routing protocol communicates between autonomous systems.
- A distance-vector routing protocol communicates a routing table periodically to directly connected neighbors while a link-state protocol communicates changes in the state of the link when changes occur.
- A hybrid routing protocol has characteristics of both link state and distance vector.
- Metric is the criteria used by a routing protocol to select the best route to a destination.
- Administrative distance is a Cisco term that determines a measure of reliability for each IP routing protocol.
- Convergence is a term used to describe a point when all routers "see" the same network topology.
- Load balancing is when a router will use multiple paths equally to forward packets to a single destination.
- Load sharing is when routers will use multiple paths (not necessarily equally) to forward packets to a single destination.

■ Route redistribution is when networks learned by one routing protocol are sent to another routing protocol.

Exercises

Refer to the following routing table and answer Exercises 5.1 through 5.5.

```
Router_B#sh ip route
Codes: C - connected, S - static, I - IGRP, R - RIP, M - mobile, B - BGP
   D - EIGRP, EX - EIGRP external, O - OSPF, IA - OSPF inter area
   N1 - OSPF NSSA external type 1, N2 - OSPF NSSA external type 2
   E1 - OSPF external type 1, E2 - OSPF external type 2, E - EGP
   i - IS-IS, L1 - IS-IS level-1, L2 - IS-IS level-2, * - candidate default
   U - per-user static route, o - ODR

Gateway of last resort is not set

   10.0.0.0/28 is subnetted, 4 subnets
R    10.10.10.16 [120/1] via 10.10.10.34, 00:00:22, Serial0
     [120/1] via 10.10.10.66, 00:00:15, Serial1
C    10.10.10.32 is directly connected, Serial0
C    10.10.10.64 is directly connected, Serial1
C    10.10.10.96 is directly connected, Serial2
```

5.1: What routing protocol is being used?

5.2: What interface will Router_B send packets to when the destination address is on network 10.10.10.96?

5.3: What is the administrative distance of this routing protocol?

5.4: How many hops will it take to get to network 10.10.10.16?

5.5: How many hops will it take to get to network 10.10.10.32?

5.6: OSPF is a link-state routing protocol. (T/F)

5.7: EIGRP is a link-state routing protocol. (T/F)

5.8: All routes to a destination are placed in a routing table. (T/F)

5.9: Describe convergence.

Answers

5.1: IP RIP

5.2: Serial 2

5.3: 120

5.4: 1 hop

5.5: 0 hops; this network is directly connected

5.6: True

5.7: False, EIGRP is a hybrid protocol

5.8: False. Only the best routes are placed in a routing table.

5.9: Convergence is the point in which all routers "see" the network topology as it exists.

CHAPTER **6**

Classful Routing Protocols & Network Topology

Objectives

■ Describe a classful routing protocol.
■ Describe a contiguous addressing scheme.

Classful routing protocols do not carry subnet mask information across different major networks. A classful router always assumes that the same subnet mask is used everywhere for the same major network. For example, if we are using the major network address of 10.0.0.0 with a subnet mask of 255.255.255.0 it is always assumed that the network 10.0.0.0 will always carry the mask of 255.255.255.0.

A Class C address has a default mask of 255.255.255.0; a classful routing protocol will always assume this mask is used for the same major network address when the update is received from another major network address.

A classful routing protocol does not communicate a subnet mask other than the default mask for that class of address, hence the name classful. A classless routing protocol will communicate the subnet mask. Chapter 8 will discuss this in greater detail.

There are two important rules to follow when using a classful routing protocol:

1. The network must be addressed in a contiguous manner.
2. Use the same mask for the same major network.

The word contiguous implies that the same major network address is carried continuously across the topology; refer to Figure 6.1. The address of 10.0.0.0 and the mask of 255.255.255.0 is used for every network.

FIGURE 6.1
Contiguous
Addressing

As shown in Figure 6.2 Router_A learns of the 10.0.4.0 subnet.

FIGURE 6.2 Router_A Routing Table

Codes: C - connected, S - static, I - IGRP, R - RIP, M - mobile, B - BGP
D - EIGRP, EX - EIGRP external, O - OSPF, IA - OSPF inter area

continued on next page

N1 - OSPF NSSA external type 1, N2 - OSPF NSSA external type 2
E1 - OSPF external type 1, E2 - OSPF external type 2, E - EGP
i - IS-IS, L1 - IS-IS level-1, L2 - IS-IS level-2, * - candidate default
U - per-user static route, o - ODR

Gateway of last resort is not set

    10.0.0.0/24 is subnetted, 3 subnets
C   10.0.3.0 is directly connected, Serial0/0
C   10.0.1.0 is directly connected, Ethernet0/0
I   10.0.4.0 [100/8576] via 10.0.3.1, 00:01:11, Serial0/0

Router_A "learns" that the subnet 10.0.4.0 is 1 hop away.

Figures 6.3 and 6.4 illustrate that IP RIP and IGRP, both classful routing protocols, will advertise subnets across the SAME major network!

Refer to the bold lines below:

FIGURE 6.3   IGRP Debug

Router_A#debug ip igrp transactions
IGRP: sending update to 255.255.255.255 via Ethernet0/0 (10.0.1.1)
    subnet 10.0.3.0, metric=8476
    subnet 10.0.4.0, metric=8576
IGRP: sending update to 255.255.255.255 via Serial0/0 (10.0.3.2)
    subnet 10.0.1.0, metric=1100
IGRP: received update from 10.0.3.1 on Serial0/0
    subnet 10.0.4.0, metric 8576 (neighbor 1100)

FIGURE 6.4   IP RIP Debug

Router_A#debug ip rip
RIP protocol debugging is on
Router_A#
RIP: sending v1 update to 255.255.255.255 via Ethernet0/0 (10.0.1.1)
    subnet 10.0.3.0, metric 1

continued on next page

RIP: sending v1 update to 255.255.255.255 via Serial0/0 (10.0.3.2)
    subnet 10.0.1.0, metric 1
RIP: received v1 update from 10.0.3.1 on Serial0/0
    10.0.4.0 in 1 hops

In a discontiguous environment a major network address will be "broken" up by another major network address. Refer to Figure 6.5.

FIGURE 6.5
Discontiguous
Addressing-1

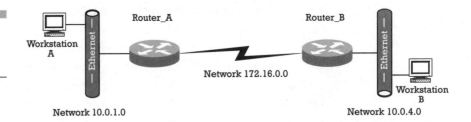

Figure 6.5 shows the "172" network in the middle of the "10" network.
    This type of topology presents a problem with a classful routing protocol. As illustrated in Figure 6.6 Router_A does not learn of network 10.0.4.0.

FIGURE 6.6   Router_A Routing Table

Router_A#sh ip route
Codes: C - connected, S - static, I - IGRP, R - RIP, M - mobile, B - BGP
    D - EIGRP, EX - EIGRP external, O - OSPF, IA - OSPF inter area
    N1 - OSPF NSSA external type 1, N2 - OSPF NSSA external type 2
    E1 - OSPF external type 1, E2 - OSPF external type 2, E - EGP
    i - IS-IS, L1 - IS-IS level-1, L2 - IS-IS level-2, * - candidate default
    U - per-user static route, o - ODR

Gateway of last resort is not set

    172.16.0.0/24 is subnetted, 1 subnets
C   172.16.1.0 is directly connected, Serial0/0
    10.0.0.0/24 is subnetted, 1 subnets
C   10.0.1.0 is directly connected, Ethernet0/0

Router_A does receive updates relating to network 10.0.0.0, but not to network 10.0.4.0. Router_A will send all packets with a destination address of 10.0.0.0 out of the Ethernet interface.

Subnets are *not* carried across different major networks.

These updates are ignored because the metric is higher than the directly connected network of 10.0.0.0.

Figures 6.7 and 6.8 show that Router_A receives an update relating to network 10.0.0.0 but assumes the default mask and discards the update as not being the best way to get to the destination.

FIGURE 6.7   IGRP Debug

```
Router_A#debug ip igrp tr
IGRP protocol debugging is on
Router_A#
IGRP: received update from 172.16.1.2 on Serial0/0
      network 10.0.0.0, metric 8576 (neighbor 1100)
IGRP: sending update to 255.255.255.255 via Ethernet0/0 (10.0.1.1).
      network 172.16.0.0, metric=8476
IGRP: sending update to 255.255.255.255 via Serial0/0 (172.16.1.1)
      network 10.0.0.0, metric=1100
```

The composite metric of 8576 is higher than the metric of a directly connected network. Therefore Router_A will discard the routing update pertaining to network 10.0.0.0 that is received from the serial interface.

FIGURE 6.8   IP RIP Debug

```
Router_A#debug ip rip
RIP protocol debugging is on
Router_A#
RIP: received v1 update from 172.16.1.2 on Serial0/0
      10.0.0.0 in 1 hops
RIP: sending v1 update to 255.255.255.255 via Ethernet0/0 (10.0.1.1)
      network 172.16.0.0, metric 1
RIP: sending v1 update to 255.255.255.255 via Serial0/0 (172.16.1.1)
      network 10.0.0.0, metric 1
```

IP RIP uses hop count as its metric therefore, 1 hop away is a higher metric than a directly connected network. The RIP update received from the serial link will be discarded.

With a discontiguous network and a classful routing protocol the routers do not see a true picture of the network topology.

Because we have a discontiguous network and a classful routing protocol Router_A gets a distorted view of the network topology. This distorted view is represented in Figure 6.9

FIGURE 6.9
Distorted View of
the Network
Topology

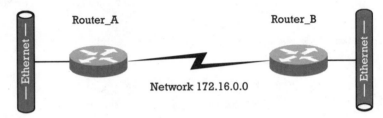

Figure 6.9 illustrates the view that Router_A has two ways to get to network 10.0.1.0. Router_A will always send a packet destined for network 10.0.0.0 to the Ethernet 0 interface.

Now let us examine another discontiguous network, but we will throw in another router. Keep in mind we have broken the rule of keeping our addressing scheme contiguous, which means we should see some problems with the routing tables. Refer to Figure 6.10.

FIGURE 6.10
Discontiguous
Addressing-2

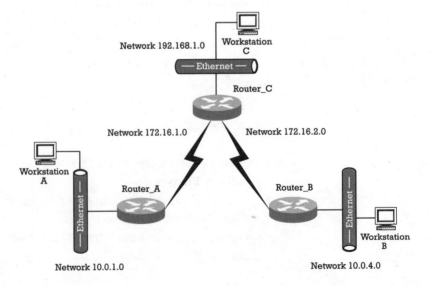

FIGURE 6.11   Router_C Routing Table

```
Router_C#sh ip route
Codes: C - connected, S - static, I - IGRP, R - RIP, M - mobile, B - BGP
    D - EIGRP, EX - EIGRP external, O - OSPF, IA - OSPF inter area
    N1 - OSPF NSSA external type 1, N2 - OSPF NSSA external type 2
    E1 - OSPF external type 1, E2 - OSPF external type 2, E - EGP
    i - IS-IS, L1 - IS-IS level-1, L2 - IS-IS level-2, * - candidate default
    U - per-user static route, o - ODR

Gateway of last resort is not set

    172.16.0.0/24 is subnetted, 2 subnets
C       172.16.1.0 is directly connected, Serial1
C       172.16.2.0 is directly connected, Serial0
```
I   10.0.0.0/8 [100/8576] via 172.16.1.1, 00:00:09, Serial1
**   [100/8576] via 172.16.2.1, 00:00:19, Serial0**

Referring to the bold lines in Figure 6.11, Router_C "thinks" it can get
to network 10.0.0.0 in two different ways, through Serial 1 or Serial 0.

Router_C has no way to distinguish between the different subnets of
"network 10" because the subnets of a classful routing protocol are not
carried across different major networks.

Since Router_C thinks it has two ways to get to network 10.0.0.0 it
will load balance the traffic over the two serial interfaces. One packet
will go out Serial 0, the next will use Serial 1, then back to Serial 0, etc.

Figure 6.12 represents pings from Router_C to network 10.0.4.1

FIGURE 6.12   Pings from Router_C

```
Router_C#ping 10.0.4.1
Type escape sequence to abort.
Sending 5, 100-byte ICMP Echos to 10.0.4.1, timeout is 2 seconds:
U!.!U
Success rate is 40 percent (2/5), round-trip min/avg/max = 4/4/4 ms
Router_C#ping 10.0.4.1
```

continued on next page

Type escape sequence to abort.

Sending 5, 100-byte ICMP Echos to 10.0.4.1, timeout is 2 seconds:

!U!.!

Success rate is 60 percent (3/5), round-trip min/avg/max = 4/4/4 ms

----

10.0.4.1 will be located with every other ping probe, resulting in a 50% average success rate.

Now we will break another rule and NOT use the same subnet mask with a classful routing protocol.

Figure 6.13 illustrates a mask of 255.255.255.0 for the serial link and a mask of 255.255.0.0 for the Ethernet links

FIGURE 6.13

Different Masks for the Same Major Network

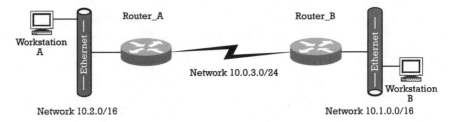

Router_A now has no way of knowing the true topology of this network. We could speculate on what will happen when Router_A attempts to route a packet, but what is the point!

The bottom line is that this IP addressing design is wrong and needs to be changed.

The routing table shows Router_A informing us that network 10.0.0.0 is variably subnetted. This is not a good thing!

FIGURE 6.14   Router_A Routing Table

Router_A#sh ip route

Codes: C - connected, S - static, I - IGRP, R - RIP, M - mobile, B - BGP

   D - EIGRP, EX - EIGRP external, O - OSPF, IA - OSPF inter area

   N1 - OSPF NSSA external type 1, N2 - OSPF NSSA external type 2

   E1 - OSPF external type 1, E2 - OSPF external type 2, E - EGP

   i - IS-IS, L1 - IS-IS level-1, L2 - IS-IS level-2, * - candidate default

   U - per-user static route, o - ODR

continued on next page

Gateway of last resort is not set

10.0.0.0/8 is variably subnetted, 2 subnets, 2 masks

C   10.2.0.0/16 is directly connected, Ethernet0/0

C   10.0.3.0/24 is directly connected, Serial0/0

A classful routing protocol presents the network designer with some severe restrictions.

Not only does the network need to be configured in a contiguous manner, but there could be a waste of IP addresses.

We will discuss these restrictions and some solutions in later chapters.

Figure 6.15 is a summary outline of classful and classless routing protocols.

FIGURE 6.15   Classful and Classless Routing Protocols

A. Classful Routing Protocols
    1. IP RIPv1
    2. IGRP
    3. IPX RIP (Novell)
    4. RTMP (Apple)

B. Classless Routing Protocols

    1. EIGRP
    2. OSPF
    3. IS-IS
    4. NLSP (Novell)
    5. IP RIPv2

Summary

- A classful routing protocol does not communicate subnet masks across different major networks.
- A contiguous addressing scheme must be used with a classful routing protocol.

Exercises

6.1: Why can we not use discontiguous addressing with a classful routing protocol?

6.2: Why must we use the same subnet mask for the same major network address?

Answers

6.1: Because a classful routing protocol does not communicate a subnet mask, we must use a contiguous addressing scheme.

6.2: Because a classful routing protocol does not communicate a subnet mask, we must use the same subnet mask for the same major network address.

CHAPTER 7

Variable Length Subnet Masking (VLSM)

Objectives

- Define VLSM.
- Describe the advantages of VLSM.

VLSM is the process by which we take a major network address and use different subnet masks at different points.

Figure 7.1 represents a topology where VLSM is not used. Throughout the entire topology the mask of 255.255.255.240 or /28 is used for network 192.16.1.0.

FIGURE 7.1

Addressing without VLSM

A classful routing protocol requires that we use the same mask for the same major network.

If we have to keep the subnet mask the same we encounter severe problems concerning addressing space.

In some cases the 255.255.255.240 mask might be the best mask for the Ethernet interfaces, but is it the best mask for the serial interfaces?

The 255.255.255.240 mask will allow 14 host addresses to be configured on each wire. We only need two hosts on the serial wire. Every time this mask is used on a serial link, 12 host addresses will be lost.

If we could use the 255.255.255.252 mask on the serial links we would have the perfect scenario, considering that this mask provides for two host addresses and that is exactly the number of hosts needed.

But if we use the /30 mask on the Ethernet links we would have a maximum of 2 hosts, which is not very practical.

VLSM allows the use of different masks for the same major network or we can say that VLSM allows us to change the length of the subnet mask for the same major network address.

VLSM will allow us to use the 255.255.255.252 mask on the serial interfaces while placing another mask on the multi-access links.

Figure 7.2 shows a mask of 255.255.255.252 on the serial links. Since this mask is only practical for serial links it has been nicknamed the *serial mask*. The 255.255.255.240 mask is still set for the Ethernet links. Since we have two different masks for the same major network we are using VLSM.

Consider the topology shown in Figure 7.3.

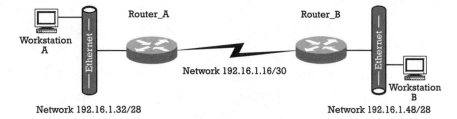

FIGURE 7.2

VLSM Addressing
Example

Network 192.16.1.16/30

Network 192.16.1.32/28   Network 192.16.1.48/28

With a single Class C address it would be impossible for us to configure all the links with an IP address without the use of VLSM.

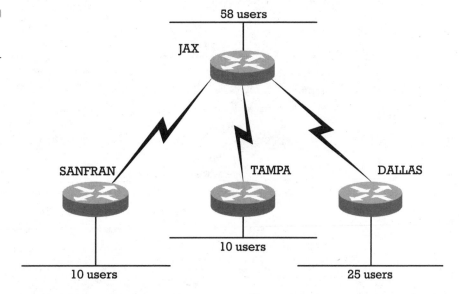

FIGURE 7.3

ARI Topology

58 users

JAX

SANFRAN   TAMPA   DALLAS

10 users

10 users   25 users

If we were to try to configure all these networks with the same mask we would run out of addressing space.

As an example, if we were to choose a mask that would allow for 58 users we would need the 255.255.255.192 mask.

This mask would only allow 2 networks to be addressed; we need 7.

VLSM makes addressing this network a simple task.

One addressing solution for ARI follows.

Serial Link Addressing

The serial mask to use is of course the 255.255.255.252 mask, since that mask provides for exactly two IP addresses, which is perfect for our needs. There are only two hosts on a serial connection; as result of using this mask, we do not waste any addresses.

Wire 199.10.11.4 to the JAX-SANFRAN link
Wire 199.10.11.8 to the JAX-TAMPA link
Wire 199.10.11.12 to the JAX-DALLAS link

IP addresses will be assigned as follows:

Router JAX

S0	199.10.11.5/30	255.255.255.252
S1	199.10.11.9/30	255.255.255.252
S2	199.10.11.13/30	255.255.255.252

At this point we have addressed 6 interfaces and used the addressing space 199.10.11.4–199.10.11.15

Now we will move on to the LAN interface.

Router SANFRAN

We need to have host addressing space for 10 users. The mask to use would be 255.255.255.240/28 if we were to use the 248 mask that would only provide for 6 addresses. The first available wire address we could use with the /28 mask would be 16. What I might do at this point is pick the next wire, which would be 32, this would leave us the lower address of 16–31 for additional serial connections in case our network grows. I could pick the 16 wire for SANFRAN; it is just a matter of preference to keep the lower addresses for the serial connections.

IP address of **E0** for **SANFRAN** will be **199.10.11.33/28**.

Router TAMPA

The same situation as SANFRAN: the next wire would be 48.

IP address of **E0** for **TAMPA** will be **199.10.11.49/28**.

Now we have burned all the addressing space up to 63, but we also have reserved the space of 16–31.

Router DALLAS

Our situation here is a little different because we need to have addressing space for 25 users.

Since the 240 mask only gave us a maximum of 14 users we will take the 255.255.255.224 which will give us a maximum of $2^5-2=30$ host addresses.

The first wire address available we can use with the 240 mask is 32, but be careful; if there is any place to make mistakes in VLSM it is right at this point. We have already used this addressing space at another location, so we will take the next wire address of 199.10.11.64.

IP address of **E0** for **DALLAS** will be **199.10.11.65/27**.

Router JAX

At this location we need addressing space for 58 users. The 240 mask only gave us 30 host addresses, so we will use the 255.255.255.192 mask. This mask will provide up to 62 users.

The first wire address for this mask would be 64, but again be careful; we already used this space for DALLAS. The next wire is 192.10.11.128.

IP address of **E0** for **JAX** is **199.10.11.129 /26**.

We have now addressed all of the router interfaces and have provided enough addressing space for all of the hosts at each location.

Address Summary

The addressing space in **bold** still remains for growth:

Addresses 199.10.11.4–15 used for serial connections
Addresses 199.10.11.16–31 not used
Addresses 199.10.11.32–63 used for SANFRAN & TAMPA
Addresses 199.10.11.64–95 used for Dallas
Addresses 199.10.11.96–127 not used
Addresses 199.10.11.128–191 used for JAX
Addresses 199.10.11.192 through 199.10.11.255 not used

IP Unnumbered

IP unnumbered is a Cisco specific IP addressing solution. Cisco allows us not to put an IP address on the serial interface, thereby saving address space. This solution would be used with a classful routing protocol. There are drawbacks to this solution; we will discuss IP unnumbered in greater detail in the configuration section.

When Can VLSM Be Used?

A classless routing protocol will allow the use of VLSM; we will cover classless routing protocols in the next chapter.

A classless routing protocol does communicate a subnet mask other than the default mask. The term classless comes from the fact that the mask does not have to be the default mask for each of the class addresses. In other words if we are using a Class B address, the mask communicated to other routers can be something other than 255.255.0.0.

Summary

- VLSM is an addressing process whereby we can use a different subnet mask for the same major network address.
- The major advantage of VLSM is that it helps preserve addressing space.
- VLSM can only be used with a classless routing protocol.

Exercises

7.1: What is VLSM?

7.2: What are the advantages of VLSM?

7.3: When can we use VLSM?

7.4: Examine Figure 7.4. Address all interfaces appropriately using the 192.16.15.0 address.

7.5: Why is the 255.255.255.252 mask considered the "serial mask"?

FIGURE 7.4

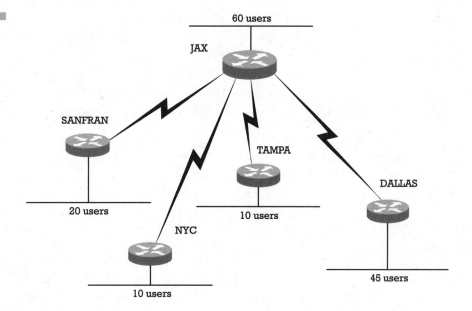

Answers

7.1: VLSM is variable-length masking, which allows different subnet masks to be used for the same major network.

7.2: VLSM preserves addressing space.

7.3: VLSM can only be used with a classless routing protocol.

7.4: One addressing solution is as follows; yours may be different:

Serial Links
Wire 192.16.15.4 to the JAX-SANFRAN link
Wire 192.16.15.8 to the JAX-NYC link
Wire 192.16.15.12 to the JAX-TAMPA link
Wire 192.16.15.16 to the JAX-DALLAS link

Router JAX Serial Addresses

S0	192.16.15.5/30	255.255.255.252
S1	192.16.15.9/30	255.255.255.252
S2	192.16.15.13/30	255.255.255.252
S3	192.16.15.17/30	255.255.255.252

Router SANFRAN

Use the mask of 255.255.255.224 on the Ethernet link.

S0 address of 192.16.15.6

E0 address of 192.16.15.65

Host address range 192.16.15.65 – 199.16.15.94

Wire address of 192.16.15.64

B/CAST 192.16.15. 95

Router NYC

Use the mask of 255.255.255.240 on the Ethernet link.

S0 address of 192.16.15.6

E0 address of 192.16.15.49

Host address range 192.16.15.49 – 199.16.15.63

Wire address of 192.16.15.48

Router TAMPA

Use the mask of 255.255.255.240 on the Ethernet link.

S0 address of 192.16.15.14

E0 address of 192.16.15.33

Host address range 192.16.15.33 – 199.16.15.47

Wire address of 192.16.15.32

Router DALLAS

Use the mask of 255.255.255.192 on the Ethernet link.

S0 address of 192.16.15.18

E0 address of 192.16.15.129

Host address range 192.16.15.129 – 199.16.15.190

Wire address of 192.16.15.128

B/CAST 199.16.15.191

Router JAX

Use the mask of 255.255.255.192 on the Ethernet link.

E0 address of 192.16.15.193

Host address range 192.16.15.193 – 199.16.15.254

Wire address of 192.16.15.192

B/CAST 192.16.15.255

7.5: The 255.255.255.252 mask is called the serial mask because it only allows for two hosts, which is only practical for serial links.

CHAPTER **8**

Classless
Routing Protocols

Objectives

■ Describe the advantages of a classless routing
protocol.

To be able to take advantage of VLSM and discontiguous network addressing we must use a routing protocol that will carry a subnet mask. Such a routing protocol is called *classless*.

Examples of classless routing protocols include Open Shortest Path First (OSPF), RIPv2, and Enhanced Interior Gateway Routing Protocol (EIGRP).

Let us take another look at the ARI scenario from Chapter 7 (Figure 8.1).

Given a single IP address and a classful routing protocol, there would be no way of configuring all hosts of ARI.

As a result, a classless routing protocol must be used.

FIGURE 8.1

ARI Topology

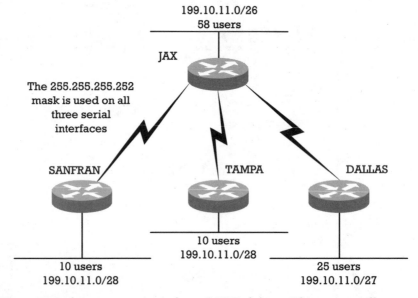

Figure 8.2 shows a portion of an OSPF debug. This output illustrates how router SANFRAN received updates relating to the serial connections and mask to TAMPA and DALLAS.

FIGURE 8.2   OSPF Debug

```
SANFRAN# debug ip ospf events
```
OSPF: Add Network Route to 192.16.15.8 Mask /30. Metric: 65, Next Hop: 192.16.15.5

continued on next page

> **OSPF: Add Network Route to 192.16.15.12 Mask /30. Metric: 65, Next Hop: 192.16.15.5**

Figures 8.3 and 8.4 show the OSPF and the EIGRP routing tables respectively, of JAX.

Router JAX "learned" all of the subnets of the 198.10.11.0 network.

FIGURE 8.3   OSPF Routing Table

```
JAX#sh ip route
Codes: C - connected, S - static, I - IGRP, R - RIP, M - mobile, B - BGP
    D - EIGRP, EX - EIGRP external, O - OSPF, IA - OSPF inter area
    N1 - OSPF NSSA external type 1, N2 - OSPF NSSA external type 2
    E1 - OSPF external type 1, E2 - OSPF external type 2, E - EGP
    i - IS-IS, L1 - IS-IS level-1, L2 - IS-IS level-2, * - candidate default
    U - per-user static route, o - ODR

Gateway of last resort is not set

    199.10.11.0/24 is variably subnetted, 7 subnets, 4 masks
O       199.10.11.64/27 [110/879] via 199.10.11.13, 00:01:03, Serial2
C       199.10.11.4/30 is directly connected, Serial0
C       199.10.11.12/30 is directly connected, Serial2
C       199.10.11.8/30 is directly connected, Serial1
C       199.10.11.128/26 is directly connected, Etherent0
O       199.10.11.32/28 [110/74] via 199.10.11.5, 00:01:03, Serial0
O       199.10.11.48/28 [110/74] via 199.10.11.9, 00:01:03, Serial1
```

FIGURE 8.4   EIGRP Routing Table

```
JAX#sh ip route
Codes: C - connected, S - static, I - IGRP, R - RIP, M - mobile, B - BGP
    D - EIGRP, EX - EIGRP external, O - OSPF, IA - OSPF inter area
    N1 - OSPF NSSA external type 1, N2 - OSPF NSSA external type 2
    E1 - OSPF external type 1, E2 - OSPF external type 2, E - EGP
```

continued on next page

i - IS-IS, L1 - IS-IS level-1, L2 - IS-IS level-2, * - candidate default
U - per-user static route, o - ODR

Gateway of last resort is not set

199.10.11.0/24 is variably subnetted, 7 subnets, 4 masks
D   199.10.11.64/27 [90/22798336] via 199.10.11.13, 00:00:40,
         Serial2
C   199.10.11.4/30 is directly connected, Serial0
C   199.10.11.12/30 is directly connected, Serial2
C   199.10.11.8/30 is directly connected, Serial1
C   199.10.11.128/26 is directly connected, Ethernet0
D   199.10.11.32/28 [90/2195456] via 199.10.11.5, 00:00:41,
         Serial0
D   199.10.11.48/28 [90/2195456] via 199.10.11.9, 00:00:40,
         Serial1

Notice that router JAX knows where each of the subnets are located.

Another advantage of using a classless routing protocol is that we can use a discontiguous addressing scheme.

This fact is illustrated in Figures 8.5 and Figure 8.6.

FIGURE 8.5

Discontiguous
Topology

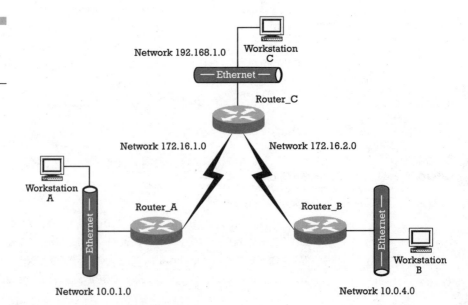

FIGURE 8.6   OSPF Routing Table

```
Router_C#sh ip route
Codes: C - connected, S - static, I - IGRP, R - RIP, M - mobile, B - BGP
       D - EIGRP, EX - EIGRP external, O - OSPF, IA - OSPF inter area
       N1 - OSPF NSSA external type 1, N2 - OSPF NSSA external type 2
       E1 - OSPF external type 1, E2 - OSPF external type 2, E - EGP
       i - IS-IS, L1 - IS-IS level-1, L2 - IS-IS level-2, * - candidate default
       U - per-user static route, o - ODR

Gateway of last resort is not set

     172.16.0.0/24 is subnetted, 2 subnets
C       172.16.1.0 is directly connected, Serial1
C       172.16.2.0 is directly connected, Serial0
     10.0.0.0/24 is subnetted, 2 subnets
O    10.0.1.0 [110/74] via 172.16.1.1, 00:02:41, Serial1
O    10.0.4.0 [110/74] via 172.16.2.1, 00:02:41, Serial0
```

Even though network 172.16.0.0 is in between network 10.0.0.0 Router_A can still distinguish which interface to use to get to either subnet of network 10.0.0.0.

A common question is "Which is the best routing protocol, OSPF or EIGRP?"

Keep in mind that OSPF is an open routing protocol, meaning that all vendors support OSPF. EIGRP on the other hand is a proprietary protocol belonging to Cisco. You must have all networking devices running the Cisco IOS to support EIGRP.

We will configure OSPF and EIGRP in later chapters.

Summary

■ A classless routing protocol allows us to use VLSM and a discontinguous addressing scheme.

Exercises

8.1: A classless routing protocol is better than a classful protocol. (T/F)

8.2: EIGRP is better than OSPF. (T/F)

8.3: Classful routing protocols can conserve IP addressing space. (T/F)

8.4: IGRP is an example of a classless routing protocol (T/F)

8.5: If we are using a discontinguous addressing scheme, a classless routing protocol must be used. (T/F)

Answers

8.1: False. It is very difficult to say which type of protocol is better. Certainly a classless protocol gives us more benefits, but it is more difficult to configure; this may present a problem for some administrators. Some older routers may have a problem with the additional processing required by using a classless protocol.

Certainly in a new environment with a well-trained staff I would opt for a classless protocol.

8.2: False. Keep in mind that EIGRP requires the Cisco IOS.

8.3: False

8.4: False.

8.5: True

CHAPTER **9**

Wild Card Masks

Objectives

■ Describe a Wild Card Mask.

No, we are not going to play poker and use wild cards. What we discuss is the concept of wild card or inverse masks.

Wild card masks are used throughout the Cisco IOS. Understanding this concept will help us with some major configuration features, which include but are not limited to:

■ Access lists
■ Route summarization
■ OSPF configuration
■ EIGRP configuration
■ Dial on Demand routing

In general wild card masks are used to identify particular networks, subnets, a host or group of hosts.

To understand a wild card mask, we should first review a subnet mask:

195.12.10.0 255.255.255.0

The above mask identifies the first 24 bits as network bits. We said that these bits could not be changed. Every time a 1 is in the mask it means do not change the corresponding bit in the address.

Everywhere there is a 0 in the mask it means the corresponding bit can be changed.

In the above example the network of 195.12.10.0 is registered to us, therefore do not change the first 24 bits. The last 8 bits can be changed to provide for subnets and host addressing.

Think of the inverse or a wild card mask working in the opposite manner.

Using the same example as above, the 255 is an octet made up of all 1's. This means the corresponding bits of the address can change. Where there are 0's these corresponding bits must remain the same as the address being tested.

In our example, it means we could have any address just as long as the last octet has a value of 0. This has no real meaning and you would never see an inverse mask of this form. So we will use an address and mask you might see.

In 192.12.10.0 0.0.0.255 the first three octets must be 192.12.10 and the last octet can have any value.

All 256 addresses of 192.12.10.0 – 192.12.10.255 would meet the criteria set by the inverse mask of 0.0.0.255.

If we had the statement:

Access-list 10 permit 192.12.10.0 0.0.0.255

All 256 (0–255) addresses listed above would be permitted.

Access-list 10 deny 143.10.2.0 0.0.0.255 would mean the subnet 143.10.2.0 would be denied.

Access-list 10 permit 123.13.2.14 0.0.0.0 identifies a single address because all 32 bits must remain the same or match the tested address.

Wild card masks, just like subnet masks, may have a value other than 0 or 255. For instance, we could have the scenario in Example 9.1:

Example 9.1

Suppose we wanted to permit the following Class C addresses:

192.12.8.2 through 192.12.15.0. We could identify the networks with the following 8 lines:

access-list 10 permit 192.12.8.0 0.0.0.255
access-list 10 permit 192.12.9.0 0.0.0.255
access-list 10 permit 192.12.10.0 0.0.0.255
access-list 10 permit 192.12.11.0 0.0.0.255
access-list 10 permit 192.12.12.0 0.0.0.255
access-list 10 permit 192.12.13.0 0.0.0.255
access-list 10 permit 192.12.14.0 0.0.0.255
access-list 10 permit 192.12.15.0 0.0.0.255

The use of a wild card mask allows us to shorten this access list to one line.

access-list 10 permit 192.12.8.0 0.0.7.255

We can easily see that the first two octets must each have a value of 192.12 and the 4th octet can have any value; but what about the 3rd octet?

TABLE 9.1

The Third Octet

	128	64	32	16	8	4	2	1	Value
Address	0	0	0	0	1	0	0	0	8
Mask	0	0	0	0	0	1	1	1	7
Possibilities									
	0	0	0	0	1	0	0	0	8
	0	0	0	0	1	0	0	1	9
	0	0	0	0	1	0	1	0	10
Addresses	0	0	0	0	1	0	1	1	11
	0	0	0	0	1	1	0	0	12
	0	0	0	0	1	1	0	1	13
	0	0	0	0	1	1	1	0	14
	0	0	0	0	1	1	1	1	15
	0	0	0	1	0	0	0	0	16

Since a value of 0 in the wild card mask means that the corresponding bits of the address must match the bits of the address being tested, and since a value of 1 in the wild card mask means that these corresponding bits can have any value, the 3rd octet can have a value between 8 and 15.

If we extend the addressing to include 16 (Example 9.1) we change the value of the fourth bit, thus not abiding by the wild card mask.

Example 9.2

What address and wild card mask would identify the following host addresses?

134.34.16.5
134.34.16.6

The first three octets will carry an inverse mask value of zero (0) because in both cases they are the same, but the 4th octet can have a value of 5 or 6.

Now we will take a close look at the 4th octet (Tables 9.2 and 9.3).

TABLE 9.2

The 4th Octet

128	64	32	16	8	4	2	1	Value	
0	0	0	0	0	1	0	1	5	
0	0	0	0	0	1	1	0	6	
0	0	0	0	0	0	1	1	3	Wild Card Mask

Table 9.2 illustrates that the first 6 bits of both addresses are the same. This alternatively means that the last two bits do not have to match. If we place a 1 in the last two bits the result is 3.

Therefore the wild card mask of 0.0.0.3 identifies 134.34.16.5 and 134.34.16.6, but these are NOT the only two addresses this wild card mask would include.

We include values of the 4th octet of 4 and 7 because if we are required to match only the first 6 bits of the 4th octet, the two bits can have any value including both being 0 or 1.

TABLE 9.3

The 4th Octet

128	64	32	16	8	4	2	1	Value
0	0	0	0	0	1	0	0	4
0	0	0	0	0	1	1	1	7

As a result, the following address and mask would identify all four of the above addresses:

134.34.16.4 0.0.0.3

It might be correctly argued that we could use other masks to identify the same addresses but other masks would include additional addresses and this may not be acceptable depending on use.

For instance, if we were to use an address and mask of 132.34.16.8 0.0.0.7 we would have identified 8 addresses. It is possible that it is not desirable to identify these additional addresses, as in the case of an access list where we might want to permit 4th octet values of 5 and 6 but not 9, 10, 11, 12, 13, 14, and 15.

Summary

■ A wild card mask can be used to identify one or more network or host addresses

Exercises

9.1: How many addresses would 145.16.15.7 0.0.0.0 identify?

9.2: How many address would 145.16.32.8 0.0.0.7 identify?

9.3: What addresses would be identified by Exercise 9.1?

9.4: What addresses would be identified by Exercise 9.2?

9.5: What address and mask would identify addresses within the following range: 192.16.16.80 through 192.16.16.95?

Answers

9.1: 1 address, because the mask says to match all 32 bits

9.2: 8 addresses

9.3: The single address of 145.16.15.7

9.4:
145.16.32.8
145.16.32.9
145.16.32.10
145.16.32.11
145.16.32.12
145.16.32.13
145.16.32.14
145.16.32.15

9.5: 192.16.16.80 0.0.0.15

CHAPTER 10

Route Summarization and Classless Interdomain Routing (CIDR)

Objectives

- Describe route summarization.
- Describe the advantages of route summarization.
- Describe a CIDR block.

Route Summarization is a technique that allows a router to have a single entry in the routing table that points to several different networks.

There are two main advantages of route summarization:

1. Reduces the size of routing tables
2. Reduces routing processing

Reducing the size of a routing table can have a positive effect on the router. If a router has fewer entries in a routing table, less memory will be required to keep track of those routes.

If a route that is being summarized goes down, that topology change will remain localized; routers that are not in the local area will not have to create new routing tables.

FIGURE 10.1

Route

Summarization

Topology

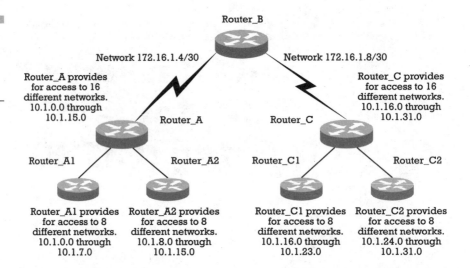

In Figure 10.1, without route summarization Router_B would have 32 separate entries in the routing table that would identify the individual networks of Routers A1, A2, C1, and C2. Router_A and Router_C each would require 16 unique router entries.

Let us also assume that if network 10.1.25.0 should go down, Router_C2 would notify Router_C, which in turn would notify Router_B that this topology change has taken place. Router_B would then communicate this change to Router_A and so on. All routers would create a new routing table based upon this new information.

With route summarization configured, Router_B would have two entries in its routing table that would, in effect, point to these 16 networks. One entry would point to Router_A for networks 10.1.0.0 through 10.1.15.0 and the other entry would point to Router_B for networks 10.1.16.0 through 10.1.31.0.

If network 10.1.25.0 should go down Router_C2 would not need to notify Router_B or Router_C that this topology change has taken place.

Route summarization can be compared to the way in which ZIP codes work.

The first digit of a ZIP code identifies a national area, a 3 for example is the southeast area, while a 9 in the first place identifies the West Coast, Alaska, and Hawaii.

So if I mail a letter to Honolulu, HI from Tallahassee, FL, Tallahassee post office employees do not care about the last four digits of the ZIP code. They know that this letter is going to the West Coast. At some point down the road a post office will look at the next two digits, which identify a sectional center. Finally the remaining two digits identify a single post office.

If you are doing a mass mailing and you bag your envelopes so that all the ZIP codes share the same first three digits you save money because this reduces the processing required by the post office to forward your letter.

In the same way Router_B does not care what specific network a packet is destined for. Router_B just needs to know what "range" the network falls into.

If Router_B receives a packet with a destination network address of 10.10.4.0, Router_B would send this packet to Router_A because the destination address falls into the range of 10.10.0.0 – 10.10.15.0.

At this point do not be worried by how the routers will be configured; we will do that in a later chapter. The objective here is to learn the concept.

Now think back to the early 60s, when the U.S. Postal Service designed the ZIP code scheme.

If they had assigned ZIP codes at random, computers and reading devices would have had to look at all 5 digits before making a forwarding decision.

For instance, suppose 10001 identified NYC and 10002 identified LA. With this type of random scheme we could not make any conclusions concerning location by looking at the first few digits.

This is the same situation if we have IP addresses that have been randomly assigned. No conclusions can be drawn, therefore the routers would be required to have each unique entry in the routing table. A router would be forced to look at all the network bits before it could make a forwarding decision.

If you design your IP addressing scheme in such a way that the first part of the address defines a region you save processing time at the router.

In the example above we have a contiguous addressing scheme. When we have addresses that are contiguous we can summarize. These networks were assigned planning to take advantage of route summarization.

If addresses are assigned haphazardly, summarization is impossible.

What makes a series of IP addresses contiguous?

When IP addresses share the same high order bits the addresses can be summarized.

Now go back to our ZIP code analogy; if we have ZIP codes 1xxxx and 9xxxx, can these envelopes be placed in the same bag en route to their destination? No, because they do not share the same high-order bits. Two envelopes with 1xxxx and 1xxxx can be put in the same bag because they do share the same high-order bits.

One can easily see the advantage of having IP addresses that share the same high-order bits. To illustrate what is meant by high-order bits we will use the 32 addresses from our example above.

There is no question that in our example the 16 high-order bits (first two octets) are the same for all 32 addresses; but do they have more than just these 16 bits in common? For a closer look at the 3rd octet, refer to Table 10.1.

3RD OCTET VALUES

TABLE 10.1	128	64	32	16	8	4	2	1	
Summarization Bits	0	0	0	0	0	0	0	0	0
for Router A and	0	0	0	0	0	0	0	1	1
Router C	0	0	0	0	0	0	1	0	2
	0	0	0	0	0	0	1	1	3
	0	0	0	0	0	1	0	0	4
	0	0	0	0	0	1	0	1	5
	0	0	0	0	0	1	1	0	6
	0	0	0	0	0	1	1	1	7
	0	0	0	0	1	0	0	0	8
	0	0	0	0	1	0	0	1	9
	0	0	0	0	1	0	1	0	10
	0	0	0	0	1	0	1	1	11
	0	0	0	0	1	1	0	0	12
	0	0	0	0	1	1	0	1	13
	0	0	0	0	1	1	1	0	14
	0	0	0	0	1	1	1	1	15
	0	0	0	1	0	0	0	0	16
	0	0	0	1	0	0	0	1	17
	0	0	0	1	0	0	1	0	18
	0	0	0	1	0	0	1	1	19
	0	0	0	1	0	1	0	0	20
	0	0	0	1	0	1	0	1	21
	0	0	0	1	0	1	1	0	22
	0	0	0	1	0	1	1	1	23
	0	0	0	1	1	0	0	0	24
	0	0	0	1	1	0	0	1	25
	0	0	0	1	1	0	1	0	26
	0	0	0	1	1	0	1	1	27
	0	0	0	1	1	1	0	0	28
	0	0	0	1	1	1	0	1	29
	0	0	0	1	1	1	1	0	30
	0	0	0	1	1	1	1	1	31
	0	0	1	0	0	0	0	0	32

Networks Connected to A1 & A2 — Router A

Networks Connected to C1 & C2 — Router C

Notice that the first 16 addresses share the same 4 high-order bits of 0000; these are the networks connected to Routers A1 and A2.

The next 16 addresses share the same 4 high order bits of 0001; these are the networks connected to Routers C1 and C2.

Simply put, Router_A will "tell" Router_B:

"If the bit pattern of the first 20 bits is 00001010 00001010 0000 send the packet to me."

Router_C will "tell" Router_B:

"If the bit pattern of the first 20 bits is 00001010 00001010 0001 send the packet to me."

It is not necessary for Router_B to look at the remaining 12 bits, just as it is not necessary for the post office to look at the entire ZIP code.

Notice that Router_C cannot summarize the "32" address because the bit pattern changes.

In the same way that Router_A and Router_C can summarize their networks to Router_B, Routers A1 and A2 can summarize their networks to Router_A.

And of course Routers C1 and C2 can summarize their networks to Router_C (Table 10.2).

With route summarization configured:

Router_A1 will be the destination router when the first 21 bits are 00001010 00001010 00000.

Router_A2 will be the destination router when the first 21 bits are 00001010 00001010 00001.

Router_C1 will be the destination router when the first 21 bits are 00001010 00001010 00010.

Router_C2 will be the destination router when the first 21 bits are 00001010 00001010 00011.

When using private addresses we can easily design our addressing scheme to use contiguous addressing to take advantage of summarization.

Classless Interdomain Routing (CIDR)

CIDR is a technique to provide multiple IP addresses in a contiguous block.

You may have heard the term "CIDR block". This refers to a set of contiguous addresses.

TABLE 10.2

Summarization Bits for Routers A1, A2, C1, and C2

128	64	32	16	8	4	2	1	
0	0	0	0	0	0	0	0	0
0	0	0	0	0	0	0	1	1
0	0	0	0	0	0	1	0	2
0	0	0	0	0	0	1	1	3
0	0	0	0	0	1	0	0	4
0	0	0	0	0	1	0	1	5
0	0	0	0	0	1	1	0	6
0	0	0	0	0	1	1	1	7
0	0	0	0	1	0	0	0	8
0	0	0	0	1	0	0	1	9
0	0	0	0	1	0	1	0	10
0	0	0	0	1	0	1	1	11
0	0	0	0	1	1	0	0	12
0	0	0	0	1	1	0	1	13
0	0	0	0	1	1	1	0	14
0	0	0	0	1	1	1	1	15
0	0	0	1	0	0	0	0	16
0	0	0	1	0	0	0	1	17
0	0	0	1	0	0	1	0	18
0	0	0	1	0	0	1	1	19
0	0	0	1	0	1	0	0	20
0	0	0	1	0	1	0	1	21
0	0	0	1	0	1	1	0	22
0	0	0	1	0	1	1	1	23
0	0	0	1	1	0	0	0	24
0	0	0	1	1	0	0	1	25
0	0	0	1	1	0	1	0	26
0	0	0	1	1	0	1	1	27
0	0	0	1	1	1	0	0	28
0	0	0	1	1	1	0	1	29
0	0	0	1	1	1	1	0	30
0	0	0	1	1	1	1	1	31
0	0	1	0	0	0	0	0	32

195.10.12.0 255.255.252.0 identifies 4 Class C addresses:

195.10.12.0
195.10.13.0
195.10.14.0
195.10.15.0

Remember what we learned earlier, that a mask identifies bits that cannot be changed. In this example if we can NOT change the most significant 6 bits of the 3rd octet that means we can change the least significant 2 bits.

Table 10.3 shows all the bit combinations the above address and mask identify:

TABLE 10.3

Combinations When the Least Significant 2 bits can be Changed

3rd Octet								
128	64	32	16	8	4	2	1	
0	0	0	0	1	1	0	0	12
0	0	0	0	1	1	0	1	13
0	0	0	0	1	1	1	0	14
0	0	0	0	1	1	1	1	15
0	0	0	1	0	0	0	0	16

I have also included the "16" address to show how the bit pattern changes and therefore is not included.

Keep the big picture in mind; if we have a CIDR block we can summarize addresses and router summarization is a good thing.

Summary

- Summarization is a process that allows a router to have a single entry that identifies multiple networks.
- Summarization reduces router processing and requires less router memory to keep track of routes.
- CIDR blocks define a contiguous set of addresses; this is required to configure route summarization.

Exercises

10.1: The following addresses can be summarized into a single address and mask. What is the address and mask that would identify these addresses ONLY?
192.16.17.16
192.16.17.17
192.16.17.18
192.16.17.19
192.16.17.20
192.16.17.21
192.16.17.22
192.16.17.23

10.2: Why is it a good thing if we can get a CIDR block from our ISP?

10.3: What does it mean when we say that addresses are contiguous?

10.4: Name two advantages of route summarization.

Answers

10.1: 192.16.17.16 0.0.0.7

10.2: A CIDR block is a set of contiguous addressing; we can summarize contiguous addressing.

10.3: Contiguous addresses share the same high order bits.

10.4: Route summarization:

  1. Reduces the size of routing tables
  2. Reduces routing processing

CHAPTER **11**

Hello Cisco!

Objectives

- Configuring a Cisco router with an IP address using the "setup dialog."
- Configuring a Cisco router with an IP address using the "configuration mode."

Now that we know how to calculate a subnet it is time to see how this address is configured on a Cisco router.

A basic understanding of the Cisco IOS and the Command Line Interface (CLI) is assumed.

There are two ways to enter the IP address on a interface.

Setup Dialog: To enter the setup dialog enter the command "setup" at the enable prompt.

Configuration Mode: To enter the configuration mode use the "configuration terminal" command.

All bolded lines in Figure 11.1 pertain to configuring an IP address.

FIGURE 11.1 The Setup Dialog

```
tallahassee#setup

       --- System Configuration Dialog ---

At any point you may enter a question mark '?' for help.
Use ctrl-c to abort configuration dialog at any prompt.
Default settings are in square brackets '[]'.

Continue with configuration dialog? [yes/no]: y

First, would you like to see the current interface summary? [yes]: y

Interface    IP-Address   OK? Method  Status                     Protocol
BRIO         unassigned   YES unset   administratively down      down
BRIO:1       unassigned   YES unset   administratively down      down
BRIO:2       unassigned   YES unset   administratively down      down
Serial0      150.20.0.2   YES NVRAM   down                       down
Serial1      20.0.0.2     YES NVRAM   down                       down
Serial2      175.20.0.2   YES NVRAM   down                       down
Serial3      unassigned   YES unset   administratively down      down
TokenRing0   unassigned   YES unset   administratively down      down

Configuring global parameters:

    Enter host name [tallahassee]:
The enable secret is a one-way cryptographic secret used
instead of the enable password when it exists.
```

continued on next page

Enter enable secret [<Use current secret>]:
The enable password is used when there is no enable secret
and when using older software and some boot images.

Enter enable password []:
Enter virtual terminal password []:
Configure SNMP Network Management? [no]:
Configure LAT? [yes]: n
Configure AppleTalk? [no]:
Configure DECnet? [no]:
Configure IP? [yes]:
    Configure IGRP routing? [yes]:
        Your IGRP autonomous system number [100]:
Configure CLNS? [no]:
Configure IPX? [no]:
Configure Vines? [no]:
Configure XNS? [no]:
Configure Apollo? [no]:
Configure bridging? [no]:
Enter ISDN BRI Switch Type [none]:

Configuring interface parameters:
Configuring interface BRI0:
    Is this interface in use? [no]:
Configuring interface Serial0:
    Is this interface in use? [yes]: y
    Configure IP on this interface? [yes]:
    Configure IP unnumbered on this interface? [no]:
        IP address for this interface [150.20.0.2]: 192.20.30.17
        Number of bits in subnet field [0]: 4
    Class C network is 192.20.30.0, 4 subnet bits; mask is /28

Configuring interface Serial1:
    Is this interface in use? [yes]:
    Configure IP on this interface? [yes]:
    Configure IP unnumbered on this interface? [no]:
        IP address for this interface [20.0.0.2]: 192.20.30.33
        Number of bits in subnet field [4]:
    Class C network is 192.20.30.0, 4 subnet bits; mask is /28

continued on next page

Configuring interface Serial2:
   Is this interface in use? [yes]:
   Configure IP on this interface? [yes]:
   Configure IP unnumbered on this interface? [no]:
      IP address for this interface [175.20.0.2]: 192.20.30.49
      Number of bits in subnet field [4]:
      Class C network is 192.20.30.0, 4 subnet bits; mask is /28

Configuring interface Serial3:
   Is this interface in use? [no]: n

Configuring interface TokenRing0:
   Is this interface in use? [no]: n

The following configuration command script was created:

```
hostname tallahassee
enable secret 5 $1$O09t$de1iCmnOqYh5Tqp.r./bV.
enable password sails
line vty 0 4
password sailing
no snmp-server
!
no appletalk routing
no decnet routing
ip routing
no clns routing
no ipx routing
no vines routing
no xns routing
no apollo routing
no bridge 1
isdn switch-type none
!
interface BRI0
shutdown
no ip address
!
interface Serial0
```

continued on next page

```
ip address 192.20.30.17 255.255.255.240
no mop enabled
!
interface Serial1
ip address 192.20.30.33 255.255.255.240
no mop enabled
!
interface Serial2
ip address 192.20.30.49 255.255.255.240
no mop enabled
!
interface Serial3
shutdown
no ip address
!
interface TokenRing0
shutdown
no ip address
!
router igrp 100
redistribute connected
network 192.20.30.0
!
end
Use this configuration? [yes/no]: y
```

Figure 11.1 shows that serial interfaces 0, 1, and 2 were configured with addresses 192.20.30.17, 192.20.30.33, and 192.20.30.49 respectively. The same mask 255.255.255.240 was configured on all three interfaces. When using the setup dialog we configure the subnet bits; in this case we are using four bits to describe subnets, hence the 255.255.255.240 mask.

When we answer yes, the setup dialog saves the configuration file to NVRAM.

TIP

The second way to configure an IP address is to use the configuration mode (Figure 11.2).

FIGURE 11.2   The Configuration Mode

san-francisco#config t

Enter configuration commands, one per line. End with CNTL/Z.

san-francisco(config)#int s0/0

san-francisco(config-if)#ip address 192.20.30.50 255.255.255.240

san-francisco(config-if)#int e0/0

san-francisco(config-if)#ip address 192.20.30.113 255.255.255.240

Figure 11.2 illustrates the configuration of a 3600 router. A 3600 is called a modular router because cards can be inserted into slots. In such a router we identify the interface by slot/port. In the case of the serial interface, slot 0 and port 0 or interfaces 0/0. On a fixed configuration router there are no slots, so to identify an interface it would simply be int s0.

Notice that when we identify interfaces the prompt does not change; be careful always to be aware of the interface that is currently identified. When configuring several interfaces it is not that difficult to lose track of the current interface.

The "configuration mode" requires the network mask, NOT the number of subnet bits, as in the case of the "setup dialog."

Addresses can be removed by using the "no form" of the command as shown in Figure 11.3.

FIGURE 11.3   Using the "no" command form

san-francisco (config) #int s0/0

san-francisco (config-if) #no ip address 192.20.30.50

255.255.255.240

san-francisco (config-if) #int e0/0

san-francisco (config-if) #no ip address 192.20.30.113

255.255.255.240

Use the "no form" of a command to remove any line of configuration.

While the setup dialog automatically saves the configuration to NVRAM, the configuration mode does not.

To save configuration changes to NVRAM, use the "copy run start" as shown in Figure 11.4.

FIGURE 11.4   Saving Configuration Changes to NVRAM

```
san-francisco#copy run start
Building configuration...
[OK]
san-francisco#
```

FIGURE 11.5   Saving Configuration changes to a TFTP Server

```
router_b>en
router_b#copy run tftp
Remote host[]? 132.10.1.2
Name of configuration file to write [router_b-confg]?
Write file router_b-confg on host 132.10.1.2? [confirm]
Building configuration...
[OK]
router_b#
```

As Figure 11.5 illustrates we will supply the router with the address of the TFTP server and the name of the file that will be used on the TFTP server. In this cast router_b-confg will be the file name; this means the default will be saved to the 132.10.1.2.

In my opinion the best way to save a configuration file, external to the router, is on a disk. This way in case we do lose the configuration of a router it is simply a case of copying and pasting the config back into the router. Use the "show run" command, block out the configuration lines and "edit-copy". Open notepad then "edit-paste". If the configuration file is lost at the console port of the router, get into configuration mode then "edit-paste to host". Of course the above example assumes a Windows platform.

Summary

The "setup dialog" can be used to configure IP addresses. This dialog requires that the number of subnet bits be identified. When the setup changes are accepted, these changes are automatically saved to NVRAM.

The "configuration mode" can also be used to configure IP addresses. This mode requires the subnet mask to be configured. All changes must be saved to NVRAM with the "copy run start" command. The configuration file may also be saved to a TFTP server or to a disk.

Exercises

11.1: What are the two modes used to configure IP addresses on a Cisco router?

11.2: The "setup" mode will automatically save configuration changes to NVRAM. (T/F)

11.3: When using the "configuration" mode what command will save configuration changes to NVRAM?

11.4: When using the "setup" mode the number of network bits is required. (T/F)

11.5: If the address of 163.24.5.5 /32 were to be configured using the "setup" mode, how would you answer the following question?

   Number of bits in subnet field [0]:

11.6: If the address of 163.24.5.5 /32 were to be configured using the "configuration" mode, what configuration line would be entered?

Answers

11.1: "setup" mode; "configuration" mode

11.2: True

11.3: "copy run start"

11.4: False; the number of subnet bits is required.

11.5:

Number of bits in subnet field [0]:14

8 bits from the 3rd octet and 6 bits from the 4th octet for a total of 14.

11.6: IP address 163.24.5.5 255.255.255.252

CHAPTER 12

Configuring
IP RIP

Objectives

- Describe the process of configuring IP RIP on a Cisco router.
- Describe the process of configuring a static route.
- Describe the process of configuring a default route.

This discussion only pertains to IP RIP v1.

Routing Information Protocol was defined in 1988, but the protocol had been in use prior to that date. RIP uses hop count as its metric. In the days when links were relatively homogeneous, hop count was an acceptable metric. In recent years, with the advent of widely used WAN links with a varying degree of bandwidth, RIP is less desirable. For instance, if a router could get to a specific network in two different ways and one of those ways was a T1 and the other was a 19200 link, RIP would have no way to distinguish between these two ways if the hop count was the same.

In later chapters we will look at alternatives to IP RIP.

As we discussed earlier, RIP is a distance-vector and classful routing protocol and consequently does not support VLSM. When RIP is used, the IP addressing scheme must be contiguous.

Below is our network topology. We will configure RIP on all routers. Keep in mind that the actual configuration itself is an easy process; the difficult part is to understand the ramifications of the configuration. As an analogy, it only takes a pilot a few minutes to get a 747 airborne, but it takes years of experience to perform such a task successfully. It may only take a few seconds to configure a routing protocol, but it takes a lot longer to completely understand the ramifications of the configuration.

Refer to Figure 12.1 and Table 12.1.

FIGURE 12.1
Four-Router
Topology

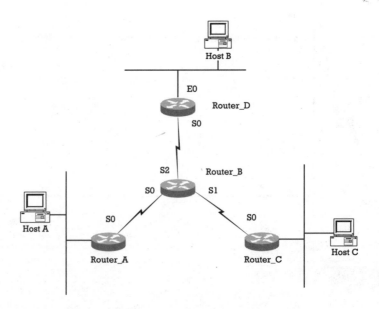

TABLE 12-1

Addresses to be used for Figure 12-1

	S0	S1	S2	E0
Router_A	10.10.8.9	N/A	N/A	10.10.1.1
Router_B	10.10.8.1	10.10.12.1	10.10.4.1	N/A
Router_C	10.10.12.9	N/A	N/A	10.10.2.1
Router_D	10.10.4.2	N/A	N/A	10.10.3.1
Mask	255.255.255.0	255.255.255.0	255.255.255.0	255.255.2̲5̲5.0

Configuration Commands

Figure 12.2 shows the commands to configure IP addresses and IP RIP on Router_D.

I have included the IP address configuration lines as a review.

The two IP RIP commands are in **bold**.

FIGURE 12.2   IP RIP Configuration Commands

Router_D# config t

Enter configuration commands, one per line. End with CNTL/Z.

Router_D(config)#int e0

Router_D(config-if)#ip address 10.10.3.1 255.255.255.0

Router_D(config-if)#int s0

Router_D(config-if)#ip address 10.10.4.2 255.255.255.0

~~Router_D(config-if)~~ **Router_D(config-if)#router rip** (INCORRECT)   Router_D(config)# Router riP

Router_D(config-router)#network 10.0.0.0

Router_D(config-router)#

Router_D#

%SYS-5-CONFIG_I: Configured from console by console

Router_D#

One of the first questions you might have is why we have not identified both subnets of the Class A address 10.0.0.0.

Remember that IP RIP is a classful routing protocol and therefore does not distinguish subnets of a network. If the address is a Class A, the mask is 255.0.0.0. Because of this fact, we need only to identify the major network.

Verifying Configuration

After Router_D is configured we should verify that our configuration is correct.

The "show run" command will help us verify that we have configured our addresses and the RIP protocol correctly.

Keep in mind that Cisco configuration statements can be truncated, therefore "sh run" is the same as "show running-config".

FIGURE 12.3   The "show run" Command

```
Router_D#show running-configuration
Building configuration...

Current configuration:
!
version 11.3
no service password-encryption
!
hostname Router_D
!
interface Ethernet0
   ip address 10.10.3.1 255.255.255.0
!
interface Serial0
   ip address 10.10.4.2 255.255.255.0
   no ip mroute-cache
   no fair-queue
   clockrate 56000
!
interface Serial 1
   no ip address
   shutdown
!
router rip
   network 10.0.0.0
!
ip classless
```

continued on next page

```
!
line con 0
line 1 8
line aux 0
line vty 0 4
!
end
```

Figure 12.3 shows that the proper addresses are configured on the correct interfaces and RIP will advertise network 10.0.0.0.

By using the command "show ip protocol" (Figure 12.4) we see that RIP is the protocol being used for network 10.0.0.0. We can also determine that Router_D is receiving RIP updates from 10.10.4.1, which is Router_B.

FIGURE 12.4   The "show ip protocol" Command

Router_D>show ip protocol
Routing Protocol is "rip"
    Sending updates every 30 seconds, next due in 3 seconds
    Invalid after 180 seconds, hold down 180, flushed after 240
    Outgoing update filter list for all interfaces is not set
    Incoming update filter list for all interfaces is not set
    Redistributing: rip
    Default version control: send version 1, receive any version

Interface	Send	Recv	Key-chain
Ethernet0	1	1 2	
Serial0	1	1 2	

Routing for Networks:
    10.0.0.0
Routing Information Sources:

Gateway	Distance	Last Update
10.10.4.1	120	00:00:10

Distance: (default is 120)

Viewing the Routing Table

Once all the routers are configured properly we can view the routing table of Router_D (Figure 12.5).

■■ ■■ ■■ ■■ ■■ ■■ ■■ ■■ ■■ ■■ ■■ ■■ ■■ ■■ ■■

FIGURE 12.5   The "show ip route" Command

Router_D#show ip route
Codes: C - connected, S - static, I - IGRP, R - RIP, M - mobile, B - BGP
   D - EIGRP, EX - EIGRP external, O - OSPF, IA - OSPF inter area
   N1 - OSPF NSSA external type 1, N2 - OSPF NSSA external type 2
   E1 - OSPF external type 1, E2 - OSPF external type 2, E - EGP
   i - IS-IS, L1 - IS-IS level-1, L2 - IS-IS level-2, * - candidate default
   U - per-user static route, o - ODR

Gateway of last resort is not set

   10.0.0.0/24 is subnetted, 6 subnets
R   10.10.1.0 [120/2] via 10.10.4.1, 00:00:25, Serial0
R   10.10.2.0 [120/2] via 10.10.4.1, 00:00:25, Serial0
C   10.10.3.0 is directly connected, Ethernet0
C   10.10.4.0 is directly connected, Serial0
R   10.10.8.0 [120/1] via 10.10.4.1, 00:00:25, Serial0
R   10.10.12.0 [120/1] via 10.10.4.1, 00:00:25, Serial0
Router_D#

Notice we have 6 routes. Two of these are connected to Router_D and are prefixed with a "C". Four routes are discovered through the RIP process; these are prefixed with an "R".

Because our address design is contiguous, the subnets of network 10.0.0.0 are communicated to its neighbors.

120 is the default administrative distance for IP RIP. The number that follows the administrative distance is the hop count to that network.

Reviewing the routing table, we see that it will take Router_D 2 hops to get to network 10.10.1.0.

There very often is confusion as to what actually is a hop. Think of it in this way; if a packet must go *through* a router to get to the destination, it is considered a hop.

In our example, Host A is 3 hops away from Host B, but Router_D is only 2 hops away from Network 10.10.1.0, since Router_D is not considered a hop.

I have only shown configuration for Router_D; to complete the configuration of the topology in Figure 12.1 all of the routers would be configured in the same manner.

In Figure 12.6 I have included, for your information, the additional configuration line for RIP v2.

RIP v2 is a classless routing protocol and therefore works in a very different way than RIP v1.

FIGURE 12.6   Configuration of IP RIP Version 2

```
Router(config-router)#router rip
Router(config-router)#version 2
Router(config-router)#network 10.0.0.0
Router(config-router)#
```

Configuring a Static Route

As we said in Chapter 5 there are times you may want to configure a static route. Please refer to Figure 12.7.

FIGURE 12.7   Configuring a Static Route

```
router_b(config)#ip route 10.10.10.5 ?
  A.B.C.D  Destination prefix mask

router_b(config)#ip route 10.10.10.5 255.255.255.0 ?
  A.B.C.D      Forwarding router's address
  BRI          ISDN Basic Rate Interface
  Null         Null interface
  Serial       Serial
  TokenRing    IEEE 802.5
router_b(config)#ip route 10.10.10.0 255.255.255.0 serial 0
router_b(config)#
```

Figure 12.7 illustrates that router_b should forward all IP packets with the destination subnet of 10.10.10.0 to its own Serial 0 interface. We also could have configured the next hop address.

When configuring a static route by using an interface, as was done in Figure 12.7, the static route will appear as a directly connected network (Figure 12.8).

FIGURE 12.8 Verifying a Static Route

```
router_b#sh ip route
Codes: C - connected, S - static, I - IGRP, R - RIP, M - mobile, B - BGP
    D - EIGRP, EX - EIGRP external, O - OSPF, IA - OSPF inter area
    N1 - OSPF NSSA external type 1, N2 - OSPF NSSA external type 2
    E1 - OSPF external type 1, E2 - OSPF external type 2, E - EGP
    i - IS-IS, L1 - IS-IS level-1, L2 - IS-IS level-2, * - candidate default
    U - per-user static route, o - ODR

Gateway of last resort is not set

    172.16.0.0/30 is subnetted, 1 subnets
C      172.16.7.4 is directly connected, Serial0
    10.0.0.0/24 is subnetted, 1 subnets
S      10.10.10.0 is directly connected, Serial0
```

Configuring a Default Route

When a default route is configured, the router will not send packets to the bit bucket when the destination route does not appear in the routing table. The packets will be sent to the default route. Refer to Figure 12.9.

FIGURE 12.9 Configuring and Verifying a Default Route

```
router_b(config)#ip default-network 172.17.0.0
router_b(config)#^Z
router_b#
```

continued on next page

```
%SYS-5-CONFIG_I: Configured from console by console
router_b#sh ip route
Codes: C - connected, S - static, I - IGRP, R - RIP, M - mobile, B - BGP
   D - EIGRP, EX - EIGRP external, O - OSPF, IA - OSPF inter area
   N1 - OSPF NSSA external type 1, N2 - OSPF NSSA external type 2
   E1 - OSPF external type 1, E2 - OSPF external type 2, E - EGP
   i - IS-IS, L1 - IS-IS level-1, L2 - IS-IS level-2, * - candidate default
   U - per-user static route, o - ODR
```

Gateway of last resort is 172.16.7.6 to network 172.17.0.0

```
R*    172.17.0.0/16 [120/1] via 172.16.7.6, 00:00:04, Serial0
      172.16.0.0/30 is subnetted, 1 subnets
C     172.16.7.4 is directly connected, Serial0
      10.0.0.0/24 is subnetted, 1 subnets
S     10.10.10.0 is directly connected, Serial0
```

Figure 12.9 illustrates that all packets whose destination address is not listed in the routing table will be sent to network 172.17.0.0, the gateway of last resort. The next-hop address is 172.16.7.6.

Summary

Configuring IP RIP is a relatively simple process requiring only a few lines of configuration.

First it is required that the protocol be configured with the "router rip" command, followed by all the major network numbers that will be advertised with the "network xx.xx.xx.xx" command.

The administrator places static routes in the routing table by using the "ip route" command.

The administrator may set a gateway of last resort or a default network by using the " ip default-network" command.

Exercises

12.1: Using Figure 12.1 and Table 12.1, what configuration steps would be required to configure Router_A with IP RIP?

12.2: Using Figure 12.1 and Table 12.1, what configuration steps would be required to configure Router_B with IP RIP?

12.3: Using Figure 12.1 and Table 12.1, what configuration steps would be required to configure Router_C with IP RIP?

12.4: What command would be used to verify the frequency of RIP updates?

12.5: What command would be used to verify IP address configuration?

12.6: What command would be used to view the routing table?

Answers

12.1:
Router_A# config t
Enter configuration commands, one per line. End with CNTL/Z.
Router_A(config)#int e0
Router_A(config-if)#ip address 10.10.1.1 255.255.255.0
Router_A(config-if)#int s0
Router_A(config-if)#ip address 10.10.8.9 255.255.255.0
Router_A(config-if)#router rip
Router_A(config-router)#network 10.0.0.0
Router_A(config-router)#
Router_A#
%SYS-5-CONFIG_I: Configured from console by console
Router_A#

12.2:
Router_B# config t
Enter configuration commands, one per line. End with CNTL/Z.

continued on next page

Router_B(config)#int s0
Router_B(config-if)#ip address 10.10.8.1 255.255.255.0
Router_B(config-if)#int s1
Router_B(config-if)#ip address 10.10.12.1 255.255.255.0
Router_B(config-if)#int s2
Router_B(config-if)#ip address 10.10.4.1 255.255.255.0

Router_B(config-if)#router rip
Router_B(config-router)#network 10.0.0.0
Router_B(config-router)#
Router_B#
%SYS-5-CONFIG_I: Configured from console by console
Router_B#

12.3:
Router_C# config t
Enter configuration commands, one per line. End with CNTL/Z.
Router_C(config)#int s0
Router_C(config-if)#ip address 10.10.12.9 255.255.255.0
Router_C(config-if)#int e0
Router_C(config-if)#ip address 10.10.2.1 255.255.255.0
Router_C(config-if)#router rip
Router_C(config-router)#network 10.0.0.0
Router_C(config-router)#
Router_C#
%SYS-5-CONFIG_I: Configured from console by console
Router_C#

12.4: "show ip protocol"

12.5: "show run"; "show ip interface" and "show interface" will also
provide information relating the IP addresses.

Router#sh ip interface e0
%SYS-5-CONFIG_I: Configured from console by console
Ethernet0 is administratively down, line protocol is down
  Internet address is 10.10.1.1/24
  Broadcast address is 255.255.255.255
  Address determined by setup command
  MTU is 1500 bytes

continued on next page

Helper address is not set

Directed broadcast forwarding is enabled

Multicast reserved groups joined: 224.0.0.9

Outgoing access list is not set

Inbound access list is not set

Proxy ARP is enabled

Security level is default

Split horizon is enabled

ICMP redirects are always sent

ICMP unreachables are always sent

ICMP mask replies are never sent

IP fast switching is enabled

IP fast switching on the same interface is disabled

IP multicast fast switching is enabled

Router Discovery is disabled

IP output packet accounting is disabled

IP access violation accounting is disabled

TCP/IP header compression is disabled

Probe proxy name replies are disabled

Gateway Discovery is disabled

Policy routing is disabled

Network address translation is disabled

Router#

Router#sh int e0

Ethernet0 is administratively down, line protocol is down

Hardware is Lance, address is 0060.09c3.df60 (bia 0060.09c3.df60)

Internet address is 10.10.1.1/24

MTU 1500 bytes, BW 10000 Kbit, DLY 1000 usec, rely 255/255,
load 1/255

Encapsulation ARPA, loopback not set, keepalive set (10 sec)

ARP type: ARPA, ARP Timeout 04:00:00

Last input never, output 2d02h, output hang never

Last clearing of "show interface" counters never

Queueing strategy: fifo

Output queue 0/40, 0 drops; input queue 0/75, 0 drops

5 minute input rate 0 bits/sec, 0 packets/sec

5 minute output rate 0 bits/sec, 0 packets/sec

continued on next page

```
O packets input, O bytes, O no buffer
Received O broadcasts, O runts, O giants, O throttles
O input errors, O CRC, O frame, O overrun, O ignored, O abort
O input packets with dribble condition detected
81 packets output, 13498 bytes, O underruns
```

12.6: "show ip route"

CHAPTER 13

Configuring IGRP

Objective

- Describe the IGRP Configuration Process.

Interior Gateway Routing Protocol (IGRP) is a Cisco proprietary protocol. Cisco defines IGRP as an advanced distance-vector routing protocol.

IGRP is also a classful routing protocol, which means it does not support VLSM.

IGRP has several unique features, which is why Cisco calls it an *advanced* routing protocol.

Those features are as follows:

1. **Scalability**—IGRP is not limited to 15 hops as is IP RIP.
2. **Event-triggered updates**—IGRP sends updates when topology changes occur.
3. **Multiple paths**—IGRP has the ability to keep track of multiple routes that have an equal as well as an unequal metric.
4. **Sophisticated metric**—IGRP uses a combination of metrics to determine the best route.

The metrics are:

- Bandwidth
- Delay
- Load
- Reliability
- Maximum Transmission Unit (MTU)

As we discussed in the previous chapter, IP RIP bases its routing decision based on hop count.

IGRP determines the best path by accounting for bandwidth as part of the metric, thereby providing for a more sophisticated determination of the best path. Refer to Chapter 5 for a review of this concept.

Refer to Figure 13.1 and Table 13.1.

TABLE 13.1

Addresses to be Used for Figure 13.1

	S0	S1	S2	E0
Router_A	10.10.8.9	N/A	N/A	10.10.1.1
Router_B	10.10.8.1	10.10.12.1	10.10.4.1	N/A
Router_C	10.10.12.9	N/A	N/A	10.10.2.1
Router_D	10.10.4.2	N/A	N/A	10.10.3.1
Mask	255.255.255.0	255.255.255.0	255.255.255.0	255.255.255.0

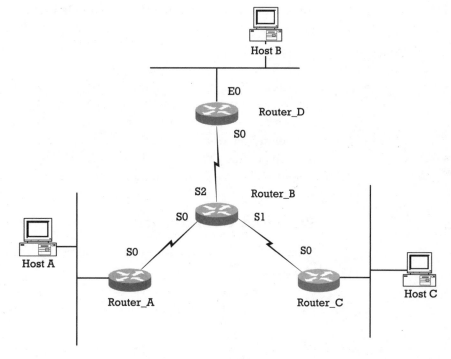

FIGURE 13.1
Four-Router
Topology

Configuration Commands

Figure 13.2 shows the commands to configure IP addresses and IGRP on Router_D.

I have included the IP address configuration lines as a review.

FIGURE 13.2   IGRP Configuration Commands

```
Router_D# config t
Enter configuration commands, one per line.  End with CNTL/Z.
Router_D(config)#int e0
Router_D(config-if)#ip address 10.10.3.1 255.255.255.0
Router_D(config-if)#int s0
Router_D(config-if)#ip address 10.10.4.2 255.255.255.0
Router_D(config-if)#router igrp 100
Router_D(config-router)#network 10.0.0.0
Router_D(config-router)#
Router_D#
```

continued on next page

%SYS-5-CONFIG_I: Configured from console by console

Router_D#

As with IP RIP, IGRP is classful so we only identify the major network address. Configuring IGRP is similar to configuring IP RIP; the one difference is we use a Autonomous System (AS) number. This AS number defines an area for which we have control. In most cases this number will remain the same throughout the topology. In our case all routers will carry an AS number of 100.

Verifying Configuration

After Router_D is configured we should verify that our configuration is correct.

The "show run" command (Figure 13.3) will help us verify that we have configured our addresses and the IGRP protocol correctly.

FIGURE 13.3   The "show run" Command

Router_D#show running-configuration
Building configuration...

Current configuration:
!
version 11.3
no service password-encryption
!
hostname Router_D
!
interface Ethernet0
  ip address 10.10.3.1 255.255.255.0
!
interface Serial0
  ip address 10.10.4.2 255.255.255.0
  no ip mroute-cache
  no fair-queue
  clockrate 56000

continued on next page

```
!
interface Serial 1
   no ip address
   shutdown
!
router igrp 100
   network 10.0.0.0
!
ip classless
!
line con 0
line 1 8
line aux 0
line vty 0 4
!
end
```

Figure 13.3 shows that the proper addresses are configured on the correct interfaces and IGRP will advertise network 10.0.0.0.

The "show ip protocol" command (Figure 13.4) will display all the IP protocols currently configured on the router.

FIGURE 13.4   The "show ip protocol" Command

Router_B#sh ip prot

Routing Protocol is "rip"

   Sending updates every 30 seconds, next due in 17 seconds
   Invalid after 180 seconds, hold down 180, flushed after 240
   Outgoing update filter list for all interfaces is not set
   Incoming update filter list for all interfaces is not set

Redistributing: rip

Default version control: send version 1, receive any version

Interface	Send	Recv	Key-chain
Serial0	1	1 2	
Serial1	1	1 2	
Serial2	1	1 2	

continued on next page

Routing for Networks:
    10.0.0.0
Routing Information Sources:

Gateway	Distance	Last Update
10.10.8.9	120	00:00:26
10.10.12.9	120	00:00:01
10.10.4.2	120	00:00:07

Distance: (default is 120)

Routing Protocol is "igrp 100"

Sending updates every 90 seconds, next due in 58 seconds
Invalid after 270 seconds, hold down 280, flushed after 630
Outgoing update filter list for all interfaces is not set
Incoming update filter list for all interfaces is not set
Default networks flagged in outgoing updates
Default networks accepted from incoming updates
IGRP metric weight K1=1, K2=0, K3=1, K4=0, K5=0
IGRP maximum hopcount 100
IGRP maximum metric variance 1

Redistributing: igrp 100

Routing for Networks:
    10.0.0.0
Routing Information Sources:

Gateway	Distance	Last Update
10.10.8.9	100	00:01:00
10.10.12.9	100	00:00:13
10.10.4.2	100	00:00:15

Distance: (default is 100)

Figure 13.4 shows that IP RIP and IGRP are both configured. The router will only use one protocol per network to determine the best path. Do you remember how the router determines which protocol to use?

Viewing the Routing Table

FIGURE 13.5   The "show ip route" Command

Router_B#show ip route
Codes: C - connected, S - static, I - IGRP, R - RIP, M - mobile, B - BGP
        D - EIGRP, EX - EIGRP external, O - OSPF, IA - OSPF inter area
        N1 - OSPF NSSA external type 1, N2 - OSPF NSSA external type 2
        E1 - OSPF external type 1, E2 - OSPF external type 2, E - EGP
        i - IS-IS, L1 - IS-IS level-1, L2 - IS-IS level-2, * - candidate default
        U - per-user static route, o - ODR

Gateway of last resort is not set

        10.0.0.0/24 is subnetted, 6 subnets
I   10.10.1.0 [100/8576] via 10.10.8.9, 00:00:26, Serial0
I   10.10.2.0 [100/8576] via 10.10.12.9, 00:00:58, Serial1
I   10.10.3.0 [100/89056] via 10.10.4.2, 00:01:07, Serial2
C   10.10.4.0 is directly connected, Serial2
C   10.10.8.0 is directly connected, Serial0
C   10.10.12.0 is directly connected, Serial1

Router_B has 3 directly connected networks and 3 routes that are discovered by the IGRP process.

The default administrative distance of IGRP is 100. Take note when viewing the configuration file that IP RIP is still configured, yet all of our routes are discovered through IGRP. The lower the administrative distance, the more reliable the routing protocol (Chapter 5). Therefore, the networks learned by the RIP process are ignored.

The metric for IGRP is the result of a calculation that IGRP performs. At this point do not be concerned with the actual number; what is important to know is the lower the number the better the route.

Summary

Configuring IGRP is a relative simple process only requiring a few lines of configuration.

First it is required that the protocol is configured with the "router igrp xx " command, where xx is the autonomous system. This is followed by all the major network numbers that will be advertised with the "network yy.yy.yy.yy" command.

Exercises

13.1: Using Figure 13.1 and Table 13.1 what configuration steps would be required to configure Router_A with IGRP?

13.2: Using Figure 13.1 and Table 13.1 what configuration steps would be required to configure Router_B with IGRP?

13.3: Using Figure 13.1 and Table 13.1 what configuration steps would be required to configure Router_C with IGRP?

13.4: What command would be used to verify the frequency of IGRP updates?

13.5: What command would be used to verify IP address configuration?

13.6: What command would be used to view the routing table?

Answers

13.1:

Router_A# config t

Enter configuration commands, one per line. End with CNTL/Z.

Router_A(config)#int e0

Router_A(config-if)#ip address 10.10.1.1 255.255.255.0

Router_A(config-if)#int s0

continued on next page

Router_A(config-if)#ip address 10.10.8.9 255.255.255.0
Router_A(config-if)#router igrp 100
Router_A(config-router)#network 10.0.0.0
Router_A(config-router)#
Router_A#
%SYS-5-CONFIG_I: Configured from console by console
Router_A#

13.2:

Router_B# config t
Enter configuration commands, one per line. End with CNTL/Z.
Router_B(config)#int s0
Router_B(config-if)#ip address 10.10.8.1 255.255.255.0
Router_B(config-if)#int s1
Router_B(config-if)#ip address 10.10.12.1 255.255.255.0
Router_B(config-if)#int s2
Router_B(config-if)#ip address 10.10.4.1 255.255.255.0

Router_B(config-if)#router igrp 100
Router_B(config-router)#network 10.0.0.0
Router_B(config-router)#
Router_B#
%SYS-5-CONFIG_I: Configured from console by console
Router_B#

13.3:

Router_C# config t
Enter configuration commands, one per line. End with CNTL/Z.
Router_C(config)#int s0
Router_C(config-if)#ip address 10.10.12.9 255.255.255.0
Router_C(config-if)#int e0
Router_C(config-if)#ip address 10.10.2.1 255.255.255.0
Router_C(config-if)#router igrp 100
Router_C(config-router)#network 10.0.0.0
Router_C(config-router)#
Router_C#
%SYS-5-CONFIG_I: Configured from console by console
Router_C#

13.4: "show ip protocol"

13.5: "show run"; "show ip interface" and "show interface" will also provide information relating the IP addresses.

Router#sh ip interface
%SYS-5-CONFIG_I: Configured from console by consolet e0
Ethernet0 is administratively down, line protocol is down
   Internet address is 10.10.1.1/24
   Broadcast address is 255.255.255.255
   Address determined by setup command
   MTU is 1500 bytes
   Helper address is not set
   Directed broadcast forwarding is enabled
   Multicast reserved groups joined: 224.0.0.9
   Outgoing access list is not set
   Inbound access list is not set
   Proxy ARP is enabled
   Security level is default
   Split horizon is enabled
   ICMP redirects are always sent
   ICMP unreachables are always sent
   ICMP mask replies are never sent
   IP fast switching is enabled
   IP fast switching on the same interface is disabled
   IP multicast fast switching is enabled
   Router Discovery is disabled
   IP output packet accounting is disabled
   IP access violation accounting is disabled
   TCP/IP header compression is disabled
   Probe proxy name replies are disabled
   Gateway Discovery is disabled
   Policy routing is disabled
   Network address translation is disabled
Router#

Router#sh int e0
Ethernet0 is administratively down, line protocol is down
   Hardware is Lance, address is 0060.09c3.df60 (bia 0060.09c3.df60)
   Internet address is 10.10.1.1/24

continued on next page

MTU 1500 bytes, BW 10000 Kbit, DLY 1000 usec, rely 255/255,
   load 1/255

Encapsulation ARPA, loopback not set, keepalive set (10 sec)

ARP type: ARPA, ARP Timeout 04:00:00

Last input never, output 2d02h, output hang never

Last clearing of "show interface" counters never

Queueing strategy: fifo

Output queue 0/40, 0 drops; input queue 0/75, 0 drops

5 minute input rate 0 bits/sec, 0 packets/sec

5 minute output rate 0 bits/sec, 0 packets/sec

   0 packets input, 0 bytes, 0 no buffer

   Received 0 broadcasts, 0 runts, 0 giants, 0 throttles

   0 input errors, 0 CRC, 0 frame, 0 overrun, 0 ignored, 0 abort

   0 input packets with dribble condition detected

   81 packets output, 13498 bytes, 0 underruns

13.6:   "show ip route"

CHAPTER **14**

Configuring OSPF

Objective

- Describe the process of configuring OSPF on a Cisco router.
- Configure a single-area topology.
- Configure a multiple-area topology with route summarization.
- Describe the difference between "stubby" and "totally stubby".
- Configure a "totally stubby" area.
- Describe IP addressing and OSPF design.

Open Shortest Path First (OSPF) is a "newer" routing protocol that was developed in the late 80s and early 90s. It is a standard and can be configured on all routers regardless of vendor. This fact is the major reason why you may not want to use EIGRP. If you have a mix of routers, for instance Bay and Cisco, OSPF will be the routing protocol to use; EIGRP requires all routers to run the Cisco IOS.

OSPF is a classless, link-state routing protocol that supports VLSM.

Single-Area Topology

FIGURE 14.1
OSPF Single-
Area–Four-Router
Topology

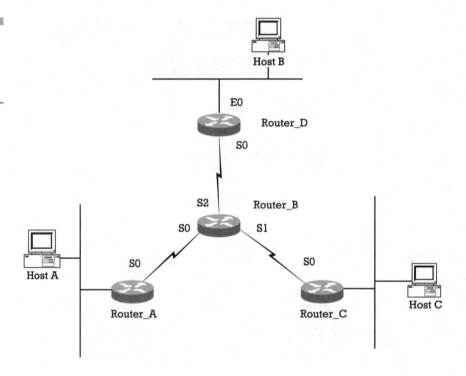

Figure 14.1 shows that we will use the "serial mask" on our serial links; as a result we will preserve address space.

TABLE 14.1

Addresses to be used for Figure 14.1

	S0	S1	S2	E0
Router_A	172.16.0.10	N/A	N/A	10.10.1.1/24
Router_B	172.16.0.9	172.16.0.13	172.16.0.5	N/A
Router_C	172.16.0.14	N/A	N/A	10.10.3.33/28
Router_D	172.16.0.6	N/A	N/A	10.10.3.17/28
Mask	255.255.255.252	255.255.255.252	255.255.255.252	

Configuration Commands

Figure 14.2 illustrates the commands to configure IP addresses and OSPF on all routers. For this first example, all networks will be configured in area 0.

We will use an OSPF process ID of 100; any number can be chosen between 1 and 65,535. The important point to remember is, when a number is chosen, use it consistently. If another process ID is chosen, redistribution will be required.

Figure 14.2 illustrates one way of configuring OSPF by identifying each interface with the appropriate area. The wild card mask of 0.0.0.0 means "match all 32 bits".

FIGURE 14.2   OSPF Configuration Commands

```
Router_D(config)#router ospf 100
Router_D(config-router)#network 10.10.3.17 0.0.0.0 area 0
Router_D(config-router)#network 172.16.0.6 0.0.0.0 area 0

Router_C(config)#router ospf 100
Router_C(config-router)#network 172.16.0.14 0.0.0.0 area 0
Router_C(config-router)#network 10.10.3.33 0.0.0.0 area 0

Router_B(config)#router ospf 100
Router_B(config-router)#network 172.16.0.9 0.0.0.0 area 0
Router_B(config-router)#network 172.16.0.13 0.0.0.0 area 0
Router_B(config-router)#network 172.16.0.5 0.0.0.0 area 0

Router_A(config)#router ospf 100
```

continued on next page

```
Router_A(config-router)#network 172.16.0.10 0.0.0.0 area 0
Router_A(config-router)#network 10.10.1.1 0.0.0.0 area 0
```

We could reduce the number of Router_B configuration commands by identifying all three directly connected networks with a single command shown in **bold**.

Router_B(config)#router ospf 100
Router_B(config-router)#network 172.16.0.0 0.0.255.255 area 0

In this case we are matching the first 16 bits since all serial connections of Router_B have the same most significant 16-bit pattern.

Verifying Configuration

FIGURE 14.3   The "show run" Command

```
Router_D#sh run
Building configuration...
Current configuration:
!
version 11.3
no service password-encryption
!
hostname Router_B
!
interface Ethernet0
    ip address 10.10.3.17 255.255.255.240
    no ip mroute-cache
    no fair-queue

interface Serial0
    ip address 172.16.0.6 255.255.255.252
    no ip mroute-cache
    no fair-queue
!
interface Serial1
```

continued on next page

```
  no ip address
!
```
router ospf 100
**   network 172.16.0.6 0.0.0.0 area 0**
**   network 10.10.3.17 0.0.0.0 area 0**
```
!
```
ip classless
```
!
line con 0
line aux 0
line vty 0 4
login
!
end
```

FIGURE 14.4   The "show ip protocol" Command

```
Router_B#sh ip prot
```
Routing Protocol is "ospf 100"
```
    Sending updates every 0 seconds
    Invalid after 0 seconds, hold down 0, flushed after 0
    Outgoing update filter list for all interfaces is not set
    Incoming update filter list for all interfaces is not set
    Redistributing: ospf 100
    Routing for Networks:
        172.16.0.9/32
        172.16.0.13/32
        172.16.0.5/32
    Routing Information Sources:
        Gateway        Distance      Last Update
        172.16.0.14        110        00:03:10
        172.16.0.10        110        00:12:19
        172.16.0.6         110        00:12:39
    Distance: (default is 110)
```

Viewing the Routing Table

FIGURE 14.5 The "show ip route" Command

Router_B#sh ip route
Codes: C - connected, S - static, I - IGRP, R - RIP, M - mobile, B - BGP
        D - EIGRP, EX - EIGRP external, O - OSPF, IA - OSPF inter area
        N1 - OSPF NSSA external type 1, N2 - OSPF NSSA external type 2
        E1 - OSPF external type 1, E2 - OSPF external type 2, E - EGP
        i - IS-IS, L1 - IS-IS level-1, L2 - IS-IS level-2, * - candidate default
        U - per-user static route, o - ODR

Gateway of last resort is not set

      172.16.0.0/30 is subnetted, 3 subnets
C   172.16.0.12 is directly connected, Serial1
C   172.16.0.8 is directly connected, Serial0
C   172.16.0.4 is directly connected, Serial2
      10.0.0.0/8 is variably subnetted, 3 subnets, 3 masks
O   10.10.1.0/24 [110/74] via 172.16.0.10, 00:09:24, Serial0
O   10.10.3.16/28 [110/879] via 172.16.0.6, 00:09:44, Serial2
O   10.10.3.32/28 [110/74] via 172.16.0.14, 00:00:16, Serial1

Router_B has 3 directly connected networks and 3 routes discovered by the OSPF process.

The default administrative distance of OSPF is 110.

The metric for OSPF is cost. Cost of each link is calculated by the following formula:

10^8/bandwidth of the link

As an example, a 10 mbps Ethernet link would have a cost of 10.

Types of OSPF Routers

■ Internal routers have all of their interfaces in the same area.
■ Area Border Routers (ABR) have interfaces in more than one area.
■ Autonomous System Border Routers (ASBR) have interfaces in more than one AS.
■ Backbone routers have an interface connected to Area 0.

Multiple-Area Topology

FIGURE 14.6
OSPF Multiple-
Area Topology

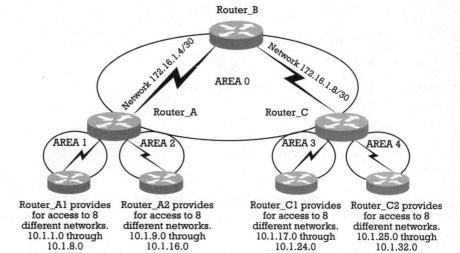

Router_A1 provides for access to 8 different networks. 10.1.1.0 through 10.1.8.0

Router_A2 provides for access to 8 different networks. 10.1.9.0 through 10.1.16.0

Router_C1 provides for access to 8 different networks. 10.1.17.0 through 10.1.24.0

Router_C2 provides for access to 8 different networks. 10.1.25.0 through 10.1.32.0

TABLE 14.2
Addresses of
Figure 14.6

	S0	S1	S2	E0–E7
Router_A	172.16.1.6	172.16.1.13	172.16.1.17	N/A
Router_B	172.16.1.5	172.16.1.9	N/A	N/A
Router_C	172.16.1.10	172.16.1.21	172.16.1.25	N/A
Router_A1	172.16.1.14	N/A	N/A	10.1.1.0 thru 10.1.8.0
Router_A2	172.16.1.18	N/A	N/A	10.1.9.0 thru 10.1.16.0
Router_C1	172.16.1.22	N/A	N/A	10.1.17.0 thur 10.1.24.2
Router_C2	172.16.1.26	N/A	N/A	10.1.25.0 thru 10.1.32.3
Mask	255.255.255.252	255.255.255.252	255.255.255.252	255.255.255.0

- Router_B is a backbone router. We could also say that Router_B is an internal router since it has all interfaces in the same area.
- Routers A and C are ABRs.
- The remaining routers are internal routers.

The configuration of Router_B will be the same as shown in Figure 14.2.

Figure 14.7 illustrates how we will use the wild card mask to identify the 32 networks of the internal routers. In each case the least significant 3 bits of the 3rd and the 4th octets can have any value.

FIGURE 14.7   Configuration of Internal Routers

Router_A1(config)router ospf 100
Router_A1(config-router)#network 10.1.0.0 0 0.7.255 area 1
Router_A1(config-router)#network 172.16.0.0 0.0.255.255 area 1

Router_A2(config)router ospf 100
Router_A2(config-router)#network 10.1.8.0 0 0.7.255 area 2
Router_A2(config-router)#network 172.16.0.0 0.0.255.255 area 2

Router_C1(config)router ospf 100
Router_C1(config-router)#network 10.1.16.0 0 0.7.255 area 3
Router_C1(config-router)#network 172.16.0.0 0.0.255.255 area 3

Router_C2(config)router ospf 100
Router_C2(config-router)#network 10.1.24.0 0 0.7.255 area 4
Router_C2(config-router)#network 172.16.0.0 0.0.255.255 area 4

FIGURE 14.8   Configuration of the Area Border Routers with Summarization

Router_A(config)router ospf 100
Router_A(config-router)#network 172.16.1.10 0.0.0.0 area 0
Router_A(config-router)#network 172.16.1.13 0.0.0.0 area 1
Router_A(config-router)#network 172.16.1.17.0.0.0.0 area 2
Router_A(config-router)#area 1 range 10.1.0.0 255.255.248.0
Router_A(config-router)#area 2 range 10.1.8.0 255.255.248.0
Router_C(config)router ospf 100
Router_C(config-router)#network 172.16.1.10 0.0.0.0 area 0
Router_C(config-router)#network 172.16.1.21 0.0.0.0 area 3
Router_C(config-router)#network 172.16.1.25 0.0.0.0 area 4
Router_C(config-router)#area 3 range 10.1.16.0 255.255.248.0
Router_C(config-router)#area 4 range 10.1.24.0 255.255.248.0

Figure 14.8 shows the configuration statements necessary to perform interarea route summarization.

Keep in mind that the range statement uses a mask, NOT a wild card mask. Therefore the mask of 255.255.248.0 means that the first 21 bits must have a value that is the same as the associated address.

As we have summarized, Router_B will NOT have to "learn" each of the 8 networks associated with each area. One entry in the routing table will identify all 8 networks. Figure 14.9 illustrates this.

FIGURE 14.9   Routing Table of Router _B

```
Router_B>sh ip route
Codes: C - connected, S - static, I - IGRP, R - RIP, M - mobile, B - BGP
       D - EIGRP, EX - EIGRP external, O - OSPF, IA - OSPF inter area
       N1 - OSPF NSSA external type 1, N2 - OSPF NSSA external type 2
       E1 - OSPF external type 1, E2 - OSPF external type 2, E - EGP
       i - IS-IS, L1 - IS-IS level-1, L2 - IS-IS level-2, * - candidate default
       U - per-user static route, o - ODR

Gateway of last resort is not set

     172.16.0.0/30 is subnetted, 3 subnets
O IA    172.16.1.12 [110/3570] via 172.16.1.6, 00:35:25, Serial0
O IA    172.16.1.16 [110/3570] via 172.16.1.6, 00:35:25, Serial0
O IA    172.16.1.20 [110/3570] via 172.16.1.6, 00:35:25, Serial1
O IA    172.16.1.24 [110/3570] via 172.16.1.6, 00:35:25, Serial1
C       172.16.1.8 is directly connected, Serial1
C       172.16.1.4 is directly connected, Serial0
     10.0.0.0/8 is variably subnetted, 3 subnets, 2 masks
O IA    10.1.8.0/21 [110/3570] via 172.16.1.6, 00:05:17, Serial0
O IA    10.1.0.0/21 [110/3570] via 172.16.1.6, 00:12:47, Serial0
O IA    10.1.16.0/21 [110/3570] via 172.16.1.10, 00:23:47, Serial1
O IA    10.1.24.0/21 [110/3570] via 172.16.1.10, 00:23:47, Serial1
```

- Router_B now "knows" to send all packets for networks 10.1.0.0 through 10.1.15.0 to the serial 0 interface.
- Router_B now "knows" to send all packets for networks 10.1.16.0 through 10.1.31.0 to the serial 0 interface.

As we mentioned earlier, there is a cost associated with each route. The total cost to get to a network is the sum of the cost of each individual link. In Figure 14.9, 3570 represents the total cost of 2–56K links.

Different Types of OSPF Routes

The different types of OSPF routes are:

- Intra-area routes are routes in the same area (IA).
- Interarea routes are routes in different areas (O).
- External routes are routes in another autonomous system.

From the perspective of Router_B, all the networks are identified as IA because they are all interarea routes; all networks discovered through the OSPF process are NOT in area 0.

Now take a look at the LAN links of Router_A1. We can see if a host is attached to one of these LAN links and that host needs to communicate with an interarea network, the traffic MUST go to the Serial 1 interface of Router_A.

Figure 14.6 illustrates that from Router_A1's perspective there are exactly 24 interarea LAN networks.

Why would it be necessary for Router_A1 to keep these 24 networks in its routing table when initially, in each case, to get to these networks all packets will go to the same interface, the Serial 1 of Router_A?

Totally Stubby Areas

Cisco has created a proprietary feature called "totally stubby".

When an area is defined as totally stubby, all routers within that area will NOT see the interarea routes. The size of the routing table will therefore be reduced.

The bolded statements of Figures 14.10 and 14.11 are all that is necessary to configure a totally stubby area.

FIGURE 14.10   Configuring an ABR Defining a "Totally Stubby" Area

Router_A(config)router ospf 100
Router_A(config-router)network 172.16.1.6 0.0.0.0 area 0

continued on next page

```
Router_A(config-router)network 172.16.1.13 0.0.0.0 area 1
Router_A(config-router)network 10.0.0.0 0.255.255.255 area 2
Router_A(config-router)area 1 stub no-summary
Router_A(config-router)area 2 stub no-summary
Router_A(config-router)area 1 range 10.1.0.0 255.255.248.0
Router_A(config-router)area 2 range 10.1.8.0 255.255.248.0
```

FIGURE 14.11 Configuring an Internal Router to be in a "Totally Stubby" Area

```
Router_A1(config)router ospf 100
Router_A1(config-router)network 172.16.1.0 0.0.0.255 area 1
Router_A1(config-router)network 10.0.0.0 0.255.255.255 area 1
Router_A1(config-router)area 1 stub
Router_A2(config)router ospf 100
Router_A2(config-router)network 172.16.1.0 0.0.0.255 area 2
Router_A2(config-router)network 10.0.0.0 0.255.255.255 area 2
Router_A2(config-router)area 2 stub
```

Figure 14.12 shows the result of configuring a "totally stubby" area. Notice that Router_A1 now has a gateway of last resort set to the Serial 1 interface of Router_A.

FIGURE 14.12 Result of Configuring a "Totally Stubby" Area

```
Router_A1>sh ip route
Codes: C - connected, S - static, I - IGRP, R - RIP, M - mobile, B - BGP
       D - EIGRP, EX - EIGRP external, O - OSPF, IA - OSPF inter area
       N1 - OSPF NSSA external type 1, N2 - OSPF NSSA external type 2
       E1 - OSPF external type 1, E2 - OSPF external type 2, E - EGP
       i - IS-IS, L1 - IS-IS level-1, L2 - IS-IS level-2, * - candidate default
       U - per-user static route, o - ODR

Gateway of last resort is 172.16.1.13 to network 0.0.0.0

   172.16.0.0/30 is subnetted, 1 subnets
```

continued on next page

C   172.16.1.12 is directly connected, Serial0/0
       10.0.0.0/24 is subnetted, 1 subnets
C   10.1.1.0 is directly connected, Ethernet0/0
O*IA 0.0.0.0/0 [110/1786] via 172.16.1.13, 02:20:55, Serial0/0
<Partial listing>

A "totally stubby" area will also hide external routes. As a result a router in a "totally stubby" area will only see intra-area routes in addition to its directly connected networks.

Multiple Autonomous Systems

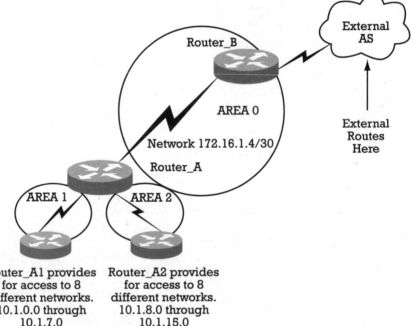

FIGURE 14.13
Multiple
Autonomous
System Topology

The same logic we used about reasoning for hiding interarea routes could be applied to the hiding of external routes. Why would it be necessary for internal routers to maintain information about external routes if there is only one way to get to them?

Stub Areas

OSPF defines a "stub" area as one in which all external routes are hidden. Interarea routes would NOT be hidden in a "stub area" configuration. In this case Router_A1 would still maintain all interarea routes. A "totally stubby" configuration offers the additional advantage of hiding not only external routes but also interarea routes.

To configure a "stub" area we would use the same configuration lines as in Figures 14.9 and 14.10, but would remove the switch "no-summary".

A stub area is a standard and not a Cisco proprietary.

IP/OSPF Addressing Design

Here is an IP addressing scheme to illustrate how the IP address can be used to define location of hosts. In our example we are going to use a private address; private addresses will be discussed in more detail in Chapter 17.

Figure 14.14 represents an organization with a home office and four remote locations.

- The 1st octet value of 10 signifies a private address.
- The 2nd octet will signify a location. For instance, we know that a host with an address of 10.4.x.x is located in NYC. Again, this is the same idea as my post office analogy; we know that a ZIP code that begins with a 9 is located on the West Coast.
- The 3rd octet represents the floor of the location. As an example, a host with the address of 10.2.3.x is located at the San Fran site on the third floor.

Since we are using OSPF we can take advantage of VLSM. Table 14.3 shows an example of addresses we can use for our serial connections.

I have chosen a 3rd-octet value of 100 to signify all serial connections. The idea is that we will not have a site with 100 floors.

All interfaces of the Jacksonville router will have a host portion value of 5. All serial interfaces of the remote routers will have a host portion value of 6.

The reason I did not choose the host values of 1 and 2 had to do with the zero subnet restrictions.

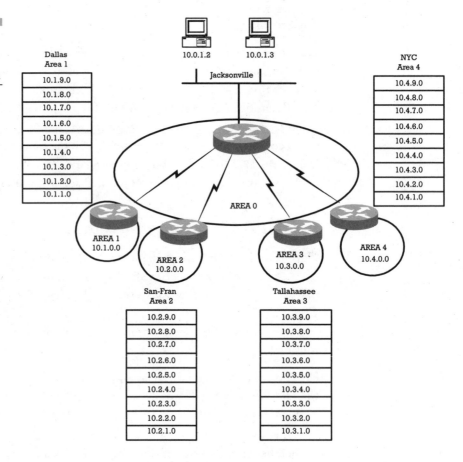

FIGURE 14.14

IP/OSPF
Addressing Design

TABLE 14.3

IP/OSPF
Addressing Serial
Connection Design

	S0	S1	S2	S3
Jacksonville	10.1.100.5	10.2.100.5	10.3.100.5	10.4.100.5
Dallas	10.1.100.6	N/A	N/A	N/A
San-Fran	N/A	10.2.100.6	N/A	N/A
Tallahassee	N/A	N/A	10.3.100.6	N/A
Jacksonville	N/A	N/A	N/A	10.4.100.5

*All serial connections will use the 255.255.255.252 mask.

Now let us consider a different logic for assigning IP addresses. Suppose that we have a lot of user movement. A user might be on the first floor today but on the fifth floor tomorrow. Maybe we could use the 3rd octet to describe department, not the floor. As an example: accounting might have a 3rd-octet value of 1, sales might have a 3rd-octet value of 2, engineering might have a 3rd-octet value of 3, etc.

Now, when there is a change of location the user can take his machine with him and there is no need for reprogramming.

In a switching environment the administrator will define a port to be associated with a VLAN. Each VLAN will represent a department. For instance the accounting department will be assigned VLAN 1, which may be made up of ports 5 and 6. When the user is moved up to the fifth floor the administrator will connect the user to port 5 or 6.

For more information about Cisco switching, I recommend the book *Cisco Catalyst LAN Switching* by Lou Rossi Jr., McGraw-Hill, New York: NY.

Summary

- OSPF is configured using a process ID and an area.
- Route summarization is configured with the "area range" command.
- A "totally stubby" area hides both external routes and interarea routes, while a "stub" area will only hide external routes.
- To configure a "totally stubby" area use the "no-summary" parameter.
- IP addressing can define location of a host.

Exercises

14.1: Using the topology of Figure 14.1 and addressing of Table 14.1 what configuration lines would be required to configure Router_C with the OSPF routing protocol?

14.2: If all routers are configured in the same area, what type of routes would an OSPF router contain in its routing table?

14.3: What type of routes would a router in a "totally stubby" area have in its routing table?

14.4: Using the topology of Figure 14.6 and addressing of Table 14.2 what configuration lines would be required to configure Router_C with the OSPF routing protocol? Route summarize all LAN routes of C1 and C2.

14.5: What would be the approximate OSPF cost of 1–56k link?

14.6: Describe the difference between a "totally stubby" and a "stub" area.

14.7: When configuring networks to belong in an area we use a wild card mask. (T/F)

14.8: When configuring route summarization we use a wild card mask. (T/F)

14.9: What is the administrative distance of OSPF?

14.10: AN ABR router may also be an internal router. (T/F)

14.11: Backbone routers must be wholly contained in Area 0. (T/F)

14.12: External routes are routes in another AS. (T/F)

Answers

14.1:
Router_C(config)#router ospf 100
Router_C(config-router)#network 10.10.3.33 0.0.0.0 area 0
Router_C(config-router)#network 172.16.0.14 0.0.0.0 area 0

The above is just one solution.

The following command line would also work because in reality all the networks 10.0.0.0 are in area 0.

Router_C(config-router)#network 10.0.0.0 0.0.0.0 area 0

14.2:
All routes would be *intra-area* routes. Of course these would be directly connected networks and possibly external networks if there were an external autonomous system.

14.3:
Only intra-area routes and a static route pointing to the gateway of last resort

14.4: Router_C Configuration Statements

Router_C(config)router ospf 100
Router_C(config-router)network 172.16.1.10 0.0.0.0 area 0
Router_C(config-router)network 172.16.1.21 0.0.0.0 area 3
Router_C(config-router)network 172.16.1.25 0.0.0.0 area 4
Router_C(config-router)area 3 stub no-summary
Router_C(config-router)area 4 stub no-summary
Router_C(config-router)area 3 range 10.1.16.0 255.255.248.0
Router_C(config-router)area 4 range 10.1.24.0 255.255.248.0

14.5: 100,000,000/56,000 = 1786

14.6: A "totally stubby" area will hide both interarea routes and external routes. A "stub" area will hide only external routes.

14.7: True

14.8: False

14.9: The administrative distance of OSPF is 110.

14.10: False; by definition an ABR is connected to multiple areas.

14.11: False; backbone routers must be connected to Area 0.

14.12: True

CHAPTER **15**

Configuring
EIGRP

Objective

■ Describe the process of Configuring Cisco's EIGRP
   on a Cisco router.

Enhanced Interior Gateway Routing Protocol (EIGRP) is a Cisco proprietary protocol. Cisco defines IGRP as an advanced distance-vector routing protocol.

EIGRP is a classless routing protocol, which means it does support VLSM.

Cisco also defines EIGRP as a hybrid routing protocol because it has characteristics of both distance-vector and link-state routing protocols. EIGRP will communicate with directly connected neighbors but NOT periodically; communication takes place only when a change occurs. As a result it is very quiet when compared to other distance-vector protocols.

EIGRP has several unique features, which may well be why Cisco calls it an advanced routing protocol.

Some of those features are:

1. **Scalability** — EIGRP is not limited to 15 hops as is IP RIP.
2. **Event Triggered Updates** — EIGRP sends updates when topology changes occur.
3. **Multiple paths** — EIGRP has the ability to keep track of multiple routes that have an equal as well as an unequal metric.
4. **Sophisticated metric**–EIGRP uses a combination of metrics to determine the best route:

   - Bandwidth
   - Delay
   - Load
   - Reliability
   - Maximum Transmission Unit (MTU)

5. EIGRP supports VLSM.
6. **Multiple Protocol Support** — EIGRP supports IP, IPX, and Appletalk. This can be a very important feature if your organization is running more than one of these protocols, especially if they are running on your serial links. Take for instance IP RIP and IPX RIP running over serial links. The routing updates of IP RIP every 30 seconds and of IPX RIP every 60 seconds will eat up a significant portion of bandwidth.

EIGRP will reduce routing traffic significantly by using one protocol to update both the IP and the IPX routing tables.

Due to the fact that EIGRP is proprietary to Cisco, the router needs to be running the Cisco IOS. OSPF is a viable alternative.

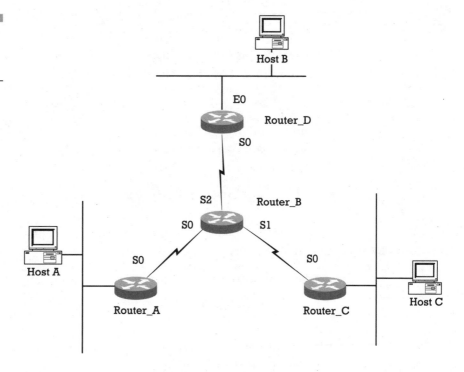

Refer to Figure 15.1 and Table 15.1.

	S0	S1	S2	E0
Router_A	10.10.8.9	N/A	N/A	10.10.1.1
Router_B	10.10.8.1	10.10.12.1	10.10.4.1	N/A
Router_C	10.10.12.9	N/A	N/A	10.10.2.1
Router_D	10.10.4.2	N/A	N/A	10.10.3.1
Mask	255.255.255.0	255.255.255.0	255.255.255.0	255.255.255.0

Configuration Commands

FIGURE 15.2   EIGRP Configuration Commands

    Router_B(config)#router eigrp 100
    Router_B(config-router)#network 10.0.0.0

Configuring EIGRP is very much the same as configuring IGRP, but
what happens behind the scenes is very different.

Verifying Configuration

FIGURE 15.3   The "show run" Command

Router_B show run

Current configuration:
!
version 11.3
no service password-encryption
!
hostname Router_B
!
interface Serial0
   ip address 10.10.8.1 255.255.255.0
   no ip mroute-cache
   no fair-queue
!
interface Serial1
   ip address 10.10.12.1 255.255.255.0
!
interface Serial2
   ip address 10.10.4.1 255.255.255.0
!
interface Serial3

continued on next page

```
    no ip address
    shutdown
!
interface TokenRing0
    no ip address
    shutdown
!
interface BRI0
    no ip address
    shutdown
!
router eigrp 100
    network 10.0.0.0
!
router rip
    network 10.0.0.0
!
router igrp 100
    network 10.0.0.0
!
ip classless
!
line con 0
line aux 0
line vty 0 4
    login
end
```

FIGURE 15.4 The "show ip protocol" Command

Router_B#sh ip prot
Routing Protocol is "rip"
    Sending updates every 30 seconds, next due in 5 seconds
    Invalid after 180 seconds, hold down 180, flushed after 240
    Outgoing update filter list for all interfaces is not set

continued on next page

Incoming update filter list for all interfaces is not set

Redistributing: rip

Default version control: send version 1, receive any version

Interface	Send	Recv	Key-chain
Serial0	1	1 2	
Serial1	1	1 2	
Serial2	1	1 2	

Routing for Networks:

    10.0.0.0

Routing Information Sources:

Gateway	Distance	Last Update
10.10.8.9	120	00:00:09
10.10.12.9	120	00:00:25
10.10.4.2	120	00:00:22

Distance: (default is 120)

Routing Protocol is "igrp 100"

Sending updates every 90 seconds, next due in 16 seconds

Invalid after 270 seconds, hold down 280, flushed after 630

Outgoing update filter list for all interfaces is not set

Incoming update filter list for all interfaces is not set

Default networks flagged in outgoing updates

Default networks accepted from incoming updates

IGRP metric weight K1=1, K2=0, K3=1, K4=0, K5=0

IGRP maximum hopcount 100

IGRP maximum metric variance 1

Redistributing: igrp 100, eigrp 100

Routing for Networks:

    10.0.0.0

Routing Information Sources:

Gateway	Distance	Last Update
10.10.8.9	100	00:00:18
10.10.12.9	100	00:00:13
10.10.4.2	100	00:00:38

Distance: (default is 100)

Routing Protocol is "eigrp 100"

Outgoing update filter list for all interfaces is not set

Incoming update filter list for all interfaces is not set

continued on next page

Default networks flagged in outgoing updates
Default networks accepted from incoming updates
EIGRP metric weight K1=1, K2=0, K3=1, K4=0, K5=0
EIGRP maximum hopcount 100
EIGRP maximum metric variance 1
Redistributing: igrp 100, eigrp 100
Automatic network summarization is in effect
Routing for Networks:
    10.0.0.0
Routing Information Sources:

Gateway	Distance	Last Update
10.10.8.9	90	00:01:31
10.10.12.9	90	00:01:31
10.10.4.2	90	00:01:31

Distance: internal 90 external 170

Viewing the Routing Table

FIGURE 15.5   The "show ip route" Command

Router_B#sh ip route
Codes: C - connected, S - static, I - IGRP, R - RIP, M - mobile, B - BGP
       D - EIGRP, EX - EIGRP external, O - OSPF, IA - OSPF inter area
       N1 - OSPF NSSA external type 1, N2 - OSPF NSSA external type 2
       E1 - OSPF external type 1, E2 - OSPF external type 2, E - EGP
       i - IS-IS, L1 - IS-IS level-1, L2 - IS-IS level-2, * - candidate default
       U - per-user static route, o - ODR

Gateway of last resort is not set

    10.0.0.0/24 is subnetted, 6 subnets
D   10.10.1.0 [90/2195456] via 10.10.8.9, 00:03:39, Serial0
D   10.10.2.0 [90/2195456] via 10.10.12.9, 00:03:39, Serial1
D   10.10.3.0 [90/22798336] via 10.10.4.2, 00:03:39, Serial2
C   10.10.4.0 is directly connected, Serial2
C   10.10.8.0 is directly connected, Serial0
C   10.10.12.0 is directly connected, Serial1

Router_B has 3 directly connected networks and 3 routes that are discovered by the EIGRP process.

The default administrative distance of EIGRP is 90. Take note when viewing the configuration file that IP RIP and IGRP are still configured, yet all of our routes are discovered through EIGRP. The lower the administrative distance, the more reliable the routing protocol. Therefore the networks learned by the RIP and IGRP processes are ignored.

The metric for EIGRP is the result of a calculation that EIGRP performs. At this point, do not be concerned with the actual number; what is important to know is the lower the number the better the route.

Since EIGRP supports VLSM we should take a look at a VLSM addressing scheme.

In Figure 15.6 we will use the same network topology but with a new addressing scheme.

FIGURE 15.6

Four Router EIGRP
Network Topology

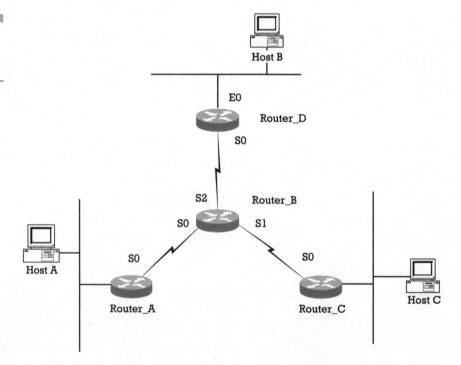

	S0	S1	S2	E0
Router_A	172.16.0.10	N/A	N/A	10.10.1.1/24
Router_B	172.16.0.9	172.16.0.13	172.16.0.5	N/A
Router_C	172.16.0.14	N/A	N/A	10.10.3.33/28
Router_D	172.16.0.6	N/A	N/A	10.10.3.17/28
Mask	255.255.255.252	255.255.255.252	255.255.255.252	

Notice we no longer have a contiguous network. The 172.16.0.0 network is in the middle of the 10.0.0.0 network. We are also using VLSM: the 10.0.0.0 network has two different masks 255.255.255.0 and 255.255.255.240.

Configuration Commands

EIGRP by default will perform auto summary; in other words, it will act as a classful routing protocol. The "no auto-summary" command (Figure 15.7) will force EIGRP into acting as a classless routing protocol.

FIGURE 15.7 The "no auto-summary" Configuration

```
Router_C(config)#int e0
Router_C(config-if)#ip address 10.10.3.33 255.255.255.240
Router_C(config-if)#int s0
Router_C(config-if)#ip address 172.16.0.14 255.255.255.252
Router_C(config-if)#router eigrp 100
Router_C(config-router)#network 10.0.0.0
Router_C(config-router)#network 172.16.0.0
Router_C(config-router)#no auto-summary
```

Verifying Configuration

FIGURE 15.8   The "show run" Command

Router_C#show run
Building configuration...
Current configuration:
!
version 11.2
no service password-encryption
no service udp-small-servers
no service tcp-small-servers
!
hostname Router_C
!
interface Ethernet0
  ip address 10.10.3.33 255.255.255.240
!
interface Ethernet1
  no ip address
  shutdown
!
interface Serial0
  ip address 172.16.0.14 255.255.255.252
  no fair-queue
  clockrate 56000
!
interface Serial1
  ip address 10.10.12.9 255.255.255.0
  shutdown
  clockrate 56000
!
router eigrp 100
  network 10.0.0.0
  network 172.16.0.0
  no auto-summary
!

continued on next page

```
router rip
   network 10.0.0.0
!
router igrp 100
   network 10.0.0.0
!
no ip classless
!
line con 0
line aux 0
line vty 0 4
   login
!
end
```

FIGURE 15.9   The "show ip prot" Command

Router_C#sh ip prot
Routing Protocol is "rip"
   Sending updates every 30 seconds, next due in 0 seconds
   Invalid after 180 seconds, hold down 180, flushed after 240
   Outgoing update filter list for all interfaces is not set
   Incoming update filter list for all interfaces is not set
   Redistributing: rip
   Default version control: send version 1, receive any version

Interface	Send	Recv	Key-chain
Ethernet0	1	1	2
Serial1	1	1	2

   Routing for Networks:
      10.0.0.0
   Routing Information Sources:

Gateway	Distance	Last Update
10.10.12.1	120	00:24:47

   Distance: (default is 120)

continued on next page

Routing Protocol is "igrp 100"
    Sending updates every 90 seconds, next due in 3 seconds
    Invalid after 270 seconds, hold down 280, flushed after 630
    Outgoing update filter list for all interfaces is not set
    Incoming update filter list for all interfaces is not set
    Default networks flagged in outgoing updates
    Default networks accepted from incoming updates
    IGRP metric weight K1=1, K2=0, K3=1, K4=0, K5=0
    IGRP maximum hopcount 100
    IGRP maximum metric variance 1
    Redistributing: igrp 100, eigrp 100
    Routing for Networks:
        10.0.0.0
    Routing Information Sources:

Gateway	Distance	Last Update
10.10.12.1	100	00:25:07

    Distance: (default is 100)

Routing Protocol is "eigrp 100"
    Outgoing update filter list for all interfaces is not set
    Incoming update filter list for all interfaces is not set
    Default networks flagged in outgoing updates
    Default networks accepted from incoming updates
    EIGRP metric weight K1=1, K2=0, K3=1, K4=0, K5=0
    EIGRP maximum hopcount 100
    EIGRP maximum metric variance 1
    Redistributing: igrp 100, eigrp 100
    Automatic network summarization is not in effect
    Routing for Networks:
        10.0.0.0
        172.16.0.0
    Routing Information Sources:

Gateway	Distance	Last Update
(this router)	5	00:16:51
10.10.12.1	90	00:24:48
172.16.0.13	90	00:08:44

    Distance: internal 90 external 170

Viewing the Routing Table

FIGURE 15.10   The "show ip route" Command

```
Router_C#sh ip route
Codes: C - connected, S - static, I - IGRP, R - RIP, M - mobile, B - BGP
       D - EIGRP, EX - EIGRP external, O - OSPF, IA - OSPF inter area
       N1 - OSPF NSSA external type 1, N2 - OSPF NSSA external type 2
       E1 - OSPF external type 1, E2 - OSPF external type 2, E - EGP
       i - IS-IS, L1 - IS-IS level-1, L2 - IS-IS level-2, * - candidate default
       U - per-user static route, o - ODR

Gateway of last resort is not set

     10.0.0.0/8 is variably subnetted, 3 subnets, 2 masks
D       10.10.1.0/24 [90/2707456] via 172.16.0.13, 00:10:06, Serial0
D       10.10.3.16/28 [90/23310336] via 172.16.0.13, 00:10:06, Serial0
C       10.10.3.32/28 is directly connected, Ethernet0
     172.16.0.0/30 is subnetted, 3 subnets
C       172.16.0.12 is directly connected, Serial0
D       172.16.0.8 [90/2681856] via 172.16.0.13, 00:10:06, Serial0
D       172.16.0.4 [90/23284736] via 172.16.0.13, 00:10:06, Serial0
```

All the subnets of network 10.0.0.0 are in **bold**.

For your information and to point out how powerful EIGRP can be, I have included a configuration of EIGRP that will route IPX and Appletalk (Figure 15.11).

IPX and Appletalk can be very chatty; EIGRP will route these protocols with a minimum amount of traffic.

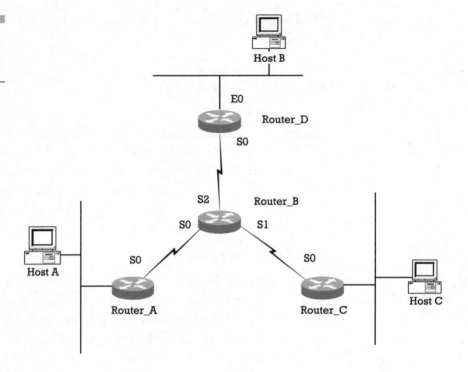

FIGURE 15.11
EIGRP Routing IPX
and Appletalk

TABLE 15.3
Appletalk & IPX
Addresses

		Appletalk Zone	Appletalk Cable	IPX Network
Router_A				
	S0	one	100-100	1
	E0	left	400-410	CAD
Router_B				
	S0	one	100-100	1
	S1	two	200-200	2
	S2	three	300-300	3
Router_C				
	S0	two	200-200	2
	E0	right	500-510	DAD
Router_D				
	S0	three	300-300	3
	E0	top	600-610	TOP

FIGURE 15.12   Router_D Configuration of EIGRP Routing IPX and Appletalk

```
Router_D#sh run
Building configuration...

Current configuration:
!
version 11.3
no service password-encryption
!
hostname Router_D
!
appletalk routing eigrp 500
appletalk route-redistribution
ipx routing 0010.7b15.bd41
!
interface Ethernet0/0
   no ip address
   appletalk cable-range 600-610 600.180
   appletalk zone top
   ipx network BAD
!
interface Serial0/0
   no ip address
   no ip mroute-cache
   appletalk cable-range 300-300 300.207
   appletalk zone three
   ipx network 3
   no fair-queue
   clockrate 56000
!
interface BRI0/0
   no ip address
   shutdown
!
interface TokenRing0/0
   no ip address
   shutdown
```

continued on next page

```
    ring-speed 16
!
interface FastEthernet1/0
  no ip address
  shutdown
!
ip classless
!
ipx router eigrp 100
  network 3
  network BAD
!
line con 0
line aux 0
line vty 0 4
  login
!
end
```

FIGURE 15.13   Appletalk Routing Table of Router_D

Router_D#sh app route

Codes: R - RTMP derived, E - EIGRP derived, C - connected, A - AURP
       S - static P - proxy
6 routes in internet

The first zone listed for each entry is its default (primary) zone.

R Net 100-100 [1/G] via 300.176, 1 sec, Serial0/0, zone one
R Net 200-200 [1/G] via 300.176, 1 sec, Serial0/0, zone two
C Net 300-300 directly connected, Serial0/0, zone three
R Net 400-410 [2/G] via 300.176, 1 sec, Serial0/0, zone left
R Net 500-510 [2/G] via 300.176, 1 sec, Serial0/0, zone right
C Net 600-610 directly connected, Ethernet0/0, zone top

FIGURE 15.14 IPX Routing Table of Router_D

```
Router_D#sh ipx route
Codes: C - Connected primary network, c - Connected secondary network
       S - Static, F - Floating static, L - Local (internal), W - IPXWAN
       R - RIP, E - EIGRP, N - NLSP, X - External, A – Aggregate
s - seconds, u - uses, U - Per-user static
6 Total IPX routes. Up to 1 parallel paths and 16 hops allowed.

No default route known.
C    3 (HDLC),              Se0/0
C    BAD (NOVELL-ETHER),    Et0/0
E    1 [2681856/0] via      3.0007.7816.fe54, age 00:03:33,
                  1u, Se0/0
E    2 [2681856/0] via      3.0007.7816.fe54, age 00:03:34,
                  1u, Se0/0
E    CAD [2707456/0] via    3.0007.7816.fe54, age 00:03:34,
                  1u, Se0/0
E    DAD [2707456/0] via    3.0007.7816.fe54, age 00:03:34,
                  1u, Se0/0
```

Summary

EIGRP is a Cisco proprietary advanced distance-vector routing protocol.

Features include the ability to use VLSM and multiple routing protocol support.

Exercises

15.1: What EIGRP command must be configured for EIGRP to "act" in a classless fashion?

15.2: What are the five metrics used by EIGRP?

15.3: What is the administrative distance for EIGRP?

15.4: What routed protocols can EIGRP route?

15.5: EIGRP must be used with a Cisco router. (T/F)

Answers

15.1: "no auto-summary"

15.2: Bandwidth, delay, load reliablity, and MTU.

15.3: 90

15.4: IP, IPX, and Appletalk

15.5: False; the Cisco IOS must be used, but not necessarily Cisco routers. It is possible to have a router under another name that uses the Cisco IOS.

CHAPTER 16

IP Access Lists

Objective

- Describe access lists.
- Describe and configure IP standard access lists.
- Describe and configure IP extended access lists.

Access Lists

Access lists can be used to control and/or manage traffic in or out of router interfaces. They can permit or deny traffic based on certain parameters. Access lists can be part of a firewall scheme.

Access lists can be used to:

■ Define interesting traffic for dial up links
■ Control routing updates
■ Define certain traffic for use with Cisco's queuing features.

In the world of IP, access lists can be defined either as standard or extended.

IP Standard Access Lists

TIP

A standard list can only key on the source IP address.

Consider the Figure 16.1 topology, Table 16.1, and the following scenario.

We wish to block all IP traffic that originates from Host B from getting to Host C, at the same time permitting Host B to communicate with all other hosts.

In another words Host B will not be allowed to communicate with Host C but will be allowed to communicate with everyone else.

TABLE 16.1

Addresses of Figure 16.1

	S0	S1	S2	E0
Router_A	172.16.0.10	N/A	N/A	10.10.1.1/24
Router_B	172.16.0.9	172.16.0.13	172.16.0.5	N/A
Router_C	172.16.0.14	N/A	N/A	10.10.3.33/28
Router_D	172.16.0.6	N/A	N/A	10.10.3.17/28
Host A				10.10.1.2/24
Host B				10.10.3.18/28
Host C				10.10.3.34/28
Mask	255.255.255.252	255.255.255.252	255.255.255.252	

FIGURE 16.1
Standard Access
List Placement

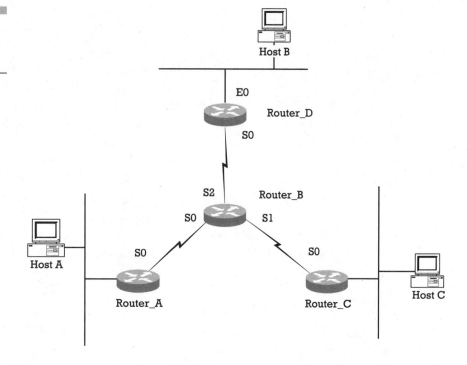

The scenario dictates that we identify the source address of 10.10.3.18. If we use a standard list we cannot identify the destination address as part of the access list; as a result we are not concerned with the actual IP address of the destination. What we need to look at is the location of Host C.

It seems likely that our access list must deny traffic with a source address of 10.10.3.18 and permit traffic with any other source address.

Where should the standard access list be placed?

If we place the list on interface E0 inbound of Router_D we would keep all traffic from Host B from going anywhere. As a result Host B would only be able to communicate with other hosts that share the same network.

If we place the list on the E0 outbound of Router_C, Host B would still be able to communicate with Host A.

Possibly we could place the access list on the outbound interface S1 of Router_B, but that would also deny Host B IP access to Router_C, which may or may not be a bad thing.

In general, a standard access list will be placed close to the destination so as not to block traffic that will go to another location.

Suppose we were to add other hosts on the network along with Host C; would Host B be able to communicate with those hosts? We will take a look at that scenario later in this chapter.

Consider what is actually going to happen when Host B attempts to communicate with Host C. The packets will travel through Router D where processing will occur, then across the serial link to Router_B, where bandwidth will be used, then again Router_B will have to process the packet, then across another serial link where more bandwidth will be burned, then to Router_C where more processing will be used *only to be denied when the packet is switched to interface E0 of Router_C.*

This is like traveling five miles down a street only to find out it is a dead end! Why not put the dead end sign at the beginning of the street so we do not have to waste time traveling the five-mile course?

In the case of standard access lists, since we cannot specify the destination, we do not know where the packet is headed, therefore we have no choice but to allow it to travel through our network.

Configuration of a Standard Access List

It takes two steps to activate an access list:

- Configure the list
- Place the list on an interface

If either step is performed without the other there will be no effect. If we configure a list and do not apply it to an interface, it will not affect traffic. If we place an access list on an interface and do not have an access list created, it will have no effect.

Every access list will be associated with a number. I have included router output in Figure 16.2, which displays the number with the associated protocol. In our case we will use a number between 1 and 99; it makes no difference what number we pick.

An access list is processed from the top down. Each line is read by the router. If the packet in question matches the parameters set in the access list, that packet will either be permitted or denied. The next packet will then be examined and the process again starts from the first line of the access list. The order in which lines are placed in the access list is of utmost importance.

To illustrate this point let us assume we have a two-line access list as follows:

Permit any
Deny host 10.10.3.18

Host 10.10.3.18 would never be denied because this address matches the first address of "any" and therefore will be permitted. As a matter of fact, the last line of this access list will NEVER be read.

It is also important to remember that the last line of every access list will deny all traffic. This is called an *implicit statement* because we DO NOT have to configure this line. The line is appended to the end of an access list as soon as we create the list. This will be an important consideration in our scenario because we want to deny only Host B. No other traffic will be denied and therefore we must explicitly permit other traffic.

An analogy to the above concepts might be a guard at a gate of a residential community. A car pulls up to the gate and must stop. The driver then will identify him or herself. The guard will begin processing the list to find the name; as the guard works down the list of names the car is still stopped; finally the name is matched as someone who may go into this community.

Now let us assume that the name is not matched on the list either as someone who is allowed access or someone who is not allowed access. Does this person get to go in? Of course not; there is always an implicit deny at the end of the guard's list.

An access list will affect performance. Just as that car must sit and wait for the guard to check the list, so a packet must wait as the router processes the list; the longer the list very possibly the longer the wait. That will depend on whether or not the packet is matched on a line toward the top or the bottom of the list. We will look at a feature of an extended access list that may help us define the list in a more efficient manner.

FIGURE 16.2   Configuring a Standard Access List

```
Router_C#config t
Enter configuration commands, one per line.  End with CNTL/Z.
Router_C(config)#access-list ?
  <1-99>      IP standard access list
```

continued on next page

```
          <100-199>   IP extended access list
          <1000-1099> IPX SAP access list
          <1100-1199> Extended 48-bit MAC address access list
          <1200-1299> IPX summary address access list
          <200-299>   Protocol type-code access list
          <300-399>   DECnet access list
          <400-499>   XNS standard access list
          <500-599>   XNS extended access list
          <600-699>   Appletalk access list
          <700-799>   48-bit MAC address access list
          <800-899>   IPX standard access list
          <900-999>   IPX extended access list

Router_C(config)#access-list 50 ?
    deny    Specify packets to reject
    permit  Specify packets to forward

Router_C(config)#access-list 50 permit ?
    Hostname or A.B.C.D  Address to match
    any               Any source host
    host              A single host address
```

Router_C(config)#access-list 50 deny 10.10.3.18 0.0.0.0
Router_C(config)#access-list 50 permit any

In Figure 16.2 I have shown the wild card mask of 0.0.0.0 which, as we have already discussed in previous chapters, means to match all 32 bits of the preceding address. This command can be shortened by using the key word host as shown below:

Router_C(config)#access-list 50 deny host 10.10.3.18

If we wanted to identify all host addresses of the subnet 10.10.3.16/28 our command would be as follows:

Router_C(config)#access-list 50 deny 10.10.3.16 0.0.0.15

This is a review of material already covered. I show it here so you can understand the importance of the inverse mask. This method certainly beats having to identify each of the possible 15 hosts with a separate line.

Verifying Access List Configuration

FIGURE 16.3   Displaying the Configured List

> **Router_C#show access-list 50**
> Standard IP access list 50
>   deny   10.10.3.18
>   permit any

The next step after the access list is configured is to place it on the appropriate interface. The list can be applied to either the inbound or the outbound direction. If we do not specify the direction, it will be applied to the outbound. I have included the key word "out" in Figure 16.4 for clarity purposes.

FIGURE 16.4   Activating an Access List

> Router_C(config)#int e0
> **Router_C(config-if)#ip access-group 50 out**

Verify the Access List has been Applied to an Interface

FIGURE 16.5   Verifying Placement and Direction with the "show interface" command

> Router_C#sh ip int e0
> Ethernet0 is up, line protocol is up
>   Internet address is 10.10.3.33/28
>   Broadcast address is 255.255.255.255
>   Address determined by setup command
>   MTU is 1500 bytes
>   Helper address is not set
>   Directed broadcast forwarding is enabled

continued on next page

Outgoing access list is 50
Inbound access list is not set
Proxy ARP is enabled
Security level is default
Split horizon is enabled
ICMP redirects are always sent
ICMP unreachables are always sent
ICMP mask replies are never sent
IP fast switching is enabled
IP fast switching on the same interface is disabled
IP multicast fast switching is enabled
Router Discovery is disabled
IP output packet accounting is disabled
IP access violation accounting is disabled
TCP/IP header compression is disabled
Probe proxy name replies are disabled
Gateway Discovery is disabled
Policy routing is disabled
Network address translation is disabled

FIGURE 16.6   Verifying Activation with the "show run" Command

Router_c#sh run
Building configuration...

Current configuration:
!
version 11.2
no service password-encryption
no service udp-small-servers
no service tcp-small-servers
!
hostname Router_C
!
appletalk routing eigrp 300
appletalk route-redistribution

continued on next page

```
ipx routing 0060.09c3.df60
!
interface Ethernet0
   ip address 10.10.3.33 255.255.255.240
   ip access-group 50 out
   appletalk cable-range 500-510 508.156
   appletalk zone right
   ipx network DAD
!
interface Ethernet1
   no ip address
   shutdown
!
interface Serial0
   ip address 172.16.0.14 255.255.255.252
   appletalk cable-range 200-200 200.216
   appletalk zone two
   appletalk protocol eigrp
   ipx network 2
   no fair-queue
!
interface Serial1
   no ip address
   shutdown
!
no ip classless
access-list 50 deny   10.10.3.18
access-list 50 permit any
!
ipx router eigrp 100
   network 2
   network DAD
!
line con 0
   exec-timeout 0 0
line aux 0
line vty 0 4
   login
end
```

IP Extended Access Lists

In our example from Figure 16.1 we denied Host B from communicating not only with Host C but with any other host that might be on the same network with Host C. In Figure 16.7 we have changed the scenario somewhat and have added another Host, C2. We still wish to block communication from Host B to Host C, but only to Host C, not Host C2.

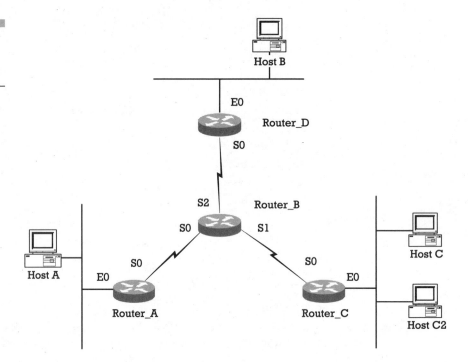

An extended IP access list has the ability to key on the following:

■ Protocol
■ IP source address
■ IP destination address
■ Port number.

Because we can now identify both source and destination addresses we can write an access list that will deny Host B from communicating with Host C only (Figure 16.8).

FIGURE 16.8 Configuring an Extended Access List

```
Router_C#config t
Enter configuration commands, one per line.  End with CNTL/Z.
Router_C(config)#access-list ?
    <1-99>       IP standard access list
    <100-199>    IP extended access list
    <1000-1099> IPX SAP access list
    <1100-1199> Extended 48-bit MAC address access list
    <1200-1299> IPX summary address access list
    <200-299>    Protocol type-code access list
    <300-399>    DECnet access list
    <400-499>    XNS standard access list
    <500-599>    XNS extended access list
    <600-699>    Appletalk access list
    <700-799>    48-bit MAC address access list
    <800-899>    IPX standard access list
    <900-999>    IPX extended access list
Router_C(config)#access-list 150 deny ip host 10.10.3.18 host
    10.10.3.34
Router_C(config)#access-list 150 permit ip any any
```

Notice the different syntax between a standard and an extended list. Now a number between 100 and 199 must be used. We must also identify a protocol, in this case IP, and a destination address, which is the IP address of Host C. Just as in the case of a standard list, the second line of the access list is needed due to the "implicit deny all" at the end of each list.

Verifying Access List Configuration

FIGURE 16.9 Displaying the Configured List

```
Extended IP access list 150
    deny  ip host 10.10.3.18 host 10.10.3.34 (16 matches)
    permit ip any any (1245 matches
```

One of the nice features of the extended access list is the fact that we can see how many times an access list line has matched a packet.

Figure 16.9 shows that 16 times Host B has attempted to communicate with Host C and 1245 times a packet matched the permit statement.

This can be very useful, especially when we have a long access list. Earlier we said that an access list will affect router performance. We would like our permit traffic to be toward the top of the list if possible. We do not really care about the traffic we are going to deny, let it wait, keep it toward the bottom of the list.

If we have several permit statements all toward the top, the fact that we can see the matches of each statement will allow us to fine tune the access list so the permit lines with the most matches can be moved higher in the list.

If a lot matches occur on deny statements they may be a policy or security problem.

Where should the extended access list be placed?

Because we can now specify the destination address, we can move the access list closer to the source address. This provides us with the benefits of reducing the processing of Router_B and Router_C. Bandwidth will also not be wasted for traffic that will ultimately be denied.

The access list should be placed on **interface E0 inbound** of Router_D.

FIGURE 16.10   Activating an Access List

```
Router_D(config)#int e0
Router_D(config-if)#ip access-group 150 in
```

Verify the Access List has been Applied to an Interface

FIGURE 16.11   Verifying Placement and Direction with the "show interface" Command

```
Router_D#sh ip int e0
Ethernet0 is up, line protocol is up
```

continued on next page

Internet address is 10.10.3.17/28
Broadcast address is 255.255.255.255
Address determined by setup command
MTU is 1500 bytes
Helper address is not set
Directed broadcast forwarding is enabled
Outgoing access list is not set
Inbound access list is 150
Proxy ARP is enabled
Security level is default
Split horizon is enabled
ICMP redirects are always sent
ICMP unreachables are always sent
ICMP mask replies are never sent
IP fast switching is enabled
IP fast switching on the same interface is disabled
IP multicast fast switching is enabled
Router Discovery is disabled
IP output packet accounting is disabled
IP access violation accounting is disabled
TCP/IP header compression is disabled
Probe proxy name replies are disabled
Gateway Discovery is disabled
Policy routing is disabled
Network address translation is disabled

Let us change our scenario once again; this time we will deny Host B from using the telnet application with Host C. Host B is allowed the use of other IP applications and protocols, we just want to *deny telnet only*.

Since an extended access list allows us to specify port numbers, we should be able to do this with no problem (Figure 16.12).

FIGURE 16.12   Configuring an Extended Access List with a Port Number

Router_C(config)#access-list 150 deny ?
    <0-255> An IP protocol number

continued on next page

eigrp	Cisco's EIGRP routing protocol
gre	Cisco's GRE tunneling
icmp	Internet Control Message Protocol
igmp	Internet Gateway Message Protocol
igrp	Cisco's IGRP routing protocol
ip	Any Internet Protocol
ipinip	IP in IP tunneling
nos	KA9Q NOS compatible IP over IP tunneling
ospf	OSPF routing protocol
tcp	**Transmission Control Protocol**
udp	User Datagram Protocol

Router_C(config)#access-list 150 deny **tcp** host 10.10.3.18 host
10.10.3.34 ?

eq	**Match only packets on a given port number**
established	Match established connections
gt	Match only packets with a greater port number
log	Log matches against this entry
log-input	Log matches against this entry, including input interface
lt	Match only packets with a lower port number
neq	Match only packets not on a given port number
precedence	Match packets with given precedence value
range	Match only packets in the range of port numbers
tos	Match packets with given TOS value
<cr>	

Router_C(config)#access-list 150 deny **tcp** host 10.10.3.18 host
10.10.3.34 **eq** ?

<0-65535>	Port number
bgp	Border Gateway Protocol (179)
chargen	Character generator (19)
cmd	Remote commands (rcmd, 514)
daytime	Daytime (13)
discard	Discard (9)
domain	Domain Name Service (53)
echo	Echo (7)
exec	Exec (rsh, 512)
finger	Finger (79)
ftp	File Transfer Protocol (21)
ftp-data	FTP data connections (used infrequently, 20)

gopher	Gopher (70)
hostname	NIC hostname server (101)
ident	Ident Protocol (113)
irc	Internet Relay Chat (194)
klogin	Kerberos login (543)
kshell	Kerberos shell (544)
login	Login (rlogin, 513)
lpd	Printer service (515)
nntp	Network News Transport Protocol (119)
pop2	Post Office Protocol v2 (109)
pop3	Post Office Protocol v3 (110)
smtp	Simple Mail Transport Protocol (25)
sunrpc	Sun Remote Procedure Call (111)
syslog	Syslog (514)
tacacs	TAC Access Control System (49)
talk	Talk (517)
telnet	**Telnet (23)**
time	Time (37)
uucp	Unix-to-Unix Copy Program (540)
whois	Nicname (43)
www	World Wide Web (HTTP, 80)

Router_C(config)#Access-list 150 deny tcp host 10.10.3.18 host
**   10.10.3.34 eq telnet**
Router_C(config)#Access-list 150 deny tcp host 10.10.3.18 host
**   10.10.3.34 eq 23**

Reviewing Figure 16.12, we see that we now identify TCP, not IP as the protocol, because telnet is a TCP protocol. Appended to the end of the line, we will identify the port number for telnet, which is 23, or use the name telnet. I have included both ways for clarity. Both ways are not required.

Other port names and numbers can be viewed by using the "?" as shown in Figure 16.12.

We are not finished yet; remember that we want Host B to be able to use other IP protocols in communication with Host C. So we need to add one more line to our access list:

Router_C(config)#access-list 150 permit ip any any

Notice we denied TCP but we are going to permit IP; if we were to permit TCP only, that would deny all IP protocol packets due to the implicit "deny all" statement at the end of the access list.

A few years ago I had a student in New York who performed a lab similar to this; as his last line he permitted TCP, not IP; he got upset when all his IP RIP routes disappeared.

Since the RIP updates use the IP protocol, they were all denied and therefore the routing table was lost.

FIGURE 16.13   Viewing the Access List

Router_C#sh access-list 150
Extended IP access list 150
deny   tcp host 10.10.3.18 host 10.10.3.34 eq telnet
permit ip any any

Summary

- A standard access list will deny an entire protocol.
- A number ranging from 1 to 99 will identify a standard access list.
- A standard access list can only key on a source address.
- A standard access list will be placed close to the destination.
- A number ranging from 100 to 199 will identify an extended access list.
- An extended access list can key on the following:

  1. Source IP address
  2. Destination IP address
  3. Protocol
  4. Port

- An extended access list will be placed close to the source.

Exercises

16.1: What type of access list may save on bandwidth and processing?

16.2: What key information can a standard list identify?

16.3: What key information can a extended list identify?

16.4: Where will a standard list most likely be placed?

16.5: Where will an extended list most likely be placed?

16.6: Access lists may be used when defining traffic to place a call. (T/F)

16.7: What port number identifies FTP?

16.8: If a 10-line access list is configured, how many lines actually make up the list?

16.9: A protocol does not need to be configured in an extended list. (T/F)

16.10: A port number does not need to be configured in an extended list. (T/F)

Answers

16.1: Extended Access List

16.2: Source IP address

16.3:
Source IP address
Destination IP address
Protocol
Port

16.4: Close to the destination

16.5: Close to the source

16.6: True

16.7: Port # 21

16.8: 11, due to the "implicit deny" statement

16.9: False; you must identify a protocol.

16.10: True; a protocol port number does not need to be configured.

CHAPTER 17

Cisco's Network Address Translation

Objective

- Explain the concept of address translation.
- Configure Cisco's network address translation (NAT).

Public Addressing

Public addresses are assigned by the InterNIC. These are addresses that can go out into the Internet and are assigned and registered to an organization.

Private Addressing

Private addresses are non-registered addresses.

TABLE 17.1

Private Addresses

Class A 10.0.0.0 (1 network)

Class B 172.16.0.0 – 172.31.0.0 (16 networks)

Class C 192.168.0.0 – 192.168.255.0 (256 networks)

The addresses in Table 17.1 have been set aside for private addressing. If an organization is not going to use the Internet, or an address translation solution will be used, these addresses are the suggested addresses that should be assigned as "inside" addresses.

Internet routers are programmed to toss any packets carrying these addresses in the bit bucket. There are no Internet police that will come and arrest you if you use a public address on the inside; but consider a packet that has a destination address to a "real" public address that happens to be the same address that your organization chose for the inside address.

How will that packet ever exit the network? The router will see the destination address and keep the packet local.

Cisco's NAT solution is used when there is a pool of public addresses. The router will translate addresses from private to public when going out to the Internet, and translate public to private on the return.

Advantages of NAT

■ Once a host has been configured with a private address, NAT can be configured without the need to change the host address. When the organization receives its pool of public addresses a few routers will be configured with these public addresses, while the host addresses remain the same.

■ NAT conserves registered public addresses.

■ NAT will also "hide" the host addresses, which in many cases can be a good thing.

Figure 17.1 presents a scenario in which the organization has received the public address of 200.200.200.0 255.255.255.0. The private address of 10.0.0.0 is being used on the inside.

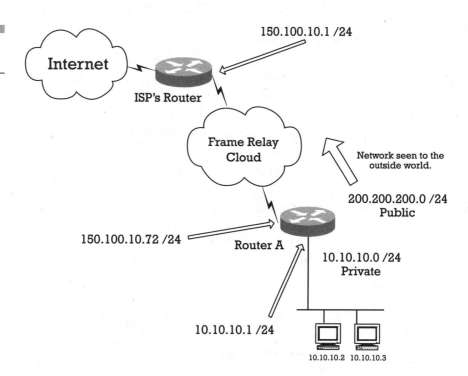

FIGURE 17.1
NAT Topology

Our goal is to configure Router A to provide us with address translation to go from a private address to the public address. We also want to advertise this public address out to the world.

Configuring NAT

The configuration commands that accomplish these goals are presented in **bold**.

FIGURE 17.2 NAT Configuration

```
Current configuration:
!
version 11.3
no service password-encryption
!
hostname router_a
!
enable secret 5 $1$.s1R$iaEqZxLnYJo2QlZi8UNaOO
enable password guess
!
ip nat pool nat-example 200.200.200.1 200.200.200.254 prefix-length
   24
ip nat inside source list 1 pool nat-example
!
interface Ethernet0/0
   ip address 200.200.200.1 255.255.255.0 secondary
   ip address 10.10.10.1 255.255.255.0
   ip nat inside
!
interface Serial0/0
   ip address 150.100.10.72 255.255.255.0
   ip nat outside
   encapsulation frame-relay
!
interface TokenRing0/0
   no ip address
   shutdown
   ring-speed 16
!
interface FastEthernet1/0
   no ip address
   shutdown
!
router rip
   network 200.200.200.0
```

continued on next page

```
        network 150.100.0.0
!
ip classless
no logging buffered
access-list 1 permit 10.10.10.0 0.0.0.255
!
!
line con 0
    exec-timeout 0 0
line aux 0
line vty 0 4
    login
!
end
```

Explanation of Router Commands

ip nat pool nat-example 200.200.200.1 200.200.200.254 prefix-length 24

This defines the pool name of "nat-example"; the first public address is 200.200.200.1 and the last address 200.200.200.254. The mask is 255.255.255.0 or /24.

ip nat inside source list 1 pool nat-example

This applies access list 1 to the pool "nat-example".

ip address 200.200.200.1 255.255.255.0 secondary

This applies the public address to the e0/0 interface as a secondary address. Since we want to advertise the public address we must configure the address.

ip nat inside

This defines the e0/0 interface as the inside address.

ip nat outside

This defines serial 0 as the outside addresses.

router rip
network 200.200.200.0

Because we configured the 200.200.200.0 address as a secondary address we can advertise it with IP RIP.

Access-list 1 permit 10.10.10.0 0.0.0.0.255

This permits the private addresses on the 10.10.10.0 subnet to be translated to the public addresses.

Keep in mind that there is always the implicit "deny all" statement at the end of every access list.

Figure 17.3 illustrates an actual translation taken after the 10.10.10.1 interface of the router and the workstation 10.10.10.2 performed a ping of the serial interface of the ISP's router.

Verifying NAT

FIGURE 17.3   Viewing the Translation Table

```
router_a#sh ip nat trans
Pro Inside global    Inside local    Outside local    Outside global
--- 200.200.200.1    10.10.10.1      ---              ---
--- 200.200.200.2    10.10.10.2      ---              ---
```

Figure 17.3 illustrates two translations. The first was the inside private address of 10.10.10.1 being translated to the inside global (public) address of 200.200.200.1; the second translation was from 10.10.10.2 to 200.200.200.2.

NAT can also be configured to "overload". The translation does not need to be on a one-to-one basis. In the example above we are permitting the 254 addresses of the 10.10.10.0 subnet to be mapped to the 254 addresses of the 200.200.200.0 network.

With the overload option we could map many to few. In such a case upper-layer protocols would be used to distinguish traffic.

NAT may also be used in an "overlapping" situation. Overlapping occurs when an organization has chosen an inside local address that was not from the private address Table 17.1.

Summary

Cisco's NAT is used to map private inside addresses to global inside public addresses.

Exercises

17.1: What is meant by an inside local address?

17.2: What is meant by an outside global address?

17.3: What is the purpose of an access list when using NAT?

17.4: How can NAT be helpful when an organization has changed ISPs?

17.5: How can NAT conserve registered IP addresses?

Answers

17.1: An inside local address is typically an address chosen from the private addresses defined by the InterNIC. This address will not go out into the public and will be translated into an inside global registered address.

17.2: An outside global address is a public registered address that will be mapped to an inside local address.

17.3: The access list defines what private local addresses can be translated into public global addresses.

17.4: When an ISP is changed, new public IP addresses need to be assigned. These new addresses can be configured on a router or routers but hosts need not be reconfigured.

17.5: Overload is a feature of NAT that allows for a many-to-few mapping. Many local private addresses can be mapped to a few public addresses.

CHAPTER 18

Hot Standby Router Protocol (HSRP)

Objectives

- Describe ARP.
- Describe the concept of HSRP.
- Configure HSRP.
- Describe the configuration of a Windows workstation.

Address Resolution Protocol (ARP)

In Chapter 1 we stated that communication between and among hosts takes place by using MAC addresses.

How does a host learn its own MAC address?

When a NIC is installed in a device, the device will read the BIA address from the NIC and place it into RAM. At that point the device knows its own MAC address.

How does a device learn the MAC address of the intended destination?

In the world of IP, this feat is accomplished by using the Address Resolution Protocol (ARP).

Refer to Figure 18.1. Let us assume that Workstation A at 192.68.5.17 has a data packet with the destination address of 172.35.6.4, which is Workstation B. For this communication to be successful Workstation A must go off its own network.

For Workstation A to go off its own network it must be configured with a default gateway. In our case the default gateway will be the E0 interface of Router_A; the IP address of the E0 interface is 192.68.5.19.

Workstation A will send an ARP request in the form of a broadcast out on to the Ethernet. All hosts connected to the Ethernet will see the broadcast, but only the host with the IP address of 192.68.5.19 will reply. Refer to Figures 18.2 and 18.3.

Figures 18.2 and 18.3 illustrate an ARP request and reply respectively. In this case Workstation A is seeking the MAC address of 192.68.5.19.

All Fs on the second line of Figure 18.2 signify a broadcast. Notice also the all 0s for the destination MAC address.

Figure 18.3 illustrates Router_A responding to the ARP request with an ARP reply that includes the MAC address of its E0 interface.

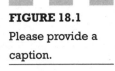

FIGURE 18.1

Please provide a caption.

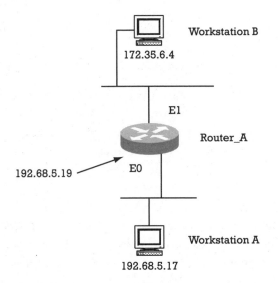

FIGURE 18.2

ARP Request

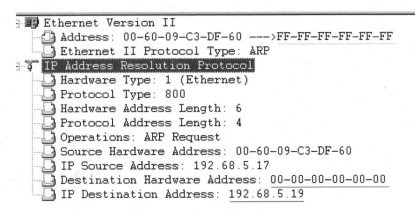

FIGURE 18.3

ARP Reply

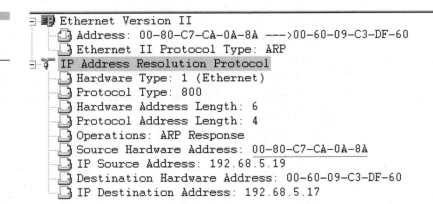

From the ARP reply, Workstation A now knows the MAC address of the default gateway is:

00-80-C7-CA-0A-8A

At this point Workstation A can send the data packet to Workstation B. But this is a step-by-step process. When Router_A receives the data packet, Router_A will switch the packet to the E1 interface. At that point Router_A may have to send an ARP request out the E1 interface to find the MAC address of Workstation B. If previous communication has occurred it may not be necessary to send an ARP; Router_A may have the MAC address stored in its ARP cache.

As data packets travel across the internetwork the IP addresses of source and destination will never change, but the MAC address will always change to reflect the current source and destination.

When a host is configured to use the IP protocol three pieces of information are required:

- IP address
- Address mask
- Default gateway

In some cases it is critical for the workstation or host to have continuous access to the network. HSRP provides a backup router to act as a default gateway.

The Concept

Refer to Figure 18.4. Cisco's Hot Standby Router Protocol (HSRP) provides Workstation A with a backup router in case its default gateway goes down. HSRP creates a virtual router with a virtual MAC address and a virtual IP address.

Many students have suggested that Windows 95 has this feature. While it is true that we can add multiple default gateways, this feature is only used at boot-up time. In other words, the host will use ARP for the first default gateway on the list; if that ARP fails it will continue down the list.

What happens when the host has successfully found the default gateway and it subsequently dies? The host will need to be re-booted.

HSRP solves this problem because it is dynamic; if the primary router dies, the secondary will take over and the host will never know the difference.

Now we should take a look at the following scenario.

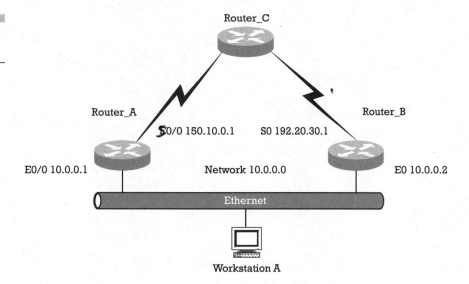

Configuring HSRP

In the following configurations Router_A will be the active router, meaning Router_A will assume all packet transfers. Router_B will be the standby router. Router_B will be ready to assume packet transfer responsibilities if Router_A goes down.

Router_A has been configured with a priority of 110, which is higher than the default priority of 100. Since no priority is configured for Router_B, Router_A will become the active router.

The IP address of 10.0.0.3 will be established as the virtual IP address. A virtual MAC address will also be selected by the Cisco IOS from a range of addresses.

The "standby preempt" command allows the router to become active.

FIGURE 18.5   Configuration for Router_A

```
version 11.3
no service password-encryption
!
hostname Router_A
!
enable secret 5 $1$.s1R$iaEqZxLnYJo2QlZi8UNaO0
enable password
!
interface Ethernet0/0
   ip address 10.0.0.1 255.0.0.0
   no ip redirects
   standby 1 priority 110
   standby 1 preempt
   standby 1 ip 10.0.0.3
!
interface Serial0/0
   ip address 150.10.0.1 255.255.0.0
   no ip mroute-cache
!
interface TokenRing0/0
   no ip address
   shutdown
   ring-speed 16
!
interface FastEthernet1/0
   no ip address
   shutdown
!
router igrp 100
   network 10.0.0.0
   network 150.10.0.0
!
ip classless
no logging buffered
!
```

continued on next page

```
line con 0
    exec-timeout 0 0
line aux 0
line vty 0 4
    login
!
end
```

FIGURE 18.6   Configuration for Router_B

```
Current configuration:
!
version 11.2
!
hostname Router_B
!
interface Ethernet0
    ip address 10.0.0.2 255.0.0.0
    no ip redirects
    standby 1 preempt
    standby 1 ip 10.0.0.3
!
interface Ethernet1
    no ip address
    shutdown
!
interface Serial0
    ip address 192.20.30.1 255.255.255.0
!
interface Serial1
    no ip address
    shutdown
!
router igrp 100
    network 10.0.0.0
    network 192.20.30.0
```

continued on next page

```
!
line con 0
line aux 0
line vty 0 4
  login
!
end
```

Figures 18.7 and 18.8 illustrate a Windows 95 configuration of the workstation.

Workstation A will be configured with a default gateway that represents the virtual IP address.

FIGURE 18.7

Configuration for
Workstation A

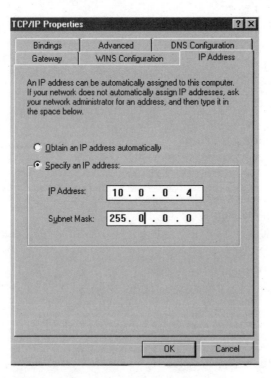

FIGURE 18.8

Configuration for
Workstation A

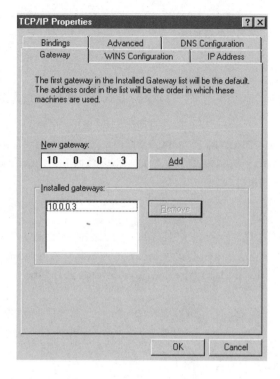

Figure 18.9 shows the result of putting the e0/0 interface in "shut" mode.

FIGURE 18.9   Router_B becomes Active

Router_A(config)#int e0/0

Router_A(config-if)#shut

Router_A(config-if)#

%STANDBY-6-STATECHANGE: Standby: 1: Ethernet0/0 state Active -> Init

%LINEPROTO-5-UPDOWN: Line protocol on Interface Ethernet0/0, changed state to down

%LINK-5-CHANGED: Interface Ethernet0/0, changed state to administratively down

Figure 18.10 shows the result of putting the e0/0 interface in "no shut" mode.

FIGURE 18.10   Router_A returns to Active State

```
Router_A(config-if)#no shut
Router_A(config-if)#
%LINEPROTO-5-UPDOWN: Line protocol on Interface Ethernet0/0,
    changed state to up

%LINK-3-UPDOWN: Interface Ethernet0/0, changed state to up
%STANDBY-6-STATECHANGE: Standby: 1: Ethernet0/0 state Listen
    -> Active
```

Figure 18.11 shows the result of a successful ping from Workstation A
and the echo reply. The echo request was initiated from Workstation A
to the fictitious IP address of the default gateway.

FIGURE 18.11   Ping Result

```
Router_B#debug ip icmp
ICMP packet debugging is on
Router_B#
ICMP: echo reply sent, src 10.0.0.3, dst 10.0.0.4
ICMP: echo reply sent, src 10.0.0.3, dst 10.0.0.4
ICMP: echo reply sent, src 10.0.0.3, dst 10.0.0.4
ICMP: echo reply sent, src 10.0.0.3, dst 10.0.0.4
Router_B#debug ip icmp
```

Summary

HSRP will provide a backup default gateway for a workstation. The
advantage is that the user will not lose connectivity to the network. Normally in such a condition the user will be off the network until the default
gateway is back up and the workstation will have to be re-booted.

Exercises

18.1: What advantage does HSRP offer?

18.2: What is the function of the active router?

18.3: What determines if the router will be the active router?

18.4: When HSRP is configured, the workstation should be configured with the IP address of the active router. (T/F)

18.5: What is the MAC address of the default gateway?

18.6: An ARP request is a broadcast. (T/F)

18.7: The ARP reply will contain the MAC address of the source. (T/F)

18.8: An ARP will contain the MAC address of the intended destination. (T/F)

Answers

18.1: HSRP provides a backup default gateway.

18.2: An active router will assume the duties of packet transfers.

18.3: The router with the highest priority will become the active router.

18.4: False; the workstation's default gateway will be the virtual IP address created when configuring HSRP.

18.5: The MAC address will be assigned from a range of addresses by the Cisco IOS.

18.6: True

18.7: True

18.8: False; there is no MAC address other than the broadcast MAC address. The reason for the ARP is to get the MAC address of the intended destination.

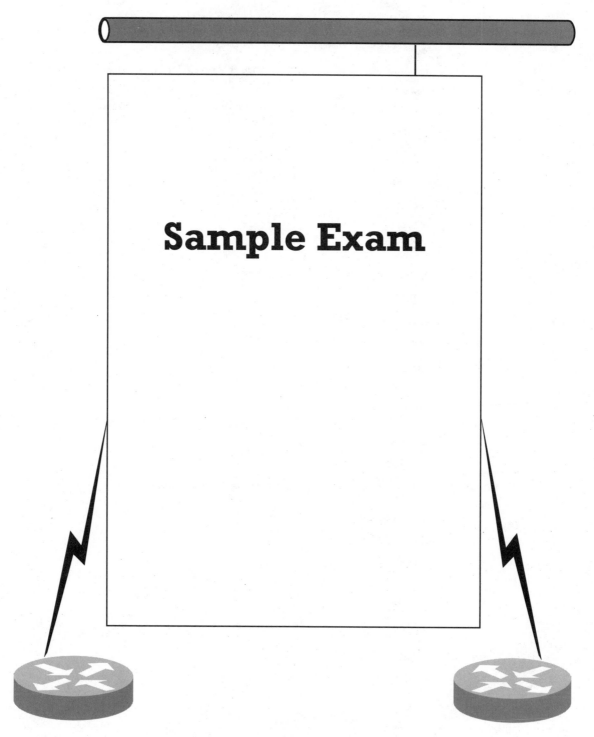

Sample Exam

Code Key

What follows is an explanation of the code letters in brackets that follow each question.

The first character represents the category of question.

A – ATM

B – bridging

C – Cisco specific

E – Ethernet

F – Frame relay

H – HDLC

I – FDDI

N – ISDN

O – OSI model

P – PPP

R – Routing

S – Switching

T – Token ring

X – X.25

x – Not applicable

The second character represents protocol or exam.

A – Appletalk

B – Banyan Vines

D – Decnet

E – EIGRP

I – IP

L – Dial on Demand

N – NLSP

O – OSPF

X – IPX

x – Not applicable

The third character represents the certification that the question will help you prepare for.

N – CCNA Exam #640-407

P – CCNP

D – CCDA & CCDP

Cisco Design Specialist Exam #9E0-004

Cisco Internetwork Design #640-025

The fourth character represents the exam.

A – CCDA Exam

D – Cisco Internetworking Design (CID) Exam

E – Relates to the two-day CCIE practical Exam

M – Cisco Monitoring and Troubleshooting Dial-up (CMTD) Exam #640-405

N – CCNA Exam #640-407

S – Switch Exam (CLSC) Exam #640-404

T – Cisco Internetworking Troubleshooting (CIT) Exam #640-406

V – Advanced Cisco Router Configuration (ACRC) Exam #640-403

As an example, when you come across a question coded "BXDx", it signifies a question that will help you gain the CCDA or CCDP certification.

If a question is coded [CIPV]:

Cisco Specific
Relating to IP
CCNP certification
Advanced exam

Since all the questions that are posted at **CCprep.com** are modeled after those that could also appear on the CCIE written test, we will not assign a specific code for this exam. As the need arises, we will add appropriate designations to this coding system.

In the future you will be able to request a practice test on-line, based on this code system. For example you may wish to build a model exam that contains 25 IP-related questions or you may want a mix of IP and IPX questions.

Question 1.   [CxNN] What command correctly displays configuration file stored in RAM?

a) show configuration
b) show running-config
c) show active-configuration file
d) write terminal
e) all of the above

Question 2.   [CxNN] What command correctly displays the configuration file stored in NVRAM?

a) show config
b) show running-config
c) show startup-config
d) write terminal
e) all of the above

Question 3.   [RINN] Which should be the subnet mask for a Class C address if 16 host are required?

a) 255.255.255. 224
b) 255.255.224.0
c) 0.0.0.224
d) 255.255.255.16
e) none of the above

Question 4.   [CxNN] After the configuration command is used when does it become effective?

a) immediately
b) after the router is rebooted
c) after you exit the configuration mode
d) depends on the change that is made
e) All of the above

Question 5.   [RINN] Which one of the following is true concerning Cisco's implementation of IP RIP and load balancing?

a) Activated by default
b) Must be configured

c) IPX does not load balance

d) Requires a Novell File Server

e) None of the above

Question 6.   [CINN] What will be the correct command on a Cisco router to set the IP address of an interface assuming you are at the "router(config-if)#" prompt?

a) ip address 192.82.4.7 255.255.255.252

b) ip address 192.82.4.7

c) ip 192.82.4.7

d) ip 192.82.4.7 255.255.255.252

e) none of the above

Question 7.   [CxNN] Which commands will display the IP address of all interfaces on a Cisco Router? (select the best answer)

a) show IP route

b) show IP address

c) show IP interface

d) show interface IP

e) display IP addresses

Question 8.   [RINN] Reverse Address Resolution Protocol (RARP) a process best described by which one of the following?

a) Where an IP host resolves its IP address by broadcasting its MAC address to the network and a RARP server assigns it an IP address.

b) Where an IP host resolves its MAC address by broadcasting to the local network its IP address.

c) Where an IP host tries to resolve the MAC address of a destination by sending a network broadcast. The destination responds to the broadcast with its MAC address.

d) Where an IP host resolves a destination IP address by sending a broadcast on the local network and the destination host responds with it's IP address.

Question 9. [RINN] Which one of the following is a link state Routing Protocol?

a) IP
b) OSPF
c) RIP
d) EIGRP

Question 10. [CxNN] Which one of the following explains the correct definition of administrative distance as it pertains to Cisco's IOS?

a) The process, by which, routers select an administrator for an autonomous system.
b) The process where a router will select the best path to a destination network.
c) The process where a router will distance itself from other routers due to it's lack of administrative experience.
d) The process where a router will prioritize routing protocols so that in the event two routing protocols have conflicting next hop addresses, the routing protocol with the lowest administrative distance will take priority.
e) The process where a router will prioritize routing protocols so that in the event two routing protocols have conflicting next hop addresses, the routing protocol with the highest administrative distance will take priority.

Question 11. [CIPM] Assuming that the s0 interface is on the outside of a Network Address Translation (NAT) router select the proper command to enable NAT on this interface.

a) ip nat enable
b) ip enable nat
c) ip enable nat outside
d) ip nat outside
e) ip nat enable outside

Question 12. [CIPV] Given the following networks and their respective subnet masks, choose the proper command or group of commands to summarize these networks to the fewest number of routes possible.

> 172.16.24.0 255.255.248.0
> 172.16.32.0 255.255.248.0
> 172.16.40.0 255.255.248.0
> 172.16.48.0 255.255.248.0
> 172.16.56.0 255.255.248.0

a) router(config)#router ospf 69
router(config-router)#area 0 range 172.16.24.0 255.255.224.0

b) router(config)#router ospf 69
router(config-router)#area 0 range 172.16.24.0 255.255.248.0
router(config-router)#area 0 range 172.16.32.0 255.255.255.0
router(config-router)#area 0 range 172.16.40.0 255.255.224.0

c) router(config)#router ospf 69
router(config-router)#area 0 range 172.16.24.0 255.255.255.248
router(config-router)#area 0 range 172.16.32.0 255.255.255.224

d) router(config)#router ospf 69
router(config-router)#area 0 range 172.16.24.0 255.255.224.0
router(config-router)#area 0 range 172.16.32.0 255.255.255.0

e) router(config)#router ospf 69
router(config-router)#area 0 range 172.16.24.0 255.255.248.0
router(config-router)#area 0 range 172.16.32.0 255.255.224.0

Question 13. [RIPV] Which of the following is true concerning EIGRP with "no auto-summary" configured?

a) EIGRP then becomes a link state routing protocol
b) EIGRP would then allow discontinuous networks to be configured
c) EIGRP could then be used to route between registered Autonomous Systems
d) none of the above

Question 14. [RINN] How many total hosts are possible with a Class C address and a subnet mask of 255.255.255.252?

a) 4
b) 30
c) 60
d) 62
e) 124

Question 15. [ROPV] Which one of the following is NOT a true statement?

a) A stub area receives LSA's for all inter-area networks
b) A totally stubby area receives LSA's for all intra-area networks
c) A totally stubby area is Cisco proprietary
d) Area 0 is always required
e) All of the above

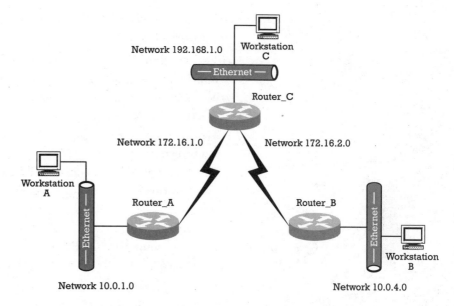

Refer to the above diagram and answer questions 16–20.

Question 16. [CIPx] Assuming IGRP is the routing protocol used for all networks on all routers.

a) Workstation A could not successfully ping both serial interfaces of Router_C

b) Workstation A could successfully ping the ethernet interface of Router_B

c) Workstation A could not successfully ping the ethernet interface of Router_C

d) Workstation A could successfully ping Workstation B

e) Workstation A could not successfully ping Workstation B

Question 17. [RIPx] Assuming IP RIP is the routing protocol used for all networks on all routers.

a) Workstation A could not successfully ping both serial interfaces of Router_C

b) Workstation A could successfully ping the Ethernet interface of Router_B

c) Workstation A could not successfully ping the Ethernet interface of Router_C

d) Workstation A could successfully ping Workstation B

e) Workstation A could not successfully ping Workstation B

Question 18. [RoPV] Assuming IP OSPF is the routing protocol used for all networks on all routers. Answer all that apply

a) Workstation A could not successfully ping both serial interfaces of Router_C

b) Workstation A could successfully ping the ethernet interface of Router_B

c) Workstation A could not successfully ping the ethernet interface of Router_C

d) Workstation A could successfully ping Workstation B

e) Workstation A could not successfully ping Workstation B

Question 19. [RINN] Assuming IGRP is the routing protocol used for all networks on all routers

a) Router_C would ping Workstation B with a 100% success rate

b) Router_C would ping Workstation B with a 50% success rate

c) Router_C would ping Workstation B with a 0% success rate

d) Router_C would ping Workstation A with a 100% success rate

e) Router_C would ping Workstation A with a 0% success rate

Question 20. [RIPx] Assuming IP RIP is the routing protocol used for all networks on all routers.

    a) Router_C would ping Workstation B with a 100% success rate

    b) Router_C would ping Workstation B with a 50% success rate

    c) Router_C would ping Workstation B with a 0% success rate

    d) Router_C would ping Workstation A with a 100% success rate

    e) Router_C would ping Workstation A with a 0% success rate

Question 21. [RxPV] Which of the following addresses can be summarized?

    a)   172.16.10.16/28
        172.16.10.48/28
        172.16.10.64/28
        172.16.10.80/28

    b)   172.16.10.0/16
        172.16.12.0/16
        172.16.14.0/16
        172.16.16.0/16

    c)   172.16.4.0/22
        172.16.8.0/22
        172.16.12.0/22
        172.16.16.0/22

    d)   172.16.10.112/30
        172.16.10.116/30
        172.16.10.120/30
        172.16.10.124/30

    e)   172.16.10.112/28
        172.16.10.116/28
        172.16.10.120/28
        172.16.10.124/28

Question 22. (CIPV) What traffic will be permitted into the serial 0 interface with the following configuration?

```
Router(config)#access-list 100 deny ip 207.239.71.1 0.0.0.0  any
Router(config)#access-list 100 permit ip 207.239.71.0 255.255.255.0
   any
Router(config)#interface serial 0
Router(config-if)#ip access-group 100 in
```

    a) All traffic from the 207.239.71.0 network
    b) All traffic from the 207.239.71.0 except 207.239.71.1
    c) No traffic will be permitted by this list
    d) None of the above

Question 23. [RINN] Consider the address of 10.6.165.0 and the mask of 255.255.224.0, what is the range of valid host addresses that sit on this wire?

    a) 10.6.165.1 to 10.6.165.254
    b) 10.6.165.0 to 10.6.165.255
    c) 10.6.160.1 to 10.6.191.255
    d) 10.6.160.1 to 10.6.191.254
    e) none of the above

Question 24. [RIPA] Classless IP addressing offers which of the following advantages over classful IP addressing?

    a) easier configuration of Classless routing protocols
    b) allows a single network addresses to carry multiple subnet masks
    c) allows the definition of subnets that contain only two host addresses
    d) allows the use of Cisco's IGRP

Question 25. [RINN] What does the address 212.10.14.63 /27 represent?

    a) host
    b) wire
    c) network
    d) broadcast
    e) none of the above

Question 26. [CINN] Which of the following are true of Administrative Distance?

a) measures the distance to a destination network
b) only applies to IGRP & EIGRP
c) measures the "reliability" of an IP routing protocol
d) the higher the value the more important the routing information

Question 27. [CINN] Which of the following is true of the following configuration line?

blue(config)#access-list 50 permit 212.10.10.1 0.0.0.0 155.10.10.1 0.0.0.0

a) would permit 212.10.10.1 access to 155.10.10.1
b) would deny all traffic other than the explicitly permitted traffic, if this was the only line of the access list
c) would permit all other traffic unless the "deny any any" command was used
d) this is an illegal command

Question 28. (CINN) Which of the following would prevent TFTP from address 172.16.16.16 to go through the Ethernet 0 interface 192.32.16.7?

a) access-list 101 deny host 172.16.16.16 1 host 192.32.16.7 eq 69
b) access-list 1 deny 172.16.16.16
c) access-list 1 deny 192.32.16.7
d) access-list 1 deny ip host 172.16.16.16 1 host 192.32.16.7 eq 69
e) none of the above

Question 29. (RIPV) Refer to the figure below.

What statement is true?

a) Host A would always be able to ping Host B successfully

b) Host A would sometimes be able to ping Host B

c) Host A would never be able to ping Host B

d) Depends on the routing protocol configured

Question 30. (RIPV) Refer to figure from Question 29. Which of the
following routing protocols could be used successfully?

a) IP RIP

b) OSPF

c) EIGRP

d) IGRP

e) The addressing scheme is wrong and never will work

Answers

Answer 1.

b) show running-config

d) write terminal

Answer 2.

a) show config

c) show startup-config

Answer 3.

a) 255.255.255.224

To calculate the number of host or networks using the formula 2^n-2 where n is the number of bits that will be used to describe the host or the network.

To answer this question we first have to determine how many host bits would we need to have at least 16 unique combinations.

Using our formula we need to have 5 host bits $2^5-2 = 30$.

This would leave us with 3 network bits therefore the mask is 224 in the fourth octet.

Answer 4.

a) immediately

After the configuration command is issued the change takes place immediately.

There are times when the router needs to be bounced, but it is very rare.

Answer 5.

a) Activated by default

Answer 6.

a) ip address 192.82.4.7 255.255.255.252

If you are not in the configuration mode, the IP address can also be set by using the setup mode.

Configuring interface Ethernet0/0:
    Is this interface in use? [yes]:
    Configure IP on this interface? [yes]:
        IP address for this interface [10.10.10.1]: 10.10.10.1
        Number of bits in subnet field [16]: 16
        Class A network is 10.0.0.0, 16 subnet bits; mask is /24

Take note when using the setup mode the mask is configured by using the number of subnet bits.

Answer 7.

c. show ip interface

Example

Router#sh ip interface
%SYS-5-CONFIG_I: Configured from console by console
Ethernet0 is administratively down, line protocol is down
    Internet address is 10.10.1.1/24
    Broadcast address is 255.255.255.255
    Address determined by setup command
    MTU is 1500 bytes
    Helper address is not set
    Directed broadcast forwarding is enabled
    Multicast reserved groups joined: 224.0.0.9
    Outgoing access list is not set
    Inbound access list is not set
    Proxy ARP is enabled
    Security level is default
    Split horizon is enabled
    ICMP redirects are always sent
    ICMP unreachables are always sent
    ICMP mask replies are never sent
    IP fast switching is enabled
    IP fast switching on the same interface is disabled
    IP multicast fast switching is enabled
    Router Discovery is disabled
    IP output packet accounting is disabled
    IP access violation accounting is disabled
    TCP/IP header compression is disabled
    Probe proxy name replies are disabled
    Gateway Discovery is disabled
    Policy routing is disabled
    Network address translation is disabled

All addresses that have IP configured will be displayed.

Answer 8.

a) Where an IP host resolves its IP address by broadcasting its MAC address to the network and a RARP server assigns it an IP address.

Choice c) describes Address Resolution Protocol (ARP). A host never has to resolve it's own MAC address. The MAC address is burned into the Network Interface card. When the host is booted the MAC address will be loaded into memory.

Answer 9.

b) OSPF

A link state routing protocol advertises, to it's neighbors, the state of the link when the state of the link changes.

Answer 10.

d) The process where a router will prioritize routing protocols so that in the event two routing protocols have conflicting next hop addresses, the routing protocol with the lowest administrative distance will take priority.

Cisco uses administrative distances (AD) to measure the reliability of the routing protocol. The lower the (AD) the more reliable the protocol.

```
Router_C#sh ip route
Codes: C - connected, S - static, I - IGRP, R - RIP, M - mobile, B - BGP
       D - EIGRP, EX - EIGRP external, O - OSPF, IA - OSPF inter area
       N1 - OSPF NSSA external type 1, N2 - OSPF NSSA external type 2
       E1 - OSPF external type 1, E2 - OSPF external type 2, E - EGP
       i - IS-IS, L1 - IS-IS level-1, L2 - IS-IS level-2, * - candidate default
       U - per-user static route, o - ODR

Gateway of last resort is not set

     172.16.0.0/24 is subnetted, 2 subnets
C       172.16.1.0 is directly connected, Serial1
C       172.16.2.0 is directly connected, Serial0
I       10.0.0.0/8 [100/8576] via 172.16.1.1, 00:00:09, Serial1
               [100/8576] via 172.16.2.1, 00:00:19, Serial0
```

The 100 in bold is the administrative distance for IGRP.

A partial list of administrative distances is included below:

Protocol	AD
EIGRP	90
IGRP	100
OSPF	110
RIP	120
BGP	180

If a router hears an IP RIP and an IGRP update for the same network the router will discard the rip information. IP RIP uses hop count as it's metric, while IGRP uses a composite metric including bandwidth and load, speed is the primary consideration.

Answer 11.

d. ip nat outside

Answer 12.

e)
```
router(config)#router ospf 69
router(config-router)#area 0 range 172.16.24.0 255.255.248.0
router(config-router)#area 0 range 172.16.32.0 255.255.224.0
```

There is no way we can manipulate the first two octets. These 16 bits uniquely describe our network. Let's examine the 3rd octet below. A 248 mask means DO NOT change the bit pattern of the most significant 5 bits. Which implies we can do what we want with the remaining 3 bits. The chart below list all the possibilities, I have also included the 36 address to show how the bit pattern will change.

	THIRD OCTET							
	128	**64**	**32**	**16**	**8**	**4**	**2**	**1**
248	1	1	1	1	1	0	0	0
24	0	0	0	1	1	0	0	0
25	0	0	0	1	1	0	0	1
26	0	0	0	1	1	0	1	0
27	0	0	0	1	1	0	1	1
28	0	0	0	1	1	1	0	0
29	0	0	0	1	1	1	0	1
30	0	0	0	1	1	1	1	0
31	0	0	0	1	1	1	1	1
32	**0**	**0**	**1**	**0**	**0**	**0**	**0**	**0**

The command area 0 range 172.16.24.0 255.255.248.0 will include the networks 24-31.

The command area 0 range 172.16.32.0 255.255.224.0 will include the networks 32-63.

	THIRD OCTET							
	128	**64**	**32**	**16**	**8**	**4**	**2**	**1**
224	1	1	1	0	0	0	0	0
32	0	0	1	0	0	0	0	0
40	**0**	**0**	**1**	**0**	**1**	**0**	**0**	**0**
48	**0**	**0**	**1**	**1**	**0**	**0**	**0**	**0**
56	**0**	**0**	**1**	**1**	**1**	**0**	**0**	**0**
64	**0**	**1**	**0**	**0**	**0**	**0**	**0**	**0**

Notice again how we have maintained the bit pattern of the first 3 bits up to a value of 64.

Answer 13.

b) EIGRP would then allow discontinuous networks to be configured

The "no auto-summary command" will force EIGRP to act as a Classless Routing Protocol. EIGRP would then have the ability to communicate a mask other than the default.

Cisco defines EIGRP as a advanced distance vector routing protocol. Mask information is communicated between hosts and therefore allows discontinuous networks to be defined.

The command "no auto-summary" is required to support discontinuous networks.

EIGRP is a internal routing protocol which means it is used to route within a autonomous system.

BGP4 is an example of a exterior routing protocol.

EIGRP also allows Variable Length Subnet Masking (VLSM) which means you can have different masks for the same major network number.

Answer 14.

e) 124

The above mask is using 6 bits to describe subnets. The formula used to determine the number of subnets is $2^6 - 2 = 62$ subnets and on each of these subnets we can have 2 hosts, there for we would have a total of 124 hosts.

Answer 15.

d) Area 0 is always required

Area 0 is not required if only one area is configured.

Answer 16.

e. Workstation A could not successfully ping Workstation B

Since Router_A is directly connected to network 10.0.0.0. Router_A will ignore the updates received from Router_C pertaining to 10.0.0.0 because the metric is higher.

Classful routing protocols only use the set prefixes of 8 bits for a Class A, 16 bits for a Class B and 24 bits for a Class C address.

IGRP is a classful routing protocol and does not communicate the subnet across different major networks. As a result there is no way Router_A can distinguish between the subnets 10.0.1.0 and 10.0.4.0.

When Workstation A pings the 10 address of Workstation B or Router_B the ICMP echo request will remain on the subnet 10.0.1.0.

Answer 17.

e) Workstation A could not successfully ping Workstation B

Since Router_A is directly connected to network 10.0.0.0 Router_A will ignore the updates received from Router_C that say's network 10.0.0.0 is 1 hop away. Classful routing protocols only use the set prefixes of 8 bits for a Class A, 16 bits for a Class B and 24 bits for a Class C address.

IP RIP is a classful routing protocol and does not communicate the subnet across different major networks. As a result there is no way Router_A can distinguish between the subnets 10.0.1.0 and 10.0.4.0.

When Workstation A pings the 10 address of Workstation B or Router_B the ICMP echo request will remain on the subnet 10.0.1.0.

Answer 18.

b) Workstation A could successfully ping the ethernet interface of Router_B
d) Workstation A could successfully ping Workstation B

A classless routing protocol can set the prefix at any length.

OSPF is a classless routing protocol and does communicate the subnet across different major networks therefore Router_A can distinguish between subnets 10.0.1.0 and 10.0.4.0.

Routing Table of Router_A

   172.16.0.0/24 is subnetted, 2 subnets
C   172.16.1.0 is directly connected, Serial0/0
O   172.16.2.0 [110/128] via 172.16.1.2, 00:01:06, Serial0/0
   10.0.0.0/24 is subnetted, 2 subnets
C   10.0.1.0 is directly connected, Ethernet0/0
**   10.0.4.0 [110/138] via 172.16.1.2, 00:01:06, Serial0/0**

Any packet with a destination address of 10.0.4.x will be sent out the Serial0/0 interface.

Answer 19.

b. Router_C would ping Workstation B with a 50% success rate

Classful routing protocols only use the set prefixes of 8 bits for a Class A, 16 bits for a Class B and 24 bits for a Class C address.

IGRP is a clssful routing protocol and does not communicate the subnet across different major networks as a result Router_C hears routing updates relating to network 10.0.0.0 from Router_A and Router_B. These updates are sent with the same metric. Therefore Router_C assumes that it can reach the 10 network by going out S0 or S1. When a ping is initiated from Router_C or Workstation C, Router_C will load balance the packets.

Refer to the routing table of Router_C below:

Gateway of last resort is not set

   172.16.0.0/24 is subnetted, 2 subnets
C   172.16.1.0 is directly connected, Serial1
C   172.16.2.0 is directly connected, Serial0
I   10.0.0.0/8 [100/8576] via 172.16.1.1, 00:00:09, Serial1
        [100/8576] via 172.16.2.1, 00:00:19, Serial0

Two pings are shown below:

Router_C#ping 10.0.4.1

Type escape sequence to abort.
Sending 5, 100-byte ICMP Echos to 10.0.4.1, timeout is 2 seconds:
U!.!U
Success rate is 40 percent (2/5), round-trip min/avg/max = 4/4/4 ms

Router_C#ping 10.0.4.1

Type escape sequence to abort.
Sending 5, 100-byte ICMP Echos to 10.0.4.1, timeout is 2 seconds:
U!.!U
Success rate is 60 percent (3/5), round-trip min/avg/max = 4/4/4 ms

10 ping probes were successful 5 times or 50%.

Answer 20.

b) Router_C would ping Workstation B with a 50% success rate

Classful routing protocols only use the set prefixes of 8 bits for a Class A, 16 bits for a Class B and 24 bits for a Class C address.

IP RIP is a classful routing protocol and does not communicate the subnet across different major networks. Router_C hears routing updates relating to network 10.0.0.0 from Router_A and Router_B. These updates are sent with the same metric of 1 hop. Therefore Router_C assumes that it can reach the 10 network by going out S0 or S1. When a ping is initiated from Router_C or Workstation C, Router_C will load balance the packets.

Refer to the routing table of Router_C below:

Gateway of last resort is not set

    172.16.0.0/24 is subnetted, 2 subnets
C   172.16.1.0 is directly connected, Serial1
C   172.16.2.0 is directly connected, Serial0
R   10.0.0.0/8 [120/1] via 172.16.1.1, 00:00:09, Serial1
         [120/1] via 172.16.2.1, 00:00:19, Serial0

Two pings are shown below:

Router_C#ping 10.0.4.1

Type escape sequence to abort.
Sending 5, 100-byte ICMP Echos to 10.0.4.1, timeout is 2 seconds:
U!.!U
Success rate is 40 percent (2/5), round-trip min/avg/max = 4/4/4 ms

Router_C#ping 10.0.4.1

Type escape sequence to abort.
Sending 5, 100-byte ICMP Echos to 10.0.4.1, timeout is 2 seconds:
!U!.!
Success rate is 60 percent (3/5), round-trip min/avg/max = 4/4/4 ms

10 ping probes were successful 5 times or 50%.

Answer 21.

d)

 172.16.10.112/3
 172.16.10.116/30
 172.16.10.120/30
 172.16.10.124/30

All of the above addresses can be summarized because the pattern of the first four bits is the same for each address; as shown below.

128	64	32	16	8	4	2	1	Value
			FOURTH OCTET					
0	1	1	1	0	0	0	0	112
0	1	1	1	0	1	0	0	116
0	1	1	1	1	0	0	0	120
0	1	1	1	1	1	0	0	124

An example of the OSPF command that would summarize these addresses is as follows:

area 0 range 172.16.10.112 255.255.255.240

Answer 22.

d) None of the above

 This is a good question to illustrate the importance of understanding the wildcard mask. A wildcard mask tells the router which bits to check (compare against the given IP) and which bits to ignore. A wildcard mask with an octet value of 0 means to check all eight bits against the corresponding octet of the given IP. A wildcard mask with an octet value of 255 means to ignore all eight bits in the corresponding octet of the given IP.

 It appears that the administrator wanted to permit the entire 207.239.71.0 network, but deny a single host. Unfortunately, the mask 255.255.255.0 was used as a WILDCARD mask against the address 207.239.71.0. The result of this access list is to permit all traffic from hosts whose fourth octet value is zero. It is possible for a host to have a fourth octet value of 0 (e.g. consider a class B network with a subnet mask of 255.255.252.0).

Answer 23.

d) 10.6.160.1 to 10.6.191.254

A mask value in the third octet means that network addresses will be a multiple of 32. Therefore network 10.6.160.0 is the wire address for this host. The next wire address is 10.6.192.0. Of course if all host bits have a value of 1 this identifies the broadcast address, therefore c) is not correct.

Answer 24.

b) allows a single network addresses to carry multiple subnet masks

c) allows the definition of subnets that contain only two host addresses

Answer 25.

d) broadcast

The /27 represents the 255.255.255.224 mask. All networks will be multiples of 32. This address represents the last address on the 32 wire it is therefore a broadcast address.

Answer 26.

c) measures the "reliability" of an IP routing protocol

Administrative Distance (AD)

Protocol	AD
EIGRP	90
IGRP	100
OSPF	110
RIP	120
BGP	180

EIGRP would be considered the most reliable protocol.

Answer 27.

d) this is an illegal command

The 50 represents a standard IP access list. Therefore only a source address can be identified.

If there is a need to identify both source and destination an access list number would have to be in the range of 100–199.

Answer 28.

b) access-list 1 deny 172.16.16.16

a) is incorrect because an extended access list must identify a protocol

c) is incorrect because it does not identify the source address

d) is incorrect because the syntax used is an extended access list yet the number 1 identifies a standard list.

b) will prevent all IP traffic from 172.16.16.16 including TFTP.

Answer 29.

d) Depends on the routing protocol configured

The major network address has been variably subnetted if we were using a Classless routing protocol there would be no problem and we should expect 100% pings. If a Classful protocol were configured then we would have a problem.

If IP RIP were configured for example the RIP updates would not be advertised out the serial interfaces due to split horizon. There fore the remote router would never "learn" about the remote subnet.

The router output below shows the update being suppressed.

```
Router_B#
debug ip rip
RIP: sending v1 update to 255.255.255.255 via Ethernet0
    (172.16.2.32) - suppressing null update
RIP: sending v1 update to 255.255.255.255 via Serial0 (172.16.4.5) -
    suppressing null update
</routerio>
```

Answer 30.

b) OSPF

c) EIGRP

Because the major network address is variably subnetted we must use a classless routing protocol.

Multicasting

Multicasting offers the ability to send data to more than one station but not to all stations. It differs from a broadcast in that a broadcast data will be sent to all stations on the network.

- Stations can be members of a multicast group.
- Class D addresses are multicast addresses.
- A Class D address will map to a MAC address.
- The first four bits of a Class D IP address are: 1110.

A Class D address expressed in dotted decimal notation will fall into the following range:

224.0.0.0 through 239.255.255.255

If a station carries a Class D address this identifies the station as being a member of a multicast group.

The Internet Assigned Numbers Authority (IANA) owns a block of Ethernet addresses which range from 01:00:5e:00:00:00 through 01:00:5e:7f:ff:ff. These MAC addresses are used for IP multicasting.

If station A sends a frame to a station B station (and station B has a Class D address), Station A will take the lower order 23 bits of the Class D address and insert them into the MAC-layer destination address.

The most significant 9 bits of the IP address are not used.

Because these 9 bits are not used in the MAC address it is possible for the resulting MAC address to point to more than one station. Therefore it becomes the responsibility of the NIC to filter out unwanted transmissions.

Refer to the example below:

224.128.64.32 or 0xe0.80.40.20
224.0.64.32 or 0xe0.00.40.20

Both of the above addresses would map to the following MAC address: 02:00:5e:00:40:20.

IP Address			
Decimal	224	128	64	32
Binary	1110 0000	1000 0000	0100 0000	0010 0000
Hex	e 0	8 0	4 0	2 0

The above address will be mapped to the following MAC address:
The first nine bits of the IP address are not used.

Binary	0000 0001	0000 0000	0101 1110	0000 0000	0100 0000	0001 0000
Hex	0 1	0 0	5 e	0 0	4 0	2 0

Since the first nine bits are not used; the most significant bit of the 2nd octet of the IP address will be dropped; therefore there is no way to distinguish whether that bit was set to 1 or 0. As a result both of the IP addresses would be mapped to the same MAC address. Even in this scenario it still beats broadcasting.

Every MAC layer address that begins with 01 will identify a multicast address.

Some multicast addresses are assigned by the IANA.

- 224.0.0.1 identifies all systems on this subnet
- 224.0.0.2 identifies all routers on this subnet
- 224.0.1.1 is used for Network Time Protocol (NTP)
- 224.0.0.9 is for RIP version 2
- 224.0.1.2 is for Silicon Graphics Dogfight Application
- 224.0.0.5 identifies routers other than Designated Routers
- 224.0.0.6 identifies Designated Routers (DR)

Internet Group Management Protocol (IGMP) is a protocol that will let routers know if any hosts on a network belong to a multicast group.

Exercises

1: Class D addresses are mapped one-to-one to an Ethernet address. (T/F)

2: Which of the following are multicast addresses?
   a) 225.8.65.7
   b) 240.10.10.1
   c) 239.10.1.3
   d) 224.9.9.3
   e) 245.6.45.3

3: If a MAC address begins with a 01:xx:xx:xx:xx:xx it is a multicast address. (T/F)

Answers

1: False

2:

    a) 225.8.65.7
    c) 239.10.1.3
    d) 224.9.9.3

The 1st octet range values for Class D addresses is from 224 through 239.

3: True

APPENDIX B

Cisco Discovery Protocol (CDP)

I have included CDP because this Cisco protocol can prove to be a very valuable tool to help troubleshoot layer 3 addressing problems. Also CDP can be used to document a Cisco network topology.

CDP is media and protocol-independent which makes this protocol so valuable. Let us assume that you have a layer 3 addressing problem, say for sake of argument, a misconfigured address on a router or a switch.

From a neighboring device we can view the layer 3 addressing with out having layer 3 connectivity.

In the example below I have intentionally addressed Router_B incorrectly, even so Router_A, using CDP, can view the addressing of Router_B.

FIGURE B-1 CDP results

```
Router_A>en
Router_A#sh ip int s0
Serial0 is up, line protocol is up
    Internet address is 172.16.4.5/30
    Broadcast address is 255.255.255.255
    Address determined by setup command
    MTU is 1500 bytes
    Helper address is not set
    Directed broadcast forwarding is enabled
    Multicast reserved groups joined: 224.0.0.9
    Outgoing access list is not set
    Inbound  access list is not set
    Proxy ARP is enabled
    Security level is default
    Split horizon is enabled
    ICMP redirects are always sent
    ICMP unreachables are always sent
    ICMP mask replies are never sent
    IP fast switching is enabled
    IP fast switching on the same interface is enabled
    IP multicast fast switching is disabled
    Router Discovery is disabled
    IP output packet accounting is disabled
    IP access violation accounting is disabled
    TCP/IP header compression is disabled
```

continued on next page

Router_A#sh cdp neighbors detail

```
---------------------------------------------------------
```

Device ID: Router_B

Entry address(es):

    IP address: 134.16.16.5 <this address should be on the 172.16.4.4

                subnet>

Platform: cisco 2521, Capabilities: Router

Interface: Serial0, Port ID (outgoing port): Serial0

Holdtime : 172 sec

Version :

Cisco Internetwork Operating System Software

IOS (tm) 2500 Software (C2500-JS-L), Version 11.3(1), RELEASE

        SOFTWARE (fc1)

Copyright (c) 1986-1997 by cisco Systems, Inc.

Compiled Mon 15-Dec-97 18:28 by richardd

```
---------------------------------
```

Device ID: receive_ntp

Entry address(es):

   IP address: 172.16.4.6

Platform: cisco 2521, Capabilities: Router

Interface: Serial0, Port ID (outgoing port): Serial0

Holdtime : 52 sec

Version :

Cisco Internetwork Operating System Software

IOS (tm) 2500 Software (C2500-JS-L), Version 11.3(1), RELEASE

        SOFTWARE (fc1)

Copyright (c) 1986-1997 by cisco Systems, Inc.

Compiled Mon 15-Dec-97 18:28 by richardd

When you suspect there may be an addressing problem us the "show cdp" neighbor command to view the addressing on the other side of the link.

CDP can also be used to document a Cisco network. I had a student a while back bring to me a beautiful diagram of his 5000 node network. The diagram was actually put together by a relatively non-technical person. By using CDP he could discover all the directly connected platforms. Then by telneting to the next router another CDP discovery could be performed. He continued in this manner to construct a diagram of the entire network.

Exercises

Refer to Figure B-1 and answer the following questions.

C.1: CDP can provide information regarding directly connected Cisco devices. (T/F)

C.2: CDP can provide information concerning router platforms of neighbors. (T/F)

C.3: CDP can provide IOS information about router neighbors. (T/F)

C.4: CDP can provide interface information about router neighbors. (T/F)

C.5: CDP can provide IP addressing information about router neighbors. (T/F)

C.6: CDP can provide IPX addressing information about router neighbors. (T/F)

C.7: CDP can provide Appletalk addressing information about router neighbors. (T/F)

Answers

C.1: True

C.2: True

C.3: True

C.4: True

C.5: True

C.6: True

C.7: True

APPENDIX C

Binary/Decimal Tables*

To translate a binary number to decimal, you need to multiply each binary digit by an appropriate power of 2. Below, we show the multipliers that are used to convert 10010111 to decimal.

$$1 \quad 0 \quad 0 \quad 1 \quad 0 \quad 1 \quad 1 \quad 1$$
$$128 \quad 64 \quad 32 \quad 16 \quad 8 \quad 4 \quad 2 \quad 1$$

Thus 10010111 is $(128)(1) + (64)(0) + (32)(0) + (16)(1) + (8)(0) + (4)(1) + (2)(1) + (1)(1)$ which equals $128 + 16 + 4 + 2 + 1 = 151$.

---

* Originally published in Feit, *TCP/IP: Architecture, Protocols, and Implementation with IPv6 and IP Security*. McGraw-Hill, 1999.

Table B.1 below lists the binary to decimal translations that are used to write subnet masks. In this case, just the set of binary numbers that have contiguous 1s on the left are translated. Note that the decimal numbers start at 128 and increase by 64, 32, 16, 8, 4, 2, and 1. Table B.2 on the pages that follow displays all 8-bit translations between binary and decimal numbers.

TABLE B.1

Subnet Mask Translation

Binary	Decimal
10000000	128
11000000	192
11100000	224
11110000	240
11111000	248
11111100	252
11111110	254
11111111	255

TABLE F.2

Binary to Decimal Translation

Binary	Decimal	Binary	Decimal	Binary	Decimal	Binary	Decimal
00000000	0	00100000	32	01000000	64	01100000	96
00000001	1	00100001	33	01000001	65	01100001	97
00000010	2	00100010	34	01000010	66	01100010	98
00000011	3	00100011	35	01000011	67	01100011	99
00000100	4	00100100	36	01000100	68	01100100	100
00000101	5	00100101	37	01000101	69	01100101	101
00000110	6	00100110	38	01000110	70	01100110	102
00000111	7	00100111	39	01000111	71	01100111	103
00001000	8	00101000	40	01001000	72	01101000	104
00001001	9	00101001	41	01001001	73	01101001	105
00001010	10	00101010	42	01001010	74	01101010	106
00001011	11	00101011	43	01001011	75	01101011	107
00001100	12	00101100	44	01001100	76	01101100	108

Binary	Decimal	Binary	Decimal	Binary	Decimal	Binary	Decimal
00001101	13	00101101	45	01001101	77	01101101	109
00001110	14	00101110	46	01001110	78	01101110	110
00001111	15	00101111	47	01001111	79	01101111	111
00010000	16	00110000	48	01010000	80	01110000	112
00010001	17	00110001	49	01010001	81	01110001	113
00010010	18	00110010	50	01010010	82	01110010	114
00010011	19	00110011	51	01010011	83	01110011	115
00010100	20	00110100	52	01010100	84	01110100	116
00010101	21	00110101	53	01010101	85	01110101	117
00010110	22	00110110	54	01010110	86	01110110	118
00010111	23	00110111	55	01010111	87	01110111	119
00011000	24	00111000	56	01011000	88	01111000	120
00011001	25	00111001	57	01011001	89	01111001	121
00011010	26	00111010	58	01011010	90	01111010	122
00011011	27	00111011	59	01011011	91	01111011	123
00011100	28	00111100	60	01011100	92	01111100	124
00011101	29	00111101	61	01011101	93	01111101	125
00011110	30	00111110	62	01011110	94	01111110	126
00011111	31	00111111	63	01011111	95	01111111	127
10000000	128	10100000	160	11000000	192	11100000	224
10000001	129	10100001	161	11000001	193	11100001	225
10000010	130	10100010	162	11000010	194	11100010	226
10000011	131	10100011	163	11000011	195	11100011	227
10000100	132	10100100	164	11000100	196	11100100	228
10000101	133	10100101	165	11000101	197	11100101	229
10000110	134	10100110	166	11000110	198	11100110	230
10000111	135	10100111	167	11000111	199	11100111	231
10001000	136	10101000	168	11001000	200	11101000	232
10001001	137	10101001	169	11001001	201	11101001	233
10001010	138	10101010	170	11001010	202	11101010	234
10001011	139	10101011	171	11001011	203	11101011	235
10001100	140	10101100	172	11001100	204	11101100	236

continued on next page

Binary	Decimal	Binary	Decimal	Binary	Decimal	Binary	Decimal
10001101	141	10101101	173	11001101	205	11101101	237
10001110	142	10101110	174	11001110	206	11101110	238
10001111	143	10101111	175	11001111	207	11101111	239
10010000	144	10110000	176	11010000	208	11110000	240
10010001	145	10110001	177	11010001	209	11110001	241
10010010	146	10110010	178	11010010	210	11110010	242
10010011	147	10110011	179	11010011	211	11110011	243
10010100	148	10110100	180	11010100	212	11110100	244
10010101	149	10110101	181	11010101	213	11110101	245
10010110	150	10110110	182	11010110	214	11110110	246
10010111	151	10110111	183	11010111	215	11110111	247
10011000	152	10111000	184	11011000	216	11111000	248
10011001	153	10111001	185	11011001	217	11111001	249
10011010	154	10111010	186	11011010	218	11111010	250
10011011	155	10111011	187	11011011	219	11111011	251
10011100	156	10111100	188	11011100	220	11111100	252
10011101	157	10111101	189	11011101	221	11111101	253
10011110	158	10111110	190	11011110	222	11111110	254
10011111	159	10111111	191	11011111	223	11111111	255

APPENDIX **D**

Glossary

255

access control list   A list defining the kinds of access granted or denied to users of an object.

address   In data communication, this is a designated identifier.

address class   Traditional method of assigning blocks of addresses to organizations.

address mask   A bit mask used to select bits from an IP address for subnet addressing.

address resolution   Conversion of an IP address into a corresponding physical address, such as ETHERNET or token ring.

address resolution protocol (ARP)   A TCP/IP protocol used to dynamically bind a high-level IP address to low-level physical hardware addresses. ARP works across single physical networks and is limited to networks that support hardware broadcast.

address space   Addresses used to uniquely identify network-accessible units, sessions, adjacent link stations, and links in a node for each network in which the node participates.

addressing   In data communication, the way in which a station selects the station to which it is to send data. An identifiable place.

AppleTalk   A networking protocol developed by Apple Computer for use with its products.

application layer   According to the ISO OSI model, this is layer 7. It provides application services.

ARPANET   The world's first packet-switching network. For many years it functioned as an Internet backbone.

autonomous system (AS)   An internetwork that is part of the Internet and has a single routing policy. Each Autonomous System is assigned an Autonomous System Number.

bandwidth   The quantity of data that can be sent across a link, typically measured in bits per second.

baud   A unit of signaling speed equal to the number of times per second that a signal changes state. If there are exactly two states, the baud rate equals the bit rate.

carrier-sense multiple access with collision detection (CSMA/CD)   A protocol utilizing equipment capable of detecting a carrier which permits multiple access to a common medium. This protocol also has the ability to detect a collision, because this type of technology is broadcast-oriented.

classless inter-domain routing (CIDR)   A method of routing used to enable the network part of IP addresses to consist of a specified number of bits.

collision   An event in which two or more devices simultaneously perform a broadcast on the same medium. This term is used in ETHERNET networks, and also in networks where broadcast technology is implemented.

collision detection   Term used to define a device that can determine when a simultaneous transmission attempt has been made.

congestion   A network state caused by one or more overloaded network devices. Congestion leads to datagram loss.

connected   To have a physical path from one point to another.

connection   A logical communication path between TCP users.

connection-oriented internetworking   A set of subnetworks connected physically and thus rendered capable of connection-oriented network service.

connection-oriented service   A type of service offered in some networks. This service has three phases: connection establishment, data transfer, and connection release.

cracker   Someone who attempts to break into computer systems, often with malicious intent.

data circuit-terminating equipment (DCE)   Equipment required to connect a DTE to a line or to a network.

data-link control (DLC)   A set of rules used by nodes at layer 2 within a network. The data link is governed by data-link protocols such as ETHERNET or token ring for example.

data-link control (DLC) protocol   Rules used by two nodes at a data-link layer to accomplish an orderly exchange of information. Examples are ETHERNET, channel, FDDI, and token ring.

data-link layer   Layer 2 of the OSI reference model. It synchronizes transmission and handles error correction for a data link.

data-link level   The conceptual level of control logic between high-level logic and a data-link protocol that maintains control of the data link.

data terminal equipment (DTE)   A source or destination for data. Often used to denote terminals or computers attached to a wide area network.

DECnet   Digital Equipment Corporation's proprietary network protocol. Versions are identified by their phase number—such as Phase IV and Phase V.

directed broadcast address   In TCP/IP-based environments, an IP address that specifies all hosts on a specific network. A single copy of a directed broadcast is routed to the specified network where it is broadcast to all machines on that network.

DIX Ethernet   Version of Ethernet developed by Digital, Intel, and Xerox.

domain name server   In TCP/IP environments, it is a protocol for matching object names and network addresses. It was designed to replace the need to update /etc/hosts files of participating entities throughout a network.

domain name system (DNS)   The online distributed database system used to map human-readable machine names into IP addresses. DNS servers throughout the connected Internet implement a hierarchical name space that allows sites freedom in assigning machine names and addresses. DNS also supports separate mappings between mail destinations and IP addresses.

dotted-decimal notation   A phrase typically found in TCP/IP network conversations. Specifically, this refers to the addressing scheme of the Internet protocol (IP). It is the representation of a 32-bit address consisting of four 8-bit numbers written in base 10 with periods separating them.

encapsulate   Generally agreed on in the internetworking community to mean surrounding one protocol with another protocol for the purpose of passing the foreign protocol through the native environment.

ETHERNET   A data-link-level protocol. It (Version 2.0) was defined by Digital Equipment Corporation, Intel Corporation, and the Xerox Corporation in 1982. It specified a data rate of 10 Mbits/s, a maximum station distance of 2.8 km, a maximum number of stations of 1024, a shielded coaxial cable using baseband signaling, functionality of CSMA/CD, and a best-effort delivery system.

exterior gateway protocol (EGP)   Routers in neighboring Autonomous Systems use this protocol to identify the set of networks that can be reached within or via each Autonomous System. EGP is being supplanted by BGP.

filter   A device or program that separates data, signals, or material in accordance with specified criteria.

firewall   A system that controls what traffic may enter and leave a site.

frame   One definition generally agreed on as being a packet as it is transmitted across a serial line. The term originated from character-oriented protocols. According to the meaning in OSI environments, it is a data structure pertaining to a particular area of data. It also consists of slots that can accept values of specific attributes.

hierarchical routing   From a TCP/IP perspective, this type of routing is based on a hierarchical addressing scheme. Most TCP/IP routing is based on a two-level hierarchy in which an IP address is divided into a network portion until the datagram reaches a gateway that can deliver it directly. The concept of subnets introduces additional levels of hierarchical routing.

hop count   (1) A measure of distance between two points in the Internet. Each hop count corresponds to one router separating a source from a destination (for example, a hop count of 3 indicates that three routers separate a source from a destination). (2) A term generally used in TCP/IP networks. The basic definition is a measure of distance between two points in an internet. A hop count of n means that n routers separate the source and the destination.

ICMP   Internet Control Message Protocol. Specific to the TCP/IP protocol suite. It is an integral part of the Internet protocol. It handles error and control messages. Routers and hosts use ICMP to send reports of problems about datagrams back to the original source that sent the datagram. ICMP also includes an echo request/reply used to test whether a destination is reachable and responding.

interior gateway protocol (IGP)   Any routing protocol used within an internetwork.

International Organization for Standardization (ISO)   An organization of national standards-making bodies from various countries established to promote development of standards to facilitate international exchange of goods and services, and develop cooperation in intellectual, scientific, technological, and economic activity.

Internet   According to different documents describing the Internet, it is a collection of networks, routers, gateways, and other networking devices that use the TCP/IP protocol suite and function as a single, cooperative virtual network. The Internet provides universal connectivity and three levels of network services: unreliable, connectionless packet delivery; reliable, full-duplex stream delivery; and application-level services such as electronic mail that build on the first two. The Internet reaches many universities, government research labs, and military installations and over a dozen countries.

Internet address   According to TCP/IP documentation, it refers to the 32-bit address assigned to the host. It is a software address that on local ("little i") internets is locally managed, but on the central ("big I") Internet is dictated to the user (entity desiring access to the Internet).

Internet Assigned Numbers Authority (IANA)   The authority responsible for controlling the assignment of a variety of parameters, such as well-known ports, multicast addresses, terminal identifiers, and system identifiers.

Internet control message protocol (ICMP)   A protocol that is required for implementation with IP. ICMP specifies error messages to be sent when datagrams are discarded or systems experience congestion. ICMP also provides several useful query services.

Internet gateway routing protocol (IGRP)   A proprietary protocol designed for Cisco routers.

Internet group management protocol (IGMP)   A protocol that is part of the multicast specification. IGMP is used to carry group membership information.

Internet packet exchange (IPX)   A Novell protocol that operates at OSI layer 3. It is used in the NetWare protocols; it is similar to IP in TCP/IP.

Internet protocol (IP)   A protocol used to route data from its source to its destination. A part of TCP/IP protocol.

IP   Internet protocol. The TCP/IP standard protocol that defines the IP datagram as the unit of information passed across an internet and provides the basis for connectionless, best-effort packet delivery service. IP includes the ICMP control and error message protocol as an integral part. The entire protocol suite is often referred to as TCP/IP because TCP and IP are the two fundamental protocols.

IP address   The 32-bit dotted-decimal address assigned to hosts that want to participate in a local TCP/IP internet or the central (connected) Internet. IP addresses are software addresses. Actually, an IP address consists of a network portion and a host portion. The partition makes routing efficient.

IP datagram   A term used with TCP/IP networks. It is a basic unit of information passed across a TCP/IP internet. An IP datagram is to an internet as a hardware packet is to a physical network. It contains a source address and a destination address along with data.

link   A medium over which nodes can communicate using a link layer protocol.

link state protocol   A routing protocol that generates routes using detailed knowledge of the topology of a network.

LLC   Logical link control. According to OSI documentation, a sublayer in the data-link layer of the OSI model. The LLC provides the basis for an unacknowledged connectionless service or connection-oriented service on the local area network.

loopback address   Address 127.0.0.1, used for communications between clients and servers that reside on the same host.

MAC address   A physical address assigned to a LAN interface.

MAC protocol   A Media Access Control protocol defines the rules that govern a system's ability to transmit and receive data on a medium.

MTU   Maximum transfer unit. The largest amount of data that can be transferred across a given physical network. For local area networks implementing ETHERNET, the MTU is determined by the network hardware. For long-haul networks that use aerial lines to inter-connect packet switches, the MTU is determined by software.

multicast   A technique that allows copies of a single packet to be passed to a selected sub-set of all possible destinations. Some hardware supports multicast by allowing a network inter-face to belong to one or more multicast groups. Broadcast is a special form of multicast in which the subset of machines to receive a copy of a packet consists of the entire set. IP sup-ports an internet multicast facility.

multicast address   According to Apple documentation, an ETHERNET address for which the node accepts packets just as it does for its permanently assigned ETHERNET hard-ware address. The low-order bit of the high-order byte is set to 1. Each node can have any number of multicast addresses, and any number of nodes can have the same multicast address. The purpose of a multicast address is to allow a group of ETHERNET nodes to receive the same transmission simultaneously, in a fashion similar to the AppleTalk broadcast service.

multicasting   A directory service agent uses this mode to chain a request to many other directory service agents.

multicast IP address   A destination IP address that can be adopted by multiple hosts. Datagrams sent to a multicast IP address will be delivered to all hosts in the group.

NetBEUI   Local area network protocol used for Microsoft LANs.

NETBIOS   A network programming interface and protocol developed for IBM-compatible personal computers.

network   A collection of computers and related devices connected together in such a way that collectively they can be more productive than standalone equipment.

network address   In general, each participating entity on a network has an address so that it can be identified when exchanging data. According to IBM documentation, in a subarea net-work, an address consists of subarea and element fields that identify a link, link station, PU, LU, or SSCP.

network layer   According to ISO documentation, it is defined as OSI layer 3. It is respon-sible for data transfer across the network. It functions independently of the network media and the topology.

octet   Eight bits (a byte).

open shortest path first (OSPF)   A routing protocol based on the least cost for routing.

packet   A term used generically in many instances. It is a small unit of control information and data that is processed by the network protocol.

physical address   An address assigned to a network interface.

physical layer   A term used in OSI circles. It refers to the lowest layer defined by the OSI model. However, layer 0 would be the lowest layer in such a model. This layer (layer 0) represents the medium, whether hard or soft.

point-to-point protocol (PPP)   A protocol for data transfer across serial links. PPP supports authentication, link configuration, and link monitoring capabilities and allows traffic for several protocols to be multiplexed across the link.

presentation layer   According to the OSI model for networks, this is layer 6. Data representation occurs here. Syntax of data such as ASCII or EBCDIC is determined at this layer.

protocol   An agreed-upon way of doing something.

proxy ARP   In TCP/IP networks, this is a technique where one machine answers ARP requests intended for another by supplying its own physical address.

RARP   Reverse address resolution protocol. A TCP/IP protocol for mapping ETHERNET addresses to IP addresses. It is used by diskless workstations who do not know their IP addresses. In essence, it asks "Who am I?" Normally, a response occurs and is cached in the host.

reverse address resolution protocol (RARP)   A protocol that enables a computer to discover its IP address by broadcasting a request on a network.

RFC   Request for comments. Proposed and accepted TCP/IP standards.

routing   The moving of data through paths in a network.

routing information protocol (RIP)   A simple protocol used to exchange information between routers. The original version was part of the XNS protocol suite.

routing policy   Rules for which traffic will be routed and how it should be routed.

routing table   A table containing information used to forward datagrams toward their destinations.

segment   A Protocol Data Unit consisting of a TCP header and optionally, some data.

Sometimes used to refer to the data portion of a TCP Protocol Data Unit.

session layer   According to the OSI reference model, this is layer 5. It coordinates the dialog between two communicating application processes.

shortest path first   A routing algorithm that uses knowledge of a network's topology in making routing decisions.

sliding window   A scenario in which a protocol permits the transmitting station to send a stream of bytes before an acknowledgment arrives.

stub network   A network that does not carry transit traffic between other networks.

subnet address   A selected number of bits from the local part of an IP address, used to identify a set of systems connected to a common link.

subnet mask   A configuration parameter that indicates how many bits of an address are used for the host part. It is expressed as a 32-bit quantity, with 1s placed in positions covering the network and subnet part of an IP address and 0s in the host part.

switch   A layer 2 device that enables many pairs of LAN devices to communicate concurrently.

T1   A digital telephony service that operates at 1.544 megabits per second. DS1 framing is used.

T3   A digital telephony service that operates at 44.746 megabits per second. DS3 framing is used.

TCP   Transmission control protocol. The TCP/IP standard transport-level protocol that provides the reliable, full-duplex, stream service on which many application protocols depend. It is connection-oriented in that before transmitting data, participants must establish a connection.

TELNET   The TCP/IP TCP standard protocol for remote terminal service.

10Base T   An ETHERNET implementation using 10 Mbits/s with baseband signaling over twisted-pair cabling.

TFTP   Trivial file transfer protocol. A TCP/IP UDP standard protocol for file transfer that uses UDP as a transport mechanism. TFTP depends only on UDP, so it can be used on machines such as diskless workstations.

token   The symbol of authority passed successively from one data station to another to indicate which station is temporarily in control of the transmission medium.

token ring   A network with a ring topology that passes tokens from one attaching device to another.

token-ring network   A ring network that allows unidirectional data transmission between data stations by a token-passing procedure.

transport layer   According to the OSI model, it is the layer that provides an end-to-end service to its users.

TTL   Time to live. A technique used in best-effort delivery systems to avoid endlessly looping packets. For example, each packet has a "time" associated with its lifetime.

well-known-port   A term used with TCP/IP networks. In TCP/IP, applications and programs that reside on top of TCP and UDP, respectively, have a designated port assigned to them. This agreed-on port is known as a well-known-port.

APPENDIX E

Acronyms and Abbreviations

3270	Reference to a 3270 data stream (arrangement of data)
3770	Reference to remote job entry
370/XA	370/eXtended Architecture
5250	Reference to a 5250 data stream (arrangement of data)
AAA	Autonomous administrative area
AAI	Administration authority identifier
AAL	ATM adaptation layer
AARP	AppleTalk address resolution protocol
AC	Access control
ACB	Application control block; access (method) control block
ACCS	Automated calling card service
ACD	Automatic call distribution
ACDF	Access control decision function
ACE	Access control (list) entry; asynchronous communication element
ACF	Access control field; advanced communications function
ACIA	Access control inner areas; asynchronous communication interface adapter
ACID	Automicity, consistency, isolation, and durability
ACK	Positive acknowledgment
ACL	Access control list
ACP	Ancillary control process
ACS	Access control store
ACSA	Access control specific area
ACSE	Association control service element
ACSP	Access control specific point
ACTLU	Activate logical unit
ACTPU	Activate physical unit
ACU	Autocalling unit
AD	Addendum document to an OSI standard
ADMD	Administrative management domain
ADP	Adapter control block; AppleTalk data stream protocol

ADPCM	Adaptive differential pulse code modulation
ADSP	AppleTalk data stream protocol
AE	Application entity
AEI	Application entity invocation
AEP	AppleTalk echo protocol
AET	Application entity title
AF	Auxiliary facility
AFI	Authority and format identifier; AppleTalk filing interface
AFP	AppleTalk filing protocol
AID	Attention identifier
AIFF	Audio interchange file format
AIX	Advanced (also Account) Interactive eXecutive
ALS	Application-layer structure
ALU	Application-layer user; arithmetic logic unit
AM	Amplitude modulation
AMI	Alternating mark inversion
ANI	Automatic number identification
ANS	American National Standard
ANSI	American National Standards Institute
AP	Application process; argument pointer
APAR	Authorized program analysis report
APB	Alpha primary bootstrap
APD	Avalanche photodiode
APDU	Application protocol data unit
API	Application program (also programming) interface
APLI	ACSE/Presentation Library Interface
APP	Applications portability profile
APPC	Advanced Program-to-Program Communication
APPL	Application program
APPN	Advanced Peer-to-Peer networking

APT	Application Process Title
ARF	Automatic reconfiguration facility
ARI	Address-recognized indicator
ARP	Address resolution protocol
ARPA	Advanced Research Projects Agency
ARQ	Automatic repeat request
ARS	Automatic route selection
AS/400	Application system/400
ASC	Accredited Standard Committee
ASCII	American Standard Code for Information Interchange
ASDC	Abstract service definition convention
ASE	Application service element
ASM	Address space manager
ASN	Abstract syntax notation
ASN.1	Abstract Syntax Notation One
ASO	Application service object
ASP	Abstract service primitive; AppleTalk session protocol; attached support processor
AST	Asynchronous system trap
ASTLVL	Asynchronous system trap level
ASTSR	Asynchronous system trap summary register
AT	Advanced Technology (IBM Computers)
ATM	Asynchronous transfer mode; abstract text method; automated teller machine
ATP	AppleTalk transaction protocol
ATS	Abstract test suite
AU	Access unit
AUI	Attachment unit interface
AVA	Attribute value assertion
AVS	APPC/VM VTAM support
AXP	A DEC hardware and operating system architecture
B-ISDN	Broadband ISDN
B8ZS	Bipolar 8-zeros substitution

BACM	Basic access control model
BAS	Basic activity subset
BASIC	Beginner's All-purpose Instruction Code
BB	Begin bracket
BC	Begin chain
BCC	Block-check character
BCN	Backward congestion notification
BCS	Basic combined subset
BCVT	Basic class virtual terminal
BECN	Backward explicit congestion notification
Bellcore	Bell Communications Research, Inc.
BER	Box event records; bit error rate
BF	Boundary function
BIS	Bracket initiation stopped
BISYNC	Binary synchronous (IBM protocol)
bits/s	bits per second
BIU	Basic information unit
BLU	Basic link unit
BMS	Basic mapping support
BMU	Basic measurement unit
BN	Backward notification; boundary node
BNN	Boundary network node
BOC	Bell Operating Company
BOM	Beginning of message
BRI	Basic rate interface
BSC	Binary synchronous communication
BSD	Berkeley standard distribution
BSS	Basic synchronization subset
BTAM	Basic telecommunications access method
BTU	Basic transmission unit
CA	Channel adapter (also attachment); certification authority

CAD	Computer-aided design
CAE	Common applications environment
CAF	Channel auxiliary facility
CAI	Computer-assisted instruction
CAR	Car area network
CASE	Common application service element
CATV	Community antenna television
CBEMA	Computer & Business Equipment Manufacturers Association
CC	Chain command
CCA	Conceptual (also "common") communication area
CCB	Connection control block; channel control block
CCIS	Common channel interoffice signaling
CCITT	Consultative Committee in International Telegraphy and Telephony
CCO	Context control object
CCR	Commitment, concurrency, and recovery
CCS	Common communications support; common channel signaling; console communication service
CCU	Central control unit; communications control unit
CCW	Channel command word
CD	Countdown counter; chain data; committee draft
CDDI	Copper-stranded distributed data interface
CDF	Configuration data flow
CDI	Change direction indicator
CDRM	Cross-domain resource manager
CDRSC	Cross-domain resource
CDS	Conceptual data storage (also store); central directory server
CEBI	Conditional end bracket indicator
CEI	Connection endpoint identifier
CEN/ELEC	Committee European de Normalization Electrotechnique
CEP	Connection endpoint
CEPT	Conference of European Postal and Telecommunications Administrations

CF	Control function
CFGR	Configuration
CGM	Computer Graphics Metafile
CHILL	CCITT High-Level Language
CHPID	Channel path identifier (ID)
CI	Computer interconnect
CICS	Customer Information Control System; customer information communication subsystem
CID	Command (also connection) identifier
CIGOS	Canadian Interest Group on Open Systems
CIM	Computer-integrated manufacturing
CIR	Commitment information rate
CLAW	Common link access to workstation
CLI	Connectionless internetworking
CLIST	Command list
CLNP	Connectionless network protocol
CLNS	Connectionless network service
CLP	Cell loss priority
CLSDST	Close destination
CLTP	Connectionless transport protocol
CLTS	Connectionless transport service
CLU	Control logical unit
CMC	Communication management configurations
CMIP	Common management information protocol
CMIS	Common management information service
CMISE	Common management information service element
CMOL	CMIP over logical link control
CMOT	CMIP over TCP/IP
CMS	Conversational monitoring system
CMT	Connection management
CN	Composite node

CNM	Communication network management
CNMA	Communication network for manufacturing applications
CNMI	Communication network management interface
CNN	Composite network node
CNOS	Change number of sessions
CNT	Communications name table
CO	Central office
COCF	Connection-oriented convergence function
CODEC	Coder/decoder
COI	Connection-oriented internetworking
COM	Continuation-of-message DMPDU
CONF	Confirm
CONS	Connection-oriented network service
COS	Class-of-service; Corporation for Open Systems
COSM	Class-of-service manager
COSS	Connection-oriented session service
COTP	Connection-oriented transport protocol
COTS	Connection-oriented transport service
CP	Control point; control program
CPCB	Control program (also point) control block
CPCS	Common part convergence sublayer
CPE	Customer premises equipment
CPF	Control program facility
CPI	Common programming interface
CPI-C	Common programming interface with C language
CPMS	Control point management services
CPU	Central processing unit
CR	Command response
CRC	Cyclical redundancy check
CRT	Cathode-ray tube
CRV	Call reference value

CS	Circuit switching; convergence sublayer; configuration services; console
CS-MUX	Circuit-switching multiplexer
CSA	Common service (also storage) area
CSALimit	Common service area (buffer use) limit
CSMA/CA	Carrier-sense multiple access with collision avoidance
CSMA/CD	Carrier-sense multiple access with collision detection
CSP	Communications scanner processor
CSS	Control, signaling, and status store
CSU	Channel service unit
CTC	Channel-to-channel
CTCA	Channel-to-channel adapter
CTCP	Communication and transport control program
CTS	Clear-to-send; common transport semantics
CUA	Channel unit address; common user access
CUG	Cluster user group
CUT	Control unit terminal
CVT	Communications vector table
DA	Destination address
DACD	Directory access control domain
DACTPU	Deactivate physical unit
DAD	Draft addendum
DAF	Framework for distributed applications; destination address field
DAP	Directory (also data) access protocol
DARPA	Defense Advanced Research Projects Agency
DAS	Dual-attachment station; dynamically assigned sockets; dual-address space
DASD	Direct-access storage device
DAT	Dynamic address translation
dB	Decibel
DBCS	Double-byte character set
DBK	Definition block
DC	Data chaining

DCA	Document-content architecture; Defense Communication Agency
DCC	Data Country Code
DCE	Data communications equipment; distributed computing environment; data circuit-terminating equipment
DCL	Digital Command Language (DEC)
DCLI	Data-link connection identifier
DCS	Defined context set
DCSS	Discontiguous shared segment
DDB	Directory database
DDCMP	Digital's (DEC's) data communications message protocol
DDDB	Distributed DDB
DDM	Distributed data management
DDN	Defense Data Network
DDName	Data definition name
DDP	Datagram delivery protocol
DDS	Digital data service
DE	Discard eligibility; directory entry
DEA	Directory entry attribute
DEC	Digital Equipment Corporation
DECdts	DEC distributed time service
DECNET	Digital equipment (DEC) network architecture
DELNI	DEC local network interconnect
DES	Data Encryption Standard
DEUNA	Digital Ethernet Unibus Network Adapter
DEV	Device address field
DFC	Data flow control
DFI	DSP format identifier
DFT	Distributed function terminal
DH	DMPDU header
DIA	Document Interchange Architecture
DIB	Directory information base

DIS	Draft International Standard
DISC	Disconnect
DISP	Draft International Standardized Profile; directory information shadowing protocol
DIT	Directory information tree
DIU	Distribution interchange unit
DIX	DEC, Intel, and Xerox
DL	Distribution list
DLC	Data-link control (also connection)
DLCEP	Data-link connection endpoint
DLCI	Data-link connection identifier
DLPDU	Data-link protocol data unit
DLS	Data-link service
DLSAP	Data-link service access point
DLSDU	Data-link service data unit
DLU	Dependent (also destination) logical unit
DLUR	Dependent logical unit requestor
DLUS	Dependent logical unit server
DM	Disconnected mode
DMA	Direct memory access
DMD	Directory management domain
DMI	Digital multiplexed interface; definition of management information
DMO	Domain management organization
DMPDU	Derived MAC protocol data unit
DMUX	Double multiplexer
DN	Distinguished name
DNA	Digital Network Architecture
DNHR	Dynamic nonhierarchical routing
DNS	Domain name service (also system)
DoD	U.S. Department of Defense
DOP	Directory operational binding management protocol

DOS	Disk operating system
DP	Draft proposal
DPG	Dedicated packet group
DPI	Dots per inch
DQDB	Distributed queue dual bus
DR	Definite response; dynamic reconfiguration
DRDA	Distributed Relational Database Architecture
DRDS	Dynamic reconfiguration data set
DRSLST	Direct search list
DS	Directory service(s); desired state
DS-n	Digital signaling level n
DSA	Directory service agent; Digital (DEC) storage architecture
DSAP	Destination service access point
DSD	Data structure definition
DSE	DSA-specific entry; data-switching exchange
DSL	Digital subscriber line
DSname	Data-set name
DSP	Directory service protocol; domain-specific part
DSS 1	Digital subscriber signaling system No. 1
DSSI	Digital (DEC) small systems (also storage systems) interconnect
DSTINIT	Data services task initialization
DSU	Digital services unit
DSUN	Distribution services unit name
DT	DMPDU trailer
DTE	Data terminal equipment
DTMF	Dual-tone multifrequency
DTR	Data terminal ready
DU	Data unit
DUA	Directory user agent
DVT	Destination vector table
E-mail	Electronic mail

EAB	Extended addressing bit
EAS	Extended area service
EB	End bracket
EBCDIC	Extended Binary-Coded Decimal Interchange Code
ECC	Enhanced error checking and correction
ECH	Echo canceller with hybrid
ECMA	European Computer Manufacturers' Association
ECO	Echo control object
ECSA	Exchange Carriers Standards Association
ED	End delimiter
EDI	Electronic Data Interchange
EDIFACT	EDI for administration, commerce, and transport
EDIM	EDI message
EDIME	EDI messaging environment
EDIMS	EDI messaging system
EDI-MS	EDI message store
EDIN	EDI notification
EDI-UA	EDI-user agent
EEI	External environment interface
EGP	Exterior gateway protocol
EIA	Electronic Industries Association
EIT	Encoded information type
ELAP	EtherTalk LAP
EMA	Enterprise management architecture
EMI	Electromagnetic interference
EN	End node
ENA	Extended network addressing
EOM	End-of-Message DMPDU
EOT	End of transmission
EP	Emulation program; echo protocol
ER	Explicit route; exception response

EREP	Environmental recording editing and printing
ERP	Error-recovery procedure
ES	End system
ESA	Enterprise system architecture; Enhanced Subarea Addressing
ESCON	Enterprise System Connection
ESF	Extended superframe format
ESH	End system hello
ES-IS	End system to intermediate system
ESS	Electronic switching system
ESTELLE	Extended State Transition Language
ETB	End-of-text block
ETR	Early token release
ETX	End of text
EVE	Extensible VAX Editor
EWOS	European Workshop on Open Systems
EXLST	Exit list
EXT	External trace (file)
FADU	File access data unit
FAS	Frame alignment sequence
FC	Frame-check; frame control (field)
FCC	Federal Communications Commission
FCI	Frame-copied indicator
FCS	Frame-check sequence
FDCO	Field definition control object
FDDI	Fiber Distributed Data Interface
FDDI-FO	FDDI follow-on
FDL	File Definition Language (DEC)
FDM	Frequency-division multiplexing
FDR	Field definition record
FDT	Formal description technique
FDX	Full-duplex

FEC	Field entry condition
FECN	Forward explicit congestion notification
FEE	Field entry event
FEI	Field entry instruction
FEICO	Field entry instruction control object
FEIR	Field entry instruction record
FEP	Front-end processor
FEPCO	Field entry pilot control object
FEPR	Field entry pilot record
FER	Field entry reaction
FFOL	FDDI follow-on LAN
FH	Frame handler
FID	Format identification
FIFO	First in, first out
FIPS	*Federal Information Processing Standard*
FM	Function management; frequency modulation
FMD	Function management data
FMH	Function management header
FN	Forward notification
FOD	Office Document Format
FQPCID	Fully qualified procedure correlation identifier
FRAD	Frame relay access device
FRFH	Frame relay frame handler
FRMR	Frame reject
FRSE	Frame relay switching equipment
FRTE	Frame relay terminal equipment
FS	Frame status field
FSG	SGML interchange format
FSK	Frequency-shift keying
FSM	Finite-state machine
F^t	Foot; fault tolerant (e.g., VAXF^t)

FTAM	File transfer and access management
FTP	File transfer protocol in TCP/IP
FX	Foreign exchange service
GAP	Gateway access protocol
Gbits	Gigabits
Gbits/s	Gigabits per second
Gbyte	Gigabyte
GCS	Group control system
GDDM	Graphical data display manager
GDMO	Guidelines for the definition of managed objects
GDS	General data stream
GEN	Generation
GFC	Generic flow control
GFI	General format indicator
GOSIP	Government OSI profile
GSA	General Services Administration
GTF	Generalized trace facility
GUI	Graphical user interface
GWNCP	Gateway NCP
GWSSCP	Gateway SSCP
H-MUX	Hybrid multiplexer
HAN	House area network
HASP	Houston Automatic Spooling Priority
HCD	Hardware configuration definition
HCS	Header check sequence
HDB3	High-density bipolar — 3 zeros
HDLC	High-level data-link control
HDX	Half-duplex (also HD)
HEC	Header error correction
hex	Hexadecimal
HFS	Hierarchical file system

HI-SAP	Hybrid isochronous–MAC service access point
HMI	Human-machine interface
HMP	Host monitoring protocol
HOB	Head of bus
HP	Hewlett-Packard
HP-SAP	Hybrid packet–MAC service access point
HRC	Hybrid ring control
HS	Half session
HSC	Hierarchical storage controller
HSLN	High-speed local network
Hz	Hertz (cycles per second)
IAB	Internet Architecture Board
IADCS	Interactivity defined context set
IAN	Integrated analog network
IAP	Inner administrative point
IAS	Interactive Application System
IBM	International Business Machines Corporation
IC	Interexchange carrier
ICA	Integrated communication adapter
ICCF	Interactive computing and control facility
ICD	International code designator
ICF	Isochronous convergence function
ICI	Interface control information
ICMP	Internet control message protocol
ICP	Interconnect control program
ICV	Integrity check value
ID	Identifier or identification
IDA	Indirect data addressing
IDI	Initial domain identifier
IDN	Integrated digital network; interface definition notation
IDP	Initial domain part; internetwork datagram packet (protocol)

IDU	Interface data unit
IEC	Interexchange carrier; International Electrotechnical Com-mission
IEEE	Institute of Electrical and Electronic Engineers
IETF	Internet Engineering Task Force
IHL	Internet header length
IIA	Information interchange architecture
ILD	Injection laser diode
ILU	Independent (also initiating) logical unit
IMAC	Isochronous media access control
IMIL	International Managed Information Library
IML	Initial microcode load
IMPDU	Initial MAC protocol data unit
IMR	Intensive mode recording
IMS	Information Management System
IMS/VS	Information Management System/Virtual Storage
IN	Intelligent network; interchange node
IND	Indication
INN	Intermediate network node
INTAP	Interoperability Technology Association for Information Processing
I/O	Input/output
IOC	Input/output control
IOCDS	Input/output configuration data set
IOCP	Input/output control (also channel or configuration) program
IONL	Internal organization of network layer
IOPD	Input/output problem determination
IP	Internet protocol
IPC	Interprocess communication
IPCS	Interactive problem control system
IPDS	Intelligent printer data stream
IPI	Initial protocol identifier
IPICS	ISP implementation conformance statement

IPL	Initial program load(er)
IPM	Interpersonal message
IPMS	Interpersonal messaging system
IPM-UA	Interpersonal messaging user agent
IPN	Interpersonal notification
IPR	Isolated pacing response
IPX	Internetwork packet exchange
IR	Internet router
IRN	Intermediate routing node
IRSG	Internet Research Steering Group
IRTF	Internet Research Task Force
IS	International Standard
ISAM	Index-sequential access method
ISC	Intersystem communications in CICS
ISCF	Intersystem control facility
ISDN	Integrated Services Digital Network
ISE	Integrate storage element
ISH	Intermediate system hello
IS-IS	Intermediate system-to-intermediate system
ISO	International Standards Organization
ISODE	ISO development environment
ISP	International Standard Profile
ISPBX	Integrated Services Private Branch Exchange
ISPF	Interactive System Productivity Facility
ISPSN	Initial synchronization point serial number
ISR	Intermediate session routing
ISSI	Interswitching system interface
ISUP	ISDN user part
IT	Information technology
ITC	Independent telephone company
ITU	International Telecommunication Union

IUCV	Interuser communication vehicle
IUT	Implementation under test
IVDT	Integrated voice/data terminal
IWU	Interworking unit
IXC	Interexchange carrier
JCL	Job Control Language
JES2, JES3	Job Entry Subsystem 2, 3
JTC	Joint Technical Committee
JTM	Job transfer and manipulation
kbits	Kilobits
kbits/s	Kilobits per second
kbyte	Kilobyte
kHz	Kilohertz
km	Kilometer
LAB	Latency adjustment buffer; line attachment base
LAN	Local area network
LANRES	Local Area Network Resource Extension Services
LANSUP	LAN adapter NDIS support
LAP	Link-access procedure (also protocol)
LAPB	Link-access procedure balanced
LAPD	Link-access procedure on the D channel
LAPM	Link-access procedure for modems
LAPS	LAN adapter and protocol support
LATA	Local access and transport area
LCF	Log control function
LCN	Logical channel number
LDDB	Local directory database
LE	Local exchange
LEC	Local exchange carrier
LED	Light-emitting diode
LEN	Low-entry networking

LFSID	Local form session identifier
LH	Link header
LI	Length indicator
LIB	Line interface base
LIC	Line interface coupler
LIDB	Line information database
LIVT	Link integrity verification test
LLAP	LocalTalk link access protocol
LLC	Logical link control
LL2	Link level 2
LME	Layer management entity
LMI	Layer (also local) management interface
LOCKD	Lock manager daemon
LOTOS	Language of Temporal Ordering Specifications
LPAR	Logical partitioned (mode)
LPD	Line printer daemon
LPDA	Link problem determination application
LPR	Line printer
LRC	Longitudinal redundancy check
LS	Link station
LSE	Local system environment
LSL	Link support layer
LSP	Link-state packet
LSS	Low-speed scanner
LT	Local termination
LU	Logical unit
m	Meters
MAC	Media (also medium) access control
MACE	Macintosh audio compression and expansion
MACF	Multiple association control function
MAN	Metropolitan area network

MAP	Manufacturing automation protocol
MAU	Media access unit; multistation access unit
MBA	MASSBUS adapter
Mbits	Megabits
Mbits/s	Megabits per second
Mbyte	Megabyte
Mbytes/s	Megabytes per second
MBZ	Must be zero
MCF	MAC convergence function
MCI	Microwave Communications, Inc.
MCP	MAC convergence protocol
MCR	Monitor console routine
MD	Management domain
MFA	Management functional areas
MFD	Master file directory
MFJ	Modified final judgment
MFS	Message formatting services in IMS
MH	Message handling (package)
MHS	Message handling service (also system)
MHz	Megahertz
mi	Mile
MIB	Management (also message) information base
MIC	Media interface connector
MID	Message identifier
MIM	Management information model
min	Minute
MIN	Multiple interaction negotiation
MIPS	Million instructions per second
MIS	Management information system
MIT	Management information tree; Massachusetts Institute of Technology
MLID	Multiple-link interface driver

MMF	Multimode fiber
MMS	Manufacturing message specification (also messaging service)
MNP	Microcom networking protocol
MOP	Maintenance operations protocol
MOSS	Maintenance and operator subsystem
MOT	Means of testing
MOTIS	Message-oriented text interchange system
MPAF	Midpage allocation field
MPC	Multipath channel
MPG	Multiple preferred guests
MPP	Multiple-protocol package
MQ	Message queue
MRO	Multiregion operation in CICS
ms	Millisecond
MS	Management services; message store
MSCP	Mass storage control protocol
MSG	Console messages
MSHP	Maintain system history program
MSN	Multiple systems networking
MSNF	Multiple systems networking facility
MSS	MAN switching system
MST	Multiplexed slotted and token ring
MSU	Management services unit
MTA	Message transfer agent
MTACP	Magnetic tape ancillary control process
MTBF	Mean time between failures
MTP	Message transfer part
MTPN	Multiprotocol Transport Networking
MTS	Message transfer system
MTSE	Message transfer service element
MTU	Maximum transfer unit

μm	Micrometer
MVC	Multicast virtual circuit
MVI	Major vector identifier
MVL	Major vector length
MVS	Multiple virtual systems
MVS/370	Multiple Virtual Storage/370 (IBM)
MVS/XA	Multiple Virtual Storage/Extended Architecture (IBM)
MVT	Multiprogramming with a variable number of tasks
NAK	Negative acknowledgment in BSC
NAU	Network-addressable (also -accessible) unit
NAUN	Nearest active upstream neighbor
NBP	Name-binding protocol
NC	Network connection; numerical controller
NCB	Node control block
NCCF	Network communications control facility
NCEP	Network connection endpoint
NCP	Network control program; network (also NetWare) core protocol
NCS	Network computing system
NCTE	Network channel-terminating equipment
NDF	NCP/EP definition facility
NDIS	Network driver interface specification
NetBIOS	Network basic input/output system
NETID	Network ID
NFS	Network file system (also server)
NIB	Node identification (also initialization) block
NIC	Network interface card
NIF	Network information file
NIS	Names information socket
NIST	National Institute of Standards and Technology
NIUF	North American ISDN Users' Forum
NJE	Network job entry

NLDM	Network logical data manager
NLM	NetWare loadable module
nm	Nanometer
NM	Network management (also model)
NMP	Network management process
NMVT	Network management vector transport
NN	Network node
NNI	Network node interface
NNT	NetView-NetView task
NOF	Node operator facility
NPA	Numbering plan area
NPCI	Network protocol control information
NPDA	Network problem determination application
NPDU	Network protocol data unit
NPM	NetView performance monitor
NPSI	Network packet-switching interface
NR	Number of receives; negative response
NREN	National Research and Education Network
NRF	Network routing facility
NRN	Nonreceipt notification
NRZ	Non-return-to-zero
NRZI	Non-return-to-zero inverted
ns	Nanosecond
NS	Network service; number of sends
NSAP	Network service access point
NSDU	Network service data unit
NSF	Network search function; National Science Foundation
NSFNET	National Science Foundation Network
NSP	Network services protocol
NTO	Network terminal option
NVLAP	National Voluntary Accreditation Program

NVP	Network voice protocol
OAF	Origination address field
OAM	Operations, administration, and maintenance
OAM&P	Operations, administration, maintenance, and provisioning
OC-n	Optical carrier level n
OCA	Open communication architectures
OCC	Other common carrier
ODA	Office (also open-) document architecture
ODI	Open data-link interface
ODIF	Office document interchange format
ODINSUP	ODI NSIS support
ODP	Open distributed processing
OIT	Object identifier tree
OIW	OSI Implementation Workshop
OLRT	Online real time
OLU	Origin(ating) logical unit
OM	Object management
Ω	Ohm
ONA	Open-network architecture
OPNDST	Open destination
O/R	Originator/recipient
OS	Operating System
OS/400	Operating System/400 for the AS/400 Computer
OSAK	OSI application kernel
OSE	Open-systems environment
OSF	Open Software Foundation
OSI	Open-systems interconnection
OSI/CS	OSI communications subsystem
OSIE	Open-systems interconnection environment
OSILL	Open-systems interconnection lower layers
OSIUL	Open-systems interconnection upper layers

OSNS	Open Systems Network Services
OSPF	Open shortest path first
P-MAC	Packet-switched media access control
PA	Prearbitrated
PABX	Private automatic branch exchange
PAD	Packet assembler/disassembler
PAF	Prearbitrated function
PAI	Protocol address information
PANS	Pretty amazing new stuff
PAP	Printer access protocol
PARC	Palo Alto (Calif.) Research Center
PBX	Private branch exchange
PC	Path control; personal computer
PCCU	Physical communications control unit
PCEP	Presentation connection endpoint
PCI	Protocol (also program) control information; program-controlled interruption; presentation context identifier
PCM	Pulse-code modulation
PCO	Points of control and observation
PCTR	Protocol conformance test report
PDAD	Proposed draft addendum
PDAU	Physical delivery access unit
PDC	Packet data channel
PDF	Program development facility
pDISP	Proposed Draft International Standard Profile
PDN	Public data network
PDP	Programmable data processor
PDS	Partitioned data set
PDU	Protocol data unit
PDV	Presentation data value
PELS	Picture elements

PEP	Partitioned emulation program
PER	Program event recording
PETS	Parameterized executable test suite
PGF	Presentation graphics feature
PH	Packet handler (or packet handling)
PhC	Physical-layer connection
PhCEP	Physical connection endpoint
PhL	Physical layer
PhPDU	Physical-layer protocol data unit
PhS	Physical-layer service
PhSAP	Physical-layer service access point
PhSDU	Physical-layer service data unit
PHY	Physical layer
PICS	Protocol information conformance statement
PIN	Positive-intrinsic negative photodiode
PING	Packet Internet Groper
PIP	Program initialization parameters
PIU	Path information unit
PIXIT	Protocol Implementation eXtra Information for Testing
PKCS	Public key cryptosystems
PLC	Programmable logic controller
PLCP	Physical-layer convergence protocol
PLP	Packet-layer (also level) protocol
PLS	Primary link station
PLU	Primary (also peripheral) logical unit
PM	Protocol machine; phase modulation
PMD	Physical-(layer)-medium-dependent
POI	Program operator interface
POP	Point of presence
POSI	Promoting Conference for OSI
POSIX	Portable Operating System Interface

POTS	Plain old telephone service
POWER	Priority output writers and execution processors and input readers
PPDU	Presentation protocol data unit
PPO	Primary program operator
PPP	Point-to-point protocol
PPSDN	Public packet-switched data network
PRI	Primary rate interface
PRMD	Private management domain
PROFS	Professional office system
PROM	Programmable read-only memory
PR/SM	Processor resource/systems manager
PS	Presentation services
PSAP	Public safety answering point; physical service access point
PSC	Public Service Commission
PSDN	Packet-switched data network
PSI	Packet-switched interface
PSID	Product-set identification
PSK	Phase-shift keying
PSN	Packet-switched network
PSPDN	Packet-switched public data network
PSTN	Public switched telephone network
PSW	Program status word
PS/2	Personal System/2 (IBM)
PS/VP	Personal System/Value Point (IBM)
PTF	Program temporary fix
PTLXAU	Public Telex Access Unit
PTN	Public telephone network
PTT	Post, Telegraph, and Telephone
PU	Physical unit
PUC	Public utility commission
PUCP	Physical unit control point

PUMS	Physical unit management services
PUT	Program update tape
PVC	Private (also permanent) virtual circuit
PVN	Private virtual network
PWSS	Programmable workstation service
P1	Protocol 1 (message transfer protocol/MHS/X.400)
P2	Protocol 2 (interpersonal messaging MHS/X.400)
P3	Protocol 3 (submission and delivery protocol/ MHS/X.400)
P5	Protocol 5 (teletext access protocol)
P7	Protocol 7 (message store access protocol in X.400)
QA	Queued arbitrated
QAF	Queued arbitrated function
QC	Quiesce complete
QEC	Quiesce at end of chain
QMF	Query management facility
QOS	Quality of service
QPSX	Queued packet and synchronous switch
QUIPU	X.500 Conformant Directory Services in ISODE
RAB	Record access block
RACF	Resource access control facility
RAM	Random-access memory
RARP	Reverse address resolution protocol
RBOC	Regional Bell Operating Company
RD	Routing domain; route redirection; request a disconnect
RDA	Relative distinguished names; remote database access
RDI	Restricted digital information
RDN	Relative distinguished name
RDT	Resource definition table
RECFMS	Record formatted maintenance statistics
REJ	Reject
REQ	Request

RESP	Response
RESYNC	Resynchronization
REXX	Restructured Extended Executor (IBM)
RFC	Request for comment
RFP	Request for proposal
RFQ	Request for price quotation
RH	Request (or response) header
RI	Ring in
RIB	Routing information base
RIF	Routing information field
RIM	Request initialization mode
RIP	Router information protocol
RISC	Reduced instruction-set computer
RJE	Remote job entry
RM	Reference model; resource manager
RMS	Record management services (for OpenVMS)
RMT	Ring management
RN	Receipt notification
RNAA	Request network address assignment
RNR	Receive not ready
RO	Ring out
RODM	Resource object data manager
ROSE	Remote-operations service element
RPC	Remote procedure call; remote procedure call in OSF/DCE
RPL	Request parameter list
RPOA	Recognized private operating agency
RQ	Request counter
RR	Receive ready
RS	Relay system
RSCS	Remote spooling communication system
RSCV	Route selection control vector

RSF	Remote support facility
RSP	Response
RSS	Route selection services
RTM	Response-time monitor
RTMP	Routing table maintenance protocol
RTR	Ready to receive
RTS	Request to send
RTSE	Reliable transfer service element
RTT	Round-trip time
RU	Request (or response) unit
S/390	IBM's System/390 Hardware Architecture
s	Second
SA	Source address (field); subarea; sequenced application
SAA	System applications architecture; specific administrative area
SAB	Subnetwork-access boundary
SABM	Set asynchronous balanced mode
SACF	Single association control function
SACK	Selective ACKnowledgment
SAF	SACF auxiliary facility
SALI	Source address length indicator
SAMBE	Set asynchronous mode balanced extended
SAO	Single association object
SAP	Service access point; service advertising protocol
SAPI	Service access point identifier
SAR	Segmentation and reassembly
SAS	Single-attachment station; statically assigned sockets
SASE	Specific application service element
SATF	Shared-access transfer facility
SATS	Selected abstract test suite
SAW	Session awareness data
SBA	Set buffer address

SBCS	Single-byte character set
SBI	Stop bracket initiation
SC	Session connection (also connector); subcommittee; session control
SCA	Systems communication architecture
SCB	Session control block
SCC	Specialized common carrier
SCCP	Signaling connection control point
SCE	System control element
SCEP	Session connection endpoint
SCIF	Single-console image facility
SCM	Session control (also connection) manager
SCP	Service control point
SCS	System conformance statement; SNA character string
SCTR	System conformance test report
SD	Start delimiter
SDDI	Shielded distributed data interface
SDH	Synchronous digital hierarchy
SDIF	Standard document interchange format
SDL	System description language
SDLC	Synchronous data-link control
SDN	Software-defined network
SDSE	Shadowed DSA entries
SDT	Start data traffic
SDU	Service data unit
SE	Session entity
SFD	Start frame delimiter
SFS	Shared file system
SFT	System fault tolerance
SG	Study group
SGFS	Special Group on Functional Standardization
SGML	Standard Generalized Markup Language

SIA	Stable implementation agreements
SIM	Set initialization mode
SIO	Start input/output
SIP	SMDS interface protocol
SLI	Suppress-length indication
SLIP	Serial-line Internet protocol
SLU	Secondary logical unit
SM	Session manager
SMAE	System management application entity
SMASE	System management application service element
SMB	Server message block
SMDR	Station message detail recording
SMDS	Switched multimegabit data service
SMF	Single-mode fiber; system management facility
SMFA	Systems management functional area
SMI	Structure of the OSI management information service; Structure of Management Information (language)
SMIB	Stored message information base
SMP	System modification program
SMS	Service management system; storage management subsystem
SMT	Station management standard
SMTP	Simple mail transfer protocol
SN	Subarea node
SNA	System Network Architecture
SNAcF	Subnetwork access function
SNAcP	Subnetwork access protocol
SNADS	SNA distribution services
SNARE	Subnetwork address routing entity
SNCP	Single-node control point
SNDCP	Subnetwork-dependent convergence protocol
SNI	Subscriber-network interface; SNA network interconnection (also interface)

SNICP	Subnetwork-independent convergence protocol
SNMP	Simple network management protocol
SNPA	Subnetwork point of attachment
SNRM	Set normal response mode
SON	Sent (or send) outside the node
SONET	Synchronous optical network
SP	Signaling point; system performance
SPAG	Standards promotion and applications group
SPC	Signaling point code
SPCS	Service point command service
SPDU	Session protocol data unit
SPE	Synchronous payload envelope
SPI	Subsequent protocol identifier
SPM	FDDI-to-SONET physical-layer mapping standard
SPSN	Synchronization-point serial number
SPX	Sequenced packet exchange
SQE	Signal-quality error
SQL	Structured Query Language
SRB	Source route bridging
SRH	SNARE request hello
SRM	System resource manager
SS	Switching system; start/stop (transmission); session services
SS6	Signaling system 6
SS7	Signaling system 7
SSA	Subschema specific area
SSAP	Source (also session) service access point
SSCP	System service control point
SSCS	Service-specific convergence sublayer
SSDU	Session service data unit
SSM	Single-segment message DMPDU
SSP	System Support Program

ST	Sequenced terminal
STACK	Start acknowledgment (message)
STM	Synchronous transfer mode; station management
STM-*n*	Synchronous transport module level *n*
STP	Shielded twisted pair; service transaction program (in LU6.2); signal transfer point
STS-*n*	Synchronous transport signal level *n*
STX	Start of text
SUT	System under test
SVA	Shared virtual area
SVC	Switched virtual circuit
SVI	Subvector identifier
SVL	Subvector length
SVP	Subvector parameters
SYN	Synchronous character in IBM's bisynchronous protocol
SYNC	Synchronization
T	Transport
TA	Terminal adapter
TAF	Terminal access facility
TAG	Technology advisory group
TAP	Trace analysis program
Tbyte	Terabyte
TC	Transport connection or technical committee
TCAM	Telecommunications access method
TCB	Task control block
TCC	Transmission control code
TCEP	Transport connection endpoint
TCM	Time-compression multiplexing
TCP	Transmission control protocol
TCP/IP	Transmission control protocol/Internet protocol
TCT	Terminal control table in CICS

TDM	Time-division multiplexing; topology database manager
TDR	Time-domain reflectometer
TE	Terminal equipment
TELNET	Remote log-on in TCP/IP
TEP	Transport endpoint
TFTP	Trivial file transfer protocol
TG	Transmission group
TH	Transmission header
THT	Token holding timer
TIC	Token-ring interface coupler
TIE	Translated image environment
TI RPC	Transport-independent RPC
TLAP	TokenTalk LAP
TLI	Transport-layer interface
TLMAU	Telematic access unit
TLV	Type, length, and value
TLXAU	Telex access unit
TMP	Text management protocol
TMS	Time-multiplexed switching
TMSCP	Tape mass storage control protocol
TOP	Technical and office protocol
TP	Transaction program (also processing); transport protocol
TP 0	TP class 0—simple
TP 1	TP class 1—basic error recovery
TP 2	TP class 2—multiplexing
TP 3	TP class 3—error recovery and multiplexing
TP 4	TP class 4—error detection and recovery
TPDU	Transport protocol data unit
TPF	Transaction processing facility
TP-PMD	Twisted-pair PMD
TPS	Two-processor switch

TPSP	Transaction processing service provider
TPSU	Transaction processing service user
TPSUI	TPSU invocation
TR	Technical report; token ring
TRA	Token-ring adapter
TRS	Topology and routing services
TRSS	Token-ring subsystem
TRT	Token rotation timer
TS	Transaction services; transport service
TSAF	Transparent services access facility
TSAP	Transport service access point
TSC	Transmission subsystem controller
TSCF	Target system control facility
TSDU	Transport service data unit
TSI	Time-slot interchange
TSO/E	Time Sharing Option/Extension
TSR	Terminate-and-stay-resident program
TSS	Transmission subsystem
TTCN	Tree and tabular combined notation
TTL	Time to live
TTP	Timed token protocol; transport test platform
TTRT	Target token rotation time
TTY	Teletype
TUP	Telephone user part
TVX	Valid transmission timer (FDDI)
TWX	Teletypewriter exchange service
TZD	Time-zone difference
UA	Unnumbered acknowledgment; user agent; unsequenced application
UART	Universal asynchronous receiver/transmitter
UCB	Unit control block; University of California, Berkeley
UCW	Unit control word

UDI	Unrestricted digital information
UDP	User datagram protocol
UI	Unnumbered information
UNI	User network interface
UOW	Unit of work
UP	Unnumbered poll
USART	Universal synchronous/asynchronous receiver/transmitter
User-ASE	User application service element
USS	Unformatted system services
UT	Unsequenced terminal
UTC	Coordinated Universal Time
UTP	Unshielded twisted pair
UUCP	UNIX-to-UNIX copy program
VAC	Value-added carrier
VAN	Value-added network
VAS	Value-added service
VAX	Virtual Address eXtended (operating system; DEC)
VAXBI	VAX bus interface
VCC	Virtual channel connection
VCI	Virtual channel identifier/indicator (DQDB)
VCNS	VTAM common network services
VDI	Video display terminal
VEST	VAX environment software translator
VIT	VTAM internal trace
VLF	Virtual look-aside facility
VLSI	Very large-scale integration
VM	Virtual machine
VMD	Virtual manufacturing device
VMDBK	Virtual machine definition block
VM/ESA	Virtual Machine/Enterprise Systems Architecture
VMS	Virtual memory system

VM/SP	Virtual machine/system product
VM/SP HPO	Virtual Machine/System Product High Performance Option
VM/XA	Virtual Machine/Extended Architecture
VPC	Virtual path connection
VPI	Virtual path indicator
VR	Virtual route
VRPWS	Virtual route pacing window size
VS	Virtual storage
VSAM	Virtual storage access method
VSCS	VM/SNA console support
VSE	Virtual Storage Extended
VSE/ESA	Virtual Storage Extended/Enterprise Systems Architecture
VT	Virtual terminal
VTAM	Virtual telecommunications access method
VTE	Virtual terminal environment
VTP	Virtual terminal protocol
VTPM	Virtual terminal protocol machine
VTSE	Virtual terminal service element
VVIEF	VAX vector instruction emulation facility
WACA	Write access connection acceptor
WACI	Write access connection initiator
WAN	Wide area network
WANDD	Wide area network device driver
WAVAR	Write access variable
WBC	Wideband channel
WD	Working document
WG	Working group
WP	Working party
X	The XWindow System
XA	Extended Architecture (IBM)

XAPIA	X.400 API Association
XCF	Cross-system coupling facility
XDF	Extended distance facility
Xdm	X display manager
XDS	X/Open Directory Services API
Xds	X display server
XI	SNA X.25 interface
XID	Exchange identification
XNS	Xerox Network Standard
XRF	Extended recovery facility
XTI	X/Open Transport Interface
ZIP	Zone information protocol
ZIS	Zone information socket
ZIT	Zone information table

APPENDIX F

RFC Listing

This section contains Requests for Comments (RFCs) in reverse numeric order.

RFC	Title
1806	Communicating Presentation Information in Internet Messages: The Content-Disposition Header, June 1995
1805	Location-Independent Data/Software Integrity Protocol, June 1995
1804	Publishing in X.500 Directory, June 1995
1803	Recommendations for an X.500 Production Directory Service, June 1995
1802	Introducing Project Long Bud: Internet Pilot Project for the Deployment of X.500 Directory Information in Support of X.400 Routing, June 1995
1801	MHS Use of the X.500 Directory to Support MHS Routing, June 1995
1800	Not yet issued
1799	Not yet issued
1798	Connection-less Lightweight Directory Access Protocol, June 1995
1797	IANA; ISI Class A Subnet Experiment, April 1995
1796	Not All RFCs Are Standards, April 1995
1795	Data Link Switching: Switch-to-Switch Protocol AIW DLSw RIG: DLSw Closed Pages, DLSw Standard Version 1.0, April 1995
1794	DNS Support for Load Balancing, 1995
1793	OSPF to Support Demand Circuits, April 1995
1792	TCP/IPX Connection Mib Specification, April 1995
1791	TCP and UDP over IPX Networks with Fixed Path MTU, April 1995
1790	An Agreement between the Internet Society and Sun Microsystems, Inc. in the Matter of ONC RPC and XDR Protocols, April 1995
1789	INETPhone: Telephone Services and Servers on Internet, April 1995
1788	Simpson, W., ICMP Domain Name Messages, April 1995
1787	Routing in a Multi-provider Internet, April 1995
1786	Representation of IP Routing Policies in a Routing Registry, March 1995
1785	TFTP Option Negotiation Analysis, March 1995
1784	TFTP Timeout Interval and Transfer Size Options, March 1995 (updates RFC 1350)
1783	TFTP Blocksize Option, March 1995 (updates RFC 1350)
1782	TFTP Option Extension, March 1995 (updates RFC 1350)
1781	Using the OSI Directory to Achieve User Friendly Naming, March 1995 (obsoletes RFC 1484)

RFC	Title
1780	Internet Official Protocol Standards, March 1995 (obsoletes RFCs 1720, 1610, 1600, 1540, 1500, 1410, 1360, 1280, 1250, 1200, 1140, and 1130)
1779	A String Representation of Distinguished Names, March 1995 (obsoletes RFC 1485)
1778	The String Representation of Standard Attribute Syntaxes, March 1995 (obsoletes RFC 1488)
1777	Lightweight Directory Access Protocol, March 1995 (obsoletes 1487)
1776	The Address Is the Message, April 1995
1775	To Be "On" the Internet, March 1995
1774	Protocol Analysis, March 1995
1773	Experience with the BGP-4 Protocol, March 1995 (obsoletes RFC 1656)
1772	Application of the Border Gateway Protocol in the Internet, March 1995 (obsoletes RFC 1655)
1771	A Border Gateway Protocol 4 (BGP-4), March 1995 (obsoletes RFC 1654)
1770	IPv4 Option for Sender Directed Multi-Destination Delivery, March 1995
1769	Simple Network Time Protocol (SNTP) March 1995
1768	Host Group Extensions for CLNP Multicasting, March 1995
1767	MIME Encapsulation of EDI Objects, March 1995
1766	Tags for the Identification of Languages, March 1995
1765	OSPF Database Overflow, March 1995
1764	The PPP XNS IDP Control Protocol (XNSCP), March 1995
1763	The PPP Banyan Vines Control Protocol (BVCP), March 1995
1762	The PPP DECnet Phase IV Control Protocol (DNCP), March 1995 (obsoletes RFC 1376)
1761	Snoop Version 2 Packet Capture File Format, February 1995
1760	The S/KEY One-Time Password System, February 1995
1759	Printer MIB, March 1995
1758	The North American Directory Forum, NADF Standing Documents: A Brief Overview, February 1995 (obsoletes 1417, 1295, 1255, 1218)
1757	Remote Network Monitoring Management Information Base, February 1995 (obsoletes RFC 1271)

RFC	Title
1756	Remote Write Protocol, January 1995
1755	ATM Signaling Support for IP over ATM, January 1995
1754	IP over ATM Working Group's Recommendations for the ATM Forum's Multiprotocol BOF Version 1, January 1995
1753	IPng Technical Requirements of the Nimrod Routing and Addressing Architecture, December 1994
1752	The Recommendation for the IP Next Generation Protocol, January 1995
1751	A Convention for Human-Readable 128-bit Keys, December 1994
1750	Randomness Recommendations for Security, December 1994
1749	IEEE 802.5 Station Source Routing MIB Using SMIv2, December 1994 (updates RFC 1748)
1748	IEEE 802.5 MIB Using SMIv2, December 1994 (obsoletes RFC 1743; updated by RFC 1749)
1747	Definitions of Managed Objects for SNA Data Link Control (SDLC) Using SMIv2, January 1995
1746	Ways to Define User Expectations, December 1994
1745	BGP4/IDRP for IP-OSPF Interaction, December 1994
1744	Observations on the Management of the Internet Address Space, December 1994
1743	IEEE 802.5 MIB Using SMIv2, December 1994 (obsoletes 1231; obsoleted by RFC 1748)
1742	AppleTalk Management Information Base II, January 1995 (obsoletes 1243)
1741	MIME Content Type for BinHex Encoded Files, December 1994
1740	MIME Encapsulation of Macintosh Files—MacMIME, December 1994
1739	A Primer on Internet and TCP/IP Tools, December 1994
1738	Uniform Resource Locators (URL), December 1994
1737	Functional Requirements for Uniform Resource Names, December 1994
1736	Functional Recommendations for Internet Resource Locators, February 1995
1735	NBMA Address Resolution Protocol (NARP), December 1994
1734	POP3 Authentication Command, December 1994
1733	Distributed Electronic Mail Models in IMAP4, December 1994
1732	Crispin, M., IMAP4 Compatibility with IMAP2 and IMAP2BIS, December 1994

RFC	Title
1731	IMAP4 Authentication Mechanisms, December 1994
1730	Internet Message Access Protocol—V.4, December 1994
1729	Using the Z39.50 Information Retrieval Protocol in the Internet Environment, December 1994
1728	Resource Transponders, December 1994
1727	A Vision of an Integrated Internet Information Service, December 1994
1726	Technical Criteria for Choosing IP: The Next Generation (IPng), December 1994
1725	Post Office Protocol—Version 3, November 1994 (obsoletes RFC 1460)
1724	RIP Version 2 MIB Extension, November 1994 (obsoletes RFC 1389)
1723	RIP Version 2 Carrying Additional Information, November 1994 (obsoletes RFC 1388; updates RFC 1058)
1722	RIP Version 2 Protocol Applicability Statement, November 1994
1721	VIP Version 2 Protocol Analysis, November 1994 (obsoletes RFC 1387)
1720	Internet Architecture Board, Internet Official Protocol Standards, November 1994 (obsoletes RFC 1610; obsoleted by RFC 1780)
1719	Not yet issued
1718	The Tao of IETF: A Guide for New Attendees of the Internet Engineering Task Force, November 1994 (obsoletes RFC 1539)
1717	The PPP Multilink Protocol (MP), November 1994
1716	Towards Requirements for IP Routers, November 1994
1715	The H Ratio for Address Assignment Efficiency, November 1994
1714	Referral Whois Protocol (RWhois) November 1994
1713	Tools for DNS Debugging, November 1994
1712	DNS Encoding of Geographical Location, November 1994
1711	Classifications in E-mail Routing, October 1994
1710	Simple Internet Protocol Plus White Paper, October 1994
1709	K-12 Internetworking Guidelines, November 1994
1708	NTP PICS PROFORMA for the Network Time Protocol Version 3, October 1994
1707	CATNIP: Common Architecture for the Internet, October 1994
1706	DNS NSAP Resource Records, October 1994 (obsoletes RFC 1637)

RFC	Title
1705	Six Virtual Inches to the Left: The Problem with IPng, October 1994
1704	On Internet Authentication, October 1994
1703	Principles of Operation for the TPC.INT Subdomain: Radio Paging—Technical Procedures, October 1994 (obsoletes RFC 1569)
1702	Generic Routing Encapsulation Over IPv4 Networks, October 1994
1701	Generic Routing Encapsulation (GRE), October 1994
1700	Assigned Numbers, October 1994 (obsoletes RFC 1340)
1699	Not yet issued
1698	Octet Sequences for Upper-Layer OSI to Support Basic Communications Applications, October 1994
1697	Relational Database Management System (RDBMS) Management Information Base (MIB) Using SMIv2, August 1994
1696	Modem Management Information Base (MIB) Using SMIv2, August 1994
1695	Definitions of Managed Objects for ATM Management Version 8.0 Using SMIv2, August 1994
1694	Definitions of Managed Objects for SMDS Interfaces Using SMIv2, August 1994 (obsoletes RFC 1304)
1693	An Extension to TCP: Partial Order Service, November 1994
1692	Transport Multiplexing Protocol (TMux), August 1994
1691	The Document Architecture for the Cornell Digital Library, August 1994
1690	Introducing the Internet Engineering and Planning Group (IEPG), August 1994
1689	A Status Report on Networked Information Retrieval: Tools and Groups, August 1994
1688	IPng Mobility Considerations, August 1994
1687	A Large Corporate User's View of IPng, August 1994
1686	IPng Requirements: A Cable Television Industry Viewpoint, August 1994
1685	Writing X.400 O/R Names, August 1994
1684	Introduction to White Pages Services Based on X.500, August 1994
1683	Multiprotocol Interoperability in IPng, August 1994
1682	IPng BSD Host Implementation Analysis, August 1994
1681	On Many Addresses per Host, August 1994
1680	IPng Support for ATM Services, August 1994

RFC	Title
1679	HPN Working Group Input to the IPng Requirements Solicitation, August 1994
1678	IPng Requirements of Large Corporate Networks, August 1994
1677	Tactical Radio Frequency Communication Requirements for IPng, August 1994
1676	INFN Requirements for an IPng, August 1994
1675	Security Concerns for IPng, August 1994
1674	A Cellular Industry View of IPng, August 1994
1673	Electric Power Research Institute Comments on IPng, August 1994
1672	Accounting Requirements for IPng, August 1994
1671	IPng White Paper on Transition and Other Considerations, August 1994
1670	Not yet issued
1669	Market Viability as a IPng Criteria, August 1994
1668	Unified Routing Requirements for IPng, August 1994
1667	Modeling and Simulation Requirements for IPng, August 1994
1666	Definitions of Managed Objects for SNA NAUs Using SMIv2, August 1994 (obsoletes RFC 1665)
1665	Definitions of Managed Objects for SNA NAUs Using SMIv2, July 1994 (obsoleted by RFC 1666)
1664	Not yet issued
1663	Reliable Transmission, July 1994
1662	PPP in HDLC-like Framing, July 1994 (obsoletes RFC 1549)
1661	The Point-to-Point Protocol, July 1994 (obsoletes RFC 1548)
1660	Definitions of Managed Objects for Parallel-printer-like Hardware Devices Using SMIv2, July 1994 (obsoletes RFC 1318)
1659	Definitions of Managed Objects for RS-232-like Hardware Devices Using SMIv2, July 1994 (obsoletes RFC 1317)
1658	Definitions of Managed Objects for Character Stream Devices Using SMIv2, July 1994 (obsoletes RFC 1316)
1657	Definitions of Managed Objects for the Fourth Version of the Border Gateway Protocol (BGP-4) Using SMIv2, July 1994
1656	BGP-4 Protocol Document Roadmap and Implementation Experience, July 1994 (obsoleted by RFC 1773)

RFC	Title
1655	Application of the Border Gateway Protocol in the Internet, July 1994
1654	A Border Gateway Protocol 4 (BGP-4), July 1994 (obsoleted by RFC 1771)
1653	SMTP Service Extension for Message Size Declaration, July 1994 (obsoletes RFC 1427)
1652	SMTP Service Extension for 8bit-MIMEtransport, July 1994 (obsoletes RFC 1426)
1651	SMTP Service Extensions, July 1994 (obsoletes RFC 1425)
1650	Definitions of Managed Objects for the Ethernet-like Interface Types Using SMIv2, August 1994
1649	Operational Requirements for X.400 Management Domains in the GO-MHS Community, July 1994
1648	Postmaster Convention for X.400 Operations, July 1994
1647	TN3270 Enhancements, July 1994
1646	TN3270 Extensions for LUname and Printer Selection, 1994
1645	Simple Network Paging Protocol—V. 2, July 1994 (obsoletes RFC 1568)
1644	T/TCP—TCP Extensions for Transactions Functional Specification, July 1994
1643	Definitions of Managed Objects for the Ethernet-like Interface Types, July 1994 (obsoletes RFC 1623)
1642	UTF-7: A Mail-Safe Transformation Format of Unicode, July 1994
1641	Using Unicode with MIME, July 1994
1640	The Process for Organization of Internet Standards Working Group (POISED), June 1994
1639	FTP Operation over Big Address Records (FOOBAR), June 1994 (obsoletes RFC 1545)
1638	PPP Bridging Control Protocol (BCP), June 1994
1637	DNS NSAP Resource Records, June 1994 (obsoletes RFC 1348; obsoleted by RFC 1706)
1636	Report of IAB Workshop on Security in the Internet Architecture, 1994
1635	How to Use Anonymous FTP, 1994
1634	Novell IPX over Various WAN Media (IPXWAN), 1994 (obsoletes RFC 1551)
1633	Integrated Services in the Internet Architecture, 1994

RFC	Title
1632	A Revised Catalog of Available X.500 Implementations, May 1994 (obsoletes RFC 1292)
1631	Not yet issued
1630	Universal Resource Identifiers in WWW, June 1994
1629	Guidelines for OSI NSAP Allocation in the Internet, 1994 (obsoletes RFC 1237)
1628	UPS Management Information Base, May 1994
1627	Network 10 Considered Harmful (Some Practices Shouldn't Be Codified), July 1994
1626	Default IP MTU for Use over ATM AAL5, May 1994
1625	WAIS over Z39.50-1988, June 1994
1624	Computation of the Internet Checksum via Incremental Update, May 1994 (updates RFC 1141)
1623	Definitions of Managed Objects for the Ethernet-like Interface Types, May 1994 (obsoletes RFC 1398; obsoleted by RFC 1643)
1622	Pip Header Processing, 1994
1621	Pip Near-term Architecture, 1994
1620	Internet Architecture Extensions for Shared Media, 1994
1619	PPP over SONET/SDH, 1994
1618	PPP over ISDN, 1994
1617	Naming and Structuring Guidelines for X.500 Directory Pilots, May 1994 (obsoletes RFC 1384)
1616	RARE WG-MSG Task Force 88, X.400 (1988) for the Academic and Research Community in Europe, 1994
1615	Migrating from X.400(84) to X.400(88), 1994
1614	Network Access to Multimedia Information, 1994
1613	Cisco Systems X.25 over TCP (XOT), 1994
1612	DNS Resolver MIB Extensions, 1994
1611	DNS Server MIB Extensions, 1994
1610	Internet Architecture Board, Internet Official Protocol Standards, July 1994 (obsoletes RFC 1600; obsoleted by RFC 1780)
1609	Charting Networks in the X.500 Directory, 1994

RFC	Title
1608	Representing IP Information in the X.500 Directory, 1994
1607	A View from the 21st Century, 1994
1606	A Historical Perspective on the Usage of IP V.9, 1994
1605	SONET to Sonnet Translation, 1994
1604	Definitions of Managed Objects for Frame Relay Service, 1994 (obsoletes RFC 1596)
1603	IETF Working Group Guidelines and Procedures, 1994
1602	Internet Architecture Board, Internet Engineering Steering Group, The Internet Standards Process — Revision 2, 1994 (obsoletes RFC 1310)
1601	Charter of the Internet Architecture Board (IAB), 1994
1600	Internet Official Protocol Standards, 1994 (obsoletes RFC 1540; obsoleted by RFC 1780)
1599	Not yet issued
1598	PPP in X.25, 1994
1597	Address Allocation for Private Internets, 1994
1596	Definitions of Managed Objects for Frame Relay Service, 1994 (obsoleted by RFC 1604)
1595	Definitions of Managed Objects for the SONET/SDH Interface Type, 1994
1594	FYI on Questions and Answers — Answers to Commonly Asked "New Internet User" Questions, 1994 (obsoletes RFC 1325)
1593	SNA APPN Node MIB, 1994
1592	Simple Network Management Protocol Distributed Protocol Interface Version 2.0, March 1994 (obsoletes RFC 1228)
1591	Domain Name System Structure and Delegation, 1994
1590	Media Type Registration Procedure, 1994 (updates RFC 1521)
1589	A Kernel Model for Precision Timekeeping, 1994
1588	White Pages Meeting Report, 1994
1587	The OSPF NSSA Option, 1994
1586	Guidelines for Running OSPF over Frame Relay Networks, 1994
1585	MOSPF: Analysis and Experience, 1994
1584	Multicast Extensions to OSPF, 1994

RFC	Title
1583	OSPF Version 2, March 1994 (obsoletes RFC 1247)
1582	Extensions to RIP to Support Demand Circuits, 1994
1581	Protocol Analysis for Extensions to RIP to Support Demand Circuits, February 1994
1580	EARN Association, Guide to Network Resource Tools, 1994
1579	Firewall-Friendly FTP, 1994
1578	FYI on Questions and Answers: Answers to Commonly Asked "Primary and Secondary School Internet User" Questions, 1994
1577	Classical IP and ARP over ATM, 1994
1576	TN3270 Current Practices, 1994
1575	An Echo Function for CLNP (ISO 8473), 1994 (obsoletes RFC 1139)
1574	Essential Tools for the OSI Internet, 1994 (obsoletes RFC 1139)
1573	Evolution of the Interfaces Group of MIB-II, 1994 (obsoletes RFC 1229)
1572	TELNET Environment Option, 1994
1571	Telnet Environment Option Interoperability Issues, 1994 (updates RFC 1408)
1570	PPP LCP Extensions, 1994 (updates RFC 1548)
1569	Principles of Operation for the TPC.INT Subdomain: Radio Paging — Technical Procedures, 1994 (obsoleted by RFC 1703)
1568	Simple Network Paging Protocol — V, 1994 (obsoleted by RFC 1645)
1567	X.500 Directory Monitoring MIB, 1994
1566	Mail Monitoring MIB, 1994
1565	Network Services Monitoring MIB, 1994
1564	DSA Metrics [OSI-DS 34 (v3)], 1994
1563	The Text/Enriched MIME Content-type, 1994 (obsoletes RFC 1523)
1562	Naming Guidelines for the AARNet X.500 Directory Service, 1993
1561	Use of ISO CLNP in TUBA Environments, December 1993
1560	The MultiProtocol Internet, December 1993
1559	DECnet Phase IV MIB Extensions (obsoletes RFC 1289), December 1993
1558	A String Representation of LDAP Search Filters, December 1993
1557	Korean Character Encoding for Internet Messages, December 1993

RFC	Title
1556	Handling of Bi-directional Texts in MIME, December 1993
1555	Hebrew Character Encoding for Internet Messages, December 1993
1554	ISO-2022-JP-2: Multilingual Extensions of ISO-2022-JP, December 1993
1553	Compressing IPX Headers over WAN Media (CIPX), December 1993
1552	The PPP Internetwork Packet Exchange Control Protocol, December 1993
1551	Novell IPX over Various WAN Media (IPXWAN) (obsoletes RFC 1362), December 1993
1550	IP: Next Generation (IPng) White Paper Solicitation, December 1993
1549	PPP in HDLC Framing, December 1993
1548	The Point-to-Point Protocol (PPP) (obsoletes RFC 1331), December 1993
1547	Requirements for an Internet Standard Point-to-Point Protocol, December 1993
1546	Host Anycasting Service, November 1993
1545	FTP Operation over Big Address Records (FOOBAR), November 1993
1544	The Content—MD5 Header Field, November 1993
1543	Instructions to RFC Authors 1993 (obsoletes RFC 1111), October 1993
1542	Clarifications and Extensions for the Bootstrap Protocol (obsoletes RFC 1532), October 1993
1541	Dynamic Host Configuration Protocol (obsoletes RFC 1531), October 1993
1540	Internet Official Protocol Standards (obsoletes RFC 1500), October 1993
1539	The Tao of IETF—A Guide for New Attendees of the Internet Engineering Task Force (obsoletes RFC 1391), October 1993
1538	Advanced SNA/IP: A Simple SNA Transport Protocol, October 1993
1537	Common DNS Data File Configuration Errors, October 1993
1536	Common DNS Implementation Errors and Suggested Fixes, October 1993
1535	A Security Problem and Proposed Correction with Widely Deployed DNS Software, October 1993
1534	Interoperation between DHCP and BOOTP, October 1993
1533	DHCP Options and BootP Vendor Extensions (obsoletes RFC 1497), October 1993
1532	Clarifications and Extensions for the Bootstrap Protocol (obsoleted by RFC 1542), October 1993
1531	Dynamic Host Configuration Protocol (obsoleted by RFC 1541), October 1993

RFC	Title
1530	Principles of Operation for the TPC.INT Subdomain: General Principles and Policy, October 1993
1529	Principles of Operation for the TPC.INT Subdomain: Remote Printing — Administrative Policies (obsoletes RFC 1486), October 1993
1528	Principles of Operation for the TPC.INT Subdomain: Remote Printing — Technical Procedures (obsoletes RFC 1486), October 1993
1527	What Should We Plan Given the Dilemma of the Network? September 1993
1526	Assignment of System Identifiers for TUBA/CLNP Hosts, September 1993
1525	Definitions of Managed Objects for Source Routing Bridges (obsoletes RFC 1286), September 1993
1524	A User Agent Configuration Mechanism for Multimedia Mail Format Information, September 1993
1523	The Text/Enriched MIME Content-type, September 1993
1522	MIME (Multipurpose Internet Mail Extensions) Part Two: Message Header Extensions for Non-ASCII Text (obsoletes RFC 1342), September 1993
1521	MIME (Multipurpose Internet Mail Extensions) Part One: Mechanisms for Specifying and Describing the Format of Internet Message Bodies (obsoletes RFC 1341), September 1993
1520	Exchanging Routing Information across Provider Boundaries in the CIDR Environment, September 1993
1519	Classless Inter-Domain Routing (CIDR): An Address Assignment and Aggregation Strategy (obsoletes RFC 1338), September 1993
1518	An Architecture for IP Address Allocation with CIDR, September 1993
1517	Applicability Statement for the Implementation of Classless Inter-Domain Routing (CIDR), September 1993
1516	Definitions of Managed Objects for IEEE 802.3 Repeater Devices (obsoletes RFC 1368), September 1993
1515	Definitions of Managed Objects for IEEE 802.3 Medium Attachment Units (MAUs), September 1993
1514	Host Resources MIB, September 1993
1513	Token Ring Extensions to the Remote Network Monitoring MIB (obsoletes RFC 1271), September 1993

RFC	Title
1512	FDDI Management Information Base (updates RFC 1285), September 1993
1511	Common Authentication Technology Overview, September 1993
1510	The Kerberos Network Authentication Service (V5), September 1993
1509	Generic Security Service API: C-bindings, September 1993
1508	Generic Security Service Application Program Interface, September 1993
1507	DASS Distributed Authentication Security Service, September 1993
1506	A Tutorial on Gatewaying between X.400 and Internet Mail, August 1993
1505	Encoding Header Field for Internet Messages (obsoletes RFC 1154), August 1993
1504	Appletalk Update-Based Routing Protocol: Enhanced Appletalk Routing, August 1993
1503	Algorithms for Automating Administration in SNMPv2 Managers, August 1993
1502	X.400 Use of Extended Character Sets, August 1993
1501	OS/2 User Group, August 1993
1500	Internet Official Protocol Standards (obsoletes RFC 1410; obsoleted by RFC 1540), August 1993
1499	Net yet issued
1498	On the Naming and Binding of Network Destinations, August 1993
1497	BOOTP Vendor Information Extensions (obsoletes RFC 1395; obsoleted by RFC 1533; updates RFC 951), August 1993
1496	Rules for Downgrading Messages from X.400/88 to X.400/84 When MIME Content-Types Are Present in the Messages (updates RFC 1328), August 1993
1495	Mapping between X.400 and RFC-822 Message Bodies (obsoletes RFC 1327), August 1993
1494	Equivalences between 1988 X.400 and RFC-822 Message Bodies, August 1993
1493	Definitions of Managed Objects for Bridges (obsoletes RFC 1286), July 1993
1492	An Access Control Protocol, Sometimes Called TACACS, July 1993
1491	A Survey of Advanced Usages of X.500, July 1993
1490	Multiprotocol Interconnect over Frame Relay (obsoletes RFC 1294), 1993
1489	Registration of a Cyrillic Character Set, July 1993
1488	The X.500 String Representation of Standard Attribute Syntaxes, July 1993
1487	X.500 Lightweight Directory Access Protocol, July 1993

RFC	Title
1486	An Experiment in Remote Printing (obsoleted by RFC 1528, RFC 1529), 1993
1485	A String Representation of Distinguished Names [OSI-DS 23 (v5)], July 1993
1484	Using the OSI Directory to Achieve User Friendly Naming [OSI-DS 24 (V1.2)], July 1993
1483	Multiprotocol Encapsulation over ATM Adaptation Layer 5, July 1993
1482	Aggregation Support in the NSFNET Policy-Based Routing Database, June 1993
1481	IAB Recommendation for an Intermediate Strategy to Address the Issue of Scaling, July 1993
1480	The US Domain (obsoletes RFC 1386), June 1993
1479	Inter-Domain Policy Routing Protocol Specification: Version 1, July 1993
1478	An Architecture for Inter-Domain Policy Routing, June 1993
1477	IDPR as a Proposed Standard, July 1993
1476	RAP: Internet Route Access Protocol, June 1993
1475	TP/IX: The Next Internet, June 1993
1474	The Definitions of Managed Objects for the Bridge Network Control Protocol of the Point-to-Point Protocol, June 1993
1473	The Definitions of Managed Objects for the IP Network Control Protocol of the Point-to-Point Protocol, 1993
1472	The Definitions of Managed Objects for the Security Protocols of the Point-to-Point Protocol, June 1993
1471	The Definitions of Managed Objects for the Link Control Protocol of the Point-to-Point Protocol, June 1993
1470	FYI on a Network Management Tool Catalog: Tools for Monitoring and Debugging PCT/IP Internets and Interconnected Devices (obsoletes RFC 1147), June 1993
1469	IP Multicast over Token-Ring Local Area Networks, 1993
1468	Japanese Character Encoding for Internet Messages, June 1993
1467	Status of CIDR Deployment in the Internet (obsoletes RFC 1367), August 1993
1466	Guidelines for Management of IP Address Space (obsoletes RFC 1366), May 1993
1465	Routing Coordination for X.400 MHS Service within a Multi Protocol/Multi Network Environment Table Format V3 for Static Routing, 1993
1464	Using the Domain Name System to Store Arbitrary String Attributes, 1993

RFC	Title
1463	FYI on Introducing the Internet—A Short Bibliography of Introductory Internetworking Readings or the Network Novice, 1993
1462	FYI on "What Is the Internet?" (also FYI 20), 1993
1461	SNMP MIB extension for Multiprotocol Interconnect over X.25, 1993
1460	Post Office Protocol—Version 3 (obsoletes RFC 1225), May 1993
1459	Internet Relay Chat Protocol, May 1993
1458	Requirements for Multicast Protocols, May 1993
1457	Security Label Framework for the Internet, May 1993
1456	Conventions for Encoding the Vietnamese Language VISCII: Vietnamese Standard Code for Information Interchange VIQR: Vietnamese Quoted-Readable Specification Revision 1.1, 1993
1455	Physical Link Security Type of Service, May 1993
1454	Comparison of Proposals for Next Version of IP, May 1993
1453	A Comment on Packet Video Remote Conferencing and the Transport/Network Layers, April 1993
1452	Coexistence between V.1 and V.2 of the Internet-standard Network Management Framework, 1993
1451	Manager-to-Manager Management Information Base, April 1993
1450	Management Information Base for Version 2 of the Simple Network Management Protocol (SNMPv2), April 1993
1449	Transport Mappings for Version 2 of the Simple Network Management Protocol (SNMPv2), April 1993
1448	Protocol Operations for Version 2 of the Simple Network Management Protocol (SNMPv2), April 1993
1447	Party MIB for Version 2 of the Simple Network Management Protocol (SNMPv2), April 1993
1446	Security Protocols for Version 2 of the Simple Network Management Protocol (SNMPv2), April 1993
1445	Administrative Model for Version 2 of the Simple Network Management Protocol (SNMPv2), 1993
1444	Conformance Statements for Version 2 of the Simple Network Management Protocol (SNMPv2), 1993

RFC Title

1443 Textual Conventions for Version 2 of the Simple Network Management Protocol (SNMPv2), April 1993

1442 Structure of Management Information for Version 2 of the Simple Network Management Protocol (SNMPv2), April 1993

1441 Introduction to Version 2 of the Internet-Standard Network Management Framework, April 1993

1440 SIFT/UFT: Sender-Initiated/Unsolicited File Transfer, July 1993

1439 The Uniqueness of Unique Identifiers, 1993

1438 Internet Engineering Task Force Statements of Boredom (SOBs), 1993

1437 The Extension of MIME Content-Types to a New Medium, 1993

1436 The Internet Gopher Protocol (a Distributed Document Search and Retrieval Protocol), March 1993

1435 IESG Advice from Experience with Path MTU Discovery, 1993

1434 Data Link Switching: Switch-to-Switch Protocol, 1993

1433 Directed ARP, 1993

1432 Recent Internet Books, March 1993

1431 DUA Metrics, February 1993

1430 A Strategic Plan for Deploying an Internet X.500 Directory Service, February 1993

1429 Listserv Distribute Protocol, February 1993

1428 Transition of InternetMail from Just-Send-8 to 8bit-SMTP/MIME, February 1993

1427 SMTP Service Extension for Message Size Declaration, February 1993

1426 SMTP Service Extension for 8bit-MIMEtransport, February 1993

1425 SMTP Service Extensions, February 1993

1424 Privacy Enhancement for Internet Electronic Mail: Part IV: Key Certification and Related Service, 1993

1423 Privacy Enhancement for Internet Electronic Mail: Part III: Algorithms, Modes, and Identifiers (obsoletes RFC 1115), 1993

1422 Privacy Enhancement for Internet Electronic Mail: Part II: Certificate-Based Key Management (obsoletes RFC 1114), 1993

1421 Privacy Enhancement for Internet Electronic Mail: Part I: Message Encryption and Authentication Procedures (obsoletes RFC 1113), 1993

RFC	Title
1420	SNMP over IPX (obsoletes RFC 1298), 1993
1419	SNMP over AppleTalk, 1993
1418	SNMP over OSI (obsoletes RFC 1161), March 1993
1417	The North American Directory Forum NADF Standing Documents: A Brief Overview (obsoletes RFC 1295, RFC 1255, RFC 1218), February 1993
1416	Telnet Authentication Option (obsoletes RFC 1409), February 1993
1415	FTP-FTAM Gateway Specification, January 1993
1414	Identification MIB, February 1993
1413	Identification Protocol (obsoletes RFC 931), 1993
1412	Telnet Authentication: SPX, 1993
1411	Telnet Authentication: Kerberos Version 4, 1993
1410	IAB Official Protocol Standards (obsoletes RFC 1360, RFC 1280, RFC 1250, RFC 1200, RFC 1100, RFC 1083, RFC 1130, RFC 1140; obsoleted by RFC 1500), 1993
1409	Telnet Authentication Option (obsoleted by RFC 1416), January 1993
1408	Telnet Environment Option, 1993
1407	Definitions of Managed Objects for the DS3/E3 Interface Type (obsoletes RFC 1233), January 1993
1406	Definitions of Managed Objects for the DS1 and E1 Interface Types (obsoletes RFC 1232), 1993
1405	Mapping between X.400 (1984/1988) and Mail-11 (DECnet mail), January 1993
1404	Model for Common Operational Statistics, January 1993
1403	BGP OSPF Interaction (obsoletes RFC 1364), 1993
1402	There's Gold in Them Thar Networks! or Searching for Treasure in All the Wrong Places (also FYI 10) (obsoletes RFC 1290), 1993
1401	Correspondence between the IAB and DISA on the Use of DNS throughout the Internet, 1993
1400	Transition and Modernization of the Internet Registration Service, March 1993
1399	Not yet issued
1398	Definitions of Managed Objects for the Ethernet-like Interface Types (obsoletes RFC 1284), 1993
1397	Default Route Advertisement in BGP2 and BGP3 Versions of the Border Gateway Protocol, 1993

RFC	Title
1396	The Process for Organization of Internet Standards — Working Group (POISED), 1993
1395	BOOTP Vendor Information Extensions (obsoletes RFC 1084, RFC 1048: obsoleted by RFC 1497; updates RFC 951), January 1993
1394	Relationship of Telex Answerback Codes to Internet Domains, January 1993
1393	Traceroute Using an IP Option, January 1993
1392	Internet Users' Glossary (also FYI 18), January 1993
1391	The Tao of IETF — A Guide for New Attendees of the Internet Engineering Task Force (obsoleted by RFC 1539) (also FYI 17), 1993
1390	Transmission of IP and ARP over FDDI Networks, January 1993
1389	RIP Version 2 MIB Extension, 1993
1388	RIP Version 2 — Carrying Additional Information (updates RFC 1058), January 1993
1387	RIP Version 2 Protocol Analysis, January 1993
1386	The US Domain (obsoleted by RFC 1480), December 1992
1385	EIP: The Extended Internet Protocol, A Framework for Maintaining Backward Compatibility, November 1992
1384	Naming Guidelines for Directory Pilots, January 1993
1383	An Experiment in DNS Based IP Routing, December 1992
1382	SNMP MIB Extension for the X.25 Packet Layer, November 1992
1381	SNMP MIB Extension for X.25 LAPB, November 1992
1380	IESG Deliberations on Routing and Addressing, November 1992
1379	Extending TCP for Transactions — Concepts, November 1992
1378	The PPP AppleTalk Control Protocol (ATCP), November 1992
1377	The PPP OSI Network Layer Control Protocol (OSINLCP), November 1992
1376	The PPP DECnet Phase IV Control Protocol (DNC), November 1992
1375	Suggestion for New Classes of IP Addresses, November 1992
1374	IP and ARP on HIPPI, October 1992
1373	PORTABLE DUAs, October 1992
1372	Telnet Remote Flow Control Option (obsoletes RFC 1080), October 1992
1371	Choosing a "Common IGP" for the IP Internet (the IESG's Recommendation to the IAB), October 1992

RFC	Title
1370	Applicability Statement for OSPF, October 1992
1369	Implementation Notes and Experience for the Internet Ethernet MIB, October 1992
1368	Definitions of Managed Objects for IEEE 802.3 Repeater Devices (obsoleted by RFC 1516), October 1992
1367	Schedule for IP Address Space Management Guidelines (obsoleted by RFC 1467), October 1992
1366	Guidelines for Management of IP Address Space (obsoleted by RFC 1466), October 1992
1365	An I Address Extension Proposal, September 1992
1364	BGP OSPF Interaction (obsoleted by RFC 1403), September 1992
1363	A Proposed Flow Specification, September 1992
1362	Novell IPX over Various WAN Media (IPXWAN) (obsoleted by RFC 1551), September 1992
1361	Simple Network Time Protocol (SNTP), August 1992
1360	IAB Official Protocol Standards (obsoletes RFCs 1280, 1250, 1100, 1083, 1130, 1140, 1200; obsoleted by RFC 1410), September 1992
1359	Connecting to the Internet: What Connecting Institutions Should Anticipate (also FYI 16), August 1992
1358	Charter of the Internet Architecture Board (IAB), August 1992
1357	A Format for E-mailing Bibliographic Records, July 1992
1356	Multiprotocol Interconnect on X.25 and ISDN in the Packet Mode (obsoletes RFC 877), August 1992
1355	Privacy and Accuracy Issues in Network Information Center Databases, August 1992
1354	IP Forwarding Table MIB, July 1992
1353	Definitions of Managed Objects for Administration of SNMP Parties, July 1992
1352	SNMP Security Protocols, July 1992
1351	SNMP Administrative Model, July 1992
1350	The TFTP Protocol (Revision 2) (obsoletes RFC 783), July 1992
1349	Type of Service in the Internet Protocol Suite (updates RFCs 1248, 1247, 1195, 1123, 1122, 1060, 791), July 1992

RFC	Title
1348	DNS NSAP RRs (updates RFCs 1034, 1035), July 1992
1347	TCP and UDP with Bigger Addresses (TUBA), A Simple Proposal for Internet Addressing and Routing, June 1992
1346	Resource Allocation, Control, and Accounting for the Use of Network Resources, June 1992
1345	Character Mnemonics & Character Sets, June 1992
1344	Implications of MIME for Internet Mail Gateways, June 1992
1343	A User Agent Configuration Mechanism for Multimedia Mail Format Information, June 1992
1342	Representation of Non-ASCII Text in Internet Message Headers (obsoleted by RFC 1522), June 1992
1341	MIME (Multipurpose Internet Mail Extensions) Mechanisms for Specifying and Describing the Format of Internet Message Bodies (obsoleted by RFC 1521), June 1992
1340	Assigned Numbers (obsoletes RFCs 1060, 1010, 990, 960, 943, 923, 900, 870, 820, 790, 776, 770, 762, 758, 755, 750, 739, 604, 503, 433, 349—IENs 127), July 1992
1339	Remote Mail Checking Protocol, June 1992
1338	Supernetting: An Address Assignment and Aggregation Strategy (obsoleted by RFC 1519), June 1992
1337	TIME-WAIT Assassination Hazards in TCP, May 1992
1336	Who's Who in the Internet—Biographies of IAB, IESG and IRSG Members (obsoletes RFC 1251, FYI 9), May 1992
1335	A Two-Tier Address Structure for the Internet: A Solution to the Problem of Address Space Exhaustion, May 1992
1334	PPP Authentication Protocols, October 1992
1333	PPP Link Quality Monitoring, May 1992
1332	The PPP Internet Protocol Control Protocol (IPCP) (obsoletes RFC 1172), May 1992
1331	The Point-to-Point Protocol (PPP) for the Transmission of Multi-protocol Datagrams over Point-to-Point Links (obsoletes RFC 1171, RFC 1172; obsoleted by RFC 1548), May 1992
1330	Recommendations for the Phase I Development of OSI Directory Services (X.500) and OSI Message Handling Services (X.400) within the ESnet Community, May 1992

RFC	Title
1329	Thoughts on Address Resolution for Dual MAC FDDI Networks, May 1992
1328	X.400 1988 to 1984 Downgrading (updated by RFC 1496), May 1992
1327	Mapping between X.400 (1988)/ISO 10021 and RFC 822 (obsoletes RFC 987, RFC 1026, RFC 1138, RFC 1148; obsoleted by RFC 1495; updates RFC 822), May 1992
1326	Mutual Encapsulation Considered Dangerous, May 1992
1325	FYI on Questions and Answers—Answers to Commonly Asked "New Internet User" Questions (obsoletes RFC 1206, FYI 4), May 1992
1324	A Discussion on Computer Network Conferencing, May 1992
1323	TCP Extensions for High Performance (obsoletes RFC 1072, RFC 1185), May 1992
1322	A Unified Approach to Inter-Domain Routing, May 1992
1321	The MD5 Message-Digest Algorithm, April 1992
1320	The MD4 Message-Digest Algorithm (obsoletes RFC 1186), April 1992
1319	The MD2 Message-Digest Algorithm, April 1992
1318	Definitions of Managed Objects for Parallel-printer-like Hardware Devices, April 1992
1317	Definitions of Managed Objects for RS-232-like Hardware Devices, April 1992
1316	Definitions of Managed Objects for Character Stream Devices, April 1992
1315	Management Information Base for Frame Relay DTEs, April 1992
1314	A File Format for the Exchange of Images in the Internet, April 1992
1313	Today's Programming for KRFC AM 1313 Internet Talk Radio, April 1992
1312	Message Send Protocol 2 (obsoletes RFC 1159), April 1992
1311	Introduction to the STD Notes, March 1992
1310	The Internet Standards Process, March 1992
1309	Technical Overview of Directory Services Using the X.500 Protocol (also FYI 14), March 1992
1308	Executive Introduction to Directory Services Using the X.500 Protocol (also FYI 13), March 1992
1307	Dynamically Switched Link Control Protocol, March 1992
1306	Experiences Supporting By-Request Circuit-Switched T3 Networks, March 1992
1305	Network Time Protocol (Version 3) Specification, Implementation and Analysis (obsoletes RFC 1119, RFC 1059, RFC 958), March 1992

RFC	Title
1304	Definitions of Managed Objects for the SIP Interface Type, February 1992
1303	A Convention for Describing SNMP-based Agents, February 1992
1302	Building a Network Information Services Infrastructure (also FYI 12), February 1992
1301	Multicast Transport Protocol, February 1992
1300	Remembrances of Things Past, February 1992
1299	Not yet issued
1298	SNMP over IPX (obsoleted by RFC 1420), February 1992
1297	NOC Internal Integrated Trouble Ticket System Functional Specification Wishlist ("NOC TT REQUIREMENTS"), January 1992
1296	Internet Growth (1981–1991), January 1992
1295	User Bill of Rights for Entries and Listings in the Public Directory (obsoleted by RFC 1417), January 1992
1294	Multiprotocol Interconnect over Frame Relay (obsoleted by RFC 1490), January 1992
1293	Inverse Address Resolution Protocol, January 1992
1292	A Catalog of Available X.500 Implementations (also FYI 11), January 1992
1291	Mid-Level networks — Potential Technical Services, December 1991
1290	There's Gold in Them Thar Networks! or Searching for Treasure in All the Wrong Places (obsoleted by RFC 1402) (also FYI 10), December 1991
1289	DECnet Phase IV MIB Extensions (obsoleted by RFC 1559), December 1991
1288	The Finger User Information Protocol (obsoletes RFC 1196, RFC 1194, RFC 742), December 1991
1287	Towards the Future Internet Architecture, December 1991
1286	Definitions of Managed Objects for Bridges (obsoleted by RFC 1493, RFC 1525), December 1991
1285	FDDI Management Information Base (updated by RFC 1512), January 1992
1284	Definitions of Managed Objects for the Ethernet-like Interface Types (obsoleted by RFC 1398), December 1991
1283	SNMP over OSI (obsoletes RFC 1161; Obsoleted by RFC 1418), December 1991
1282	BSD Rlogin (obsoletes RFC 1258), December 1991
1281	Guidelines for the Secure Operation of the Internet, November 1991

RFC	Title
1280	IAB Official Protocol Standards (obsoletes RFCs 1250, 1100, 1083, 1130, 1140, 1200; obsoleted by RFC 1360), March 1992
1279	X.500 and Domains, November 1991
1278	A String Encoding of Presentation Address, November 1991
1277	Encoding Network Addresses to Support Operation over Non-OSI Lower Layers, November 1991
1276	Replication and Distributed Operations Extensions to Provide an Internet Directory Using X.500, November 1991
1275	Replication Requirements to Provide an Internet Directory Using X.500, November 1991
1274	The COSINE and Internet X.500 Schema, November 1991
1273	A Measurement Study of Changes in Service-level Reachability in the Global TCP/IP Internet, November 1991
1272	Internet Accounting: Background, November 1991
1271	Remote Network Monitoring Management Information Base (obsoleted by RFC 1513), November 1991
1270	SNMP Communications Services, October 1991
1269	Definitions of Managed Objects for the Border Gateway Protocol (Version 3), October 1991
1268	Application of the Border Gateway Protocol in the Internet (obsoletes RFC 1164), October 1991
1267	A Border Gateway Protocol 3 (BGP-3) (obsoletes RFC 1105, RFC 1163), October 1991
1266	Experience with the BGP Protocol, October 1991
1265	BGP Protocol Analysis, October 1991
1264	Internet Routing Protocol Standardization Criteria, October 1991
1263	TCP Extensions Considered Harmful, October 1991
1262	Guidelines for Internet Measurement Activities, October 1991
1261	Transition of NIC Services, September 1991
1260	Not yet issued
1259	Building the Open Road: The NREN as Test-bed for the National Public Network, September 1991

RFC	Title
1258	BSD Rlogin (obsoleted by RFC 1282), September 1991
1257	Isochronous Applications Do Not Require Jitter-controlled Networks, September 1991
1256	ICMP Router Discovery Messages, September 1991
1255	Naming Scheme for c = US (obsoletes RFC 1218; obsoleted by RFC 1417), September 1991
1254	Gateway Congestion Control Survey, August 1991
1253	OSPF Version 2: Management Information Base (obsoletes RFC 1252), August 1991
1252	OSPF Version 2: Management Information Base (obsoletes RFC 1248; obsoleted by RFC 1253), August 1991
1251	Who's Who in the Internet: Biographies of IAB, IESG and IRSG Members (obsoleted by RFC 1336) (also FYI 9), August 1991
1250	IAB Official Protocol Standards (obsoletes RFC 1200; obsoleted by RFC 1360), August 1991
1249	DIXIE Protocol Specification, August 1991
1248	OSPF Version 2: Management Information Base (obsoleted by RFC 1252; updated by RFC 1349), July 1991
1247	OSPF Version 2 (obsoletes RFC 1131; updated by RFC 1349), July 1991
1246	Experience with the OSPF Protocol, July 1991
1245	OSPF Protocol Analysis, July 1991
1244	Site Security Handbook (also FYI 8), July 1991
1243	Appletalk Management Information Base, July 1991
1242	Benchmarking Terminology for Network Interconnection Devices, July 1991
1241	Scheme for an Internet Encapsulation Protocol: Version 1, July 1991
1240	OSI Connectionless Transport Services on Top of UDP: Version 1, June 1991
1239	Reassignment of Experimental MIBs to Standard MIBs (updates RFC 1229, RFC 1230, RFC 1231, RFC 1232, RFC 1233), June 1991
1238	CLNS MIB for Use with Connectionless Network Protocol (ISO 8473) and End System to Intermediate System (ISO 9542) (obsoletes RFC 1162), June 1991
1237	Guideline for OSI NSAP Allocation in the Internet, July 1991
1236	IP to X.121 Address Mapping for DDN IP to X 121 Address Mapping for DDN, June 1991

RFC	Title
1235	Coherent File Distribution Protocol, June 1991
1234	Tunneling IPX Traffic through IP Networks, June 1991
1233	Definitions of Managed Objects for the DS3 Interface Type (obsoleted by RFC 1407; updated by RFC 1239), May 1991
1232	Definitions of Managed Objects for the DS1 Interface Type (obsoleted by RFC 1406; updated by RFC 1239), May 1991
1231	IEEE 802.5 Token Ring MIB (updated by RFC 1239), May 1991
1230	IEEE 802.4 Token Bus MIB (updated by RFC 1239), May 1991
1229	Extensions to the Generic-Interface MIB (updated by RFC 1239), May 1991
1228	SNMP-DPI: Simple Network Management Protocol Distributed Program Interface, May 1991
1227	SNMP MUX Protocol and MIB, May 1991
1226	Internet Protocol Encapsulation of AX.25 Frames Internet Protocol Encapsulation of AX 25 Frames, May 1991
1225	Post Office Protocol: Version 3 (obsoletes RFC 1081; obsoleted by RFC 1460), May 1991
1224	Techniques for Managing Asynchronously Generated Alerts, May 1991
1223	OSI CLNS and LLC1 Protocols on Network Systems HYPERchannel, May 1991
1222	Advancing the NSFNET Routing Architecture, May 1991
1221	Host Access Protocol (HAP) Specification: Version 2 (updates RFC 907), April 1991
1220	Point-to-Point Protocol Extensions for Bridging, April 1991
1219	On the Assignment of Subnet Numbers, April 1991
1218	Naming Scheme for c = US (obsoleted by RFC 1417), April 1991
1217	Memo from the Consortium for Slow Commotion Research (CSCR), April 1991
1216	Gigabit Network Economics and Paradigm Shifts, April 1991
1215	Convention for Defining Traps for Use with the SNMP, March 1991
1214	OSI Internet Management: Management Information Base, April 1991
1213	Management Information Base for Network Management of TCP/IP-based Internets: MIB-II (obsoletes RFC 1158), March 1991
1212	Concise MIB Definitions, March 1991

RFC	Title
1211	Problems with the Maintenance of Large Mailing Lists, March 1991
1210	Network and Infrastructure User Requirements for Transatlantic Research Collaboration: Brussels, July 16–18, and Washington, July 24–25, 1990, March 1991
1209	Transmission of IP Datagrams over the SMDS Service, March 1991
1208	Glossary of Networking Terms, March 1991
1207	FYI on Questions and Answers: Answers to Commonly Asked "Experienced Internet User" Questions, February 1991
1206	FYI on Questions and Answers: Answers to Commonly Asked "New Internet User" Questions (obsoletes RFC 1177; obsoleted by RFC 1325), February 1991
1205	5250 Telnet Interface, February 1991
1204	Message Posting Protocol (MPP), February 1991
1203	Interactive Mail Access Protocol: Version 3 (obsoletes RFC 1064), February 1991
1202	Directory Assistance Service, February 1991
1201	Transmitting IP Traffic over ARCNET Networks (obsoletes RFC 1051), February 1991
1200	Defense Advanced Research Projects Agency, Internet Activities Board; DARPA IAB Official Protocol Standards (obsoletes RFC 1104; obsoleted by RFC 1360), April 1991
1199	RFC Numbers 1100–1199, December 1991
1198	FYI on the X Window System (Also FYI 6), January 1991
1197	Using ODA for Translating Multimedia Information, December 1990
1196	Finger User Information Protocol (obsoletes RFC 1194; obsoleted by RFC 1288), December 1990
1195	Use of OSI IS-IS for Routing in TCP/IP and Dual Environments (updated by RFC 1349), December 1990
1194	Finger User Information Protocol (obsoletes RFC 742; obsoleted by RFC 1288), November 1990
1193	Client Requirements for Real-time Communication Services, November 1990
1192	Commercialization of the Internet Summary Report, November 1990
1191	Path MTU Discovery (obsoletes RFC 1063), November 1990
1190	Experimental Internet Stream Protocol: Version 2 (ST-11) (obsoletes IEN 119), October 1990

RFC	Title
1189	Common Management Information Services and Protocols for the Internet (CMOT and CMIP) (obsoletes RFC 1095), October 1990
1188	Proposed Standard for the Transmission of IP Datagrams over FDDI Networks (obsoletes RFC 1103), October 1990
1187	Bulk Table Retrieval with the SNMP, October 1990
1186	MD4 Message Digest Algorithm (obsoleted by RFC 1320), October 1990
1185	TCP Extension for High-speed Paths (obsoleted by RFC 1323), October 1990
1184	Telnet Linemode Option (obsoletes RFC 1116), October 1990
1183	New DNS RR definitions (updates RFC 1034, RFC 1035), October 1990
1182	Not yet issued
1181	RIPE Terms of Reference, September 1990
1180	TCP/IP Tutorial, January 1991
1179	Line Printer Daemon Protocol, August 1990
1178	Choosing a Name for Your Computer (also FYI 5), August 1990
1177	FYI on Questions and Answers: Answers to Commonly Asked "New Internet User" Questions (obsoleted by RFC 1206), August 1990
1176	Interactive Mail Access Protocol: Version 2 (obsoletes RFC 1064), August 1990
1175	FYI on Where to Start: A Bibliography of Internetworking Information (also FYI 3), August 1990
1174	IAB Recommended Policy on Distributing Internet Identifier Assignment and IAB Recommended Policy Change to Internet "Connected" Status, August 1990
1173	Responsibilities of Host and Network Managers: A Summary of the "Oral Tradition" of the Internet, August 1990
1172	Point-to-Point Protocol (PPP) Initial Configuration Options (obsoleted by RFC 1332), July 1990
1171	Point-to-Point Protocol for the Transmission of Multi-protocol Datagrams over Point-to-Point Links (obsoletes RFC 1134; obsoleted by RFC 1331), July 1990
1170	Public Key Standards and Licenses, January 1991
1169	Explaining the Role of GOSIP, August 1990
1168	Intermail and Commercial Mail Relay Services, July 1990
1167	Thoughts on the National Research and Education Network, July 1990

RFC	Title
1166	Internet Numbers (obsoletes RFC 1117, RFC 1062, RFC 1020), July 1990
1165	Network Time Protocol (NTP) over the OSI Remote Operations Service, June 1990
1164	Application of the Border Gateway Protocol in the Internet (obsoleted by RFC 1268), June 1990
1163	Border Gateway Protocol (BGP) (obsoletes RFC 1105; obsoleted by RFC 1267), June 1990
1162	Connectionless Network Protocol (ISO 8473) and End System to Intermediate System (ISO 9542) Management Information Base (obsoleted by RFC 1238), June 1990
1161	SNMP over OSI (obsoleted by RFC 1283), June 1990
1160	Internet Activities Board (obsoletes RFC 1120), May 1990
1159	Message Send Protocol (obsoleted by RFC 1312), June 1990
1158	Management Information Base for Network Management of TCP/IP-based Internets: MIB-II (obsoleted by RFC 1213), May 1990
1157	Simple Network Management Protocol (SNMP) (obsoletes RFC 1098), May 1990
1156	Management Information Base for Network Management of TCP/IP-based Internets (obsoletes RFC 1066), May 1990
1155	Structure and Identification of Management Information for TCP/IP-based Internets (obsoletes RFC 1065), May 1990
1154	Encoding Header Field for Internet Messages (obsoleted by RFC 1505), April 1990
1153	Digest Message Format, April 1990
1152	Workshop Report: Internet Research Steering Group Workshop on Very-high-speed Networks, April 1990
1151	Version 2 of the Reliable Data Protocol (RDP) (updates RFC 908), April 1990
1150	FYI on FYI: Introduction to the FYI Notes (also FYI 1), March 1990
1149	Standard for the Transmission of IP Datagrams on Avian Carriers, April 1990
1148	Mapping between X.400 (1988)/ISO 10021 and RFC 822 (obsoleted by RFC 1327; updates RFC 822, RFC 987, RFC 1026, RFC 1138), March 1990
1147	FYI on a Network Management Tool Catalog: Tools for Monitoring and Debugging TCP/IP Internets and Inter Connected Devices (also FYI 2) (obsoleted by RFC 1470), April 1990

RFC	Title
1146	TCP Alternate Checksum Options (obsoletes RFC 1145), March 1990
1145	TCP Alternate Checksum Options (obsoleted by RFC 1146), February 1990
1144	Compressing TCP/IP Headers for Low-speed Serial Links, February 1990
1143	Q Method of Implementing Telnet Option Negotiation, February 1990
1142	OSI IS-IS Intra-domain Routing Protocol, February 1990
1141	Incremental Updating of the Internet Checksum (updates RFC 1071), January 1990
1140	DARPA IAB Official Protocol Standards (obsoletes RFC 1130; obsoleted by RFC 1360), May 1990
1139	Echo Function for ISO 8473, January 1990
1138	Mapping between X.400 (1988)/ISO 10021 and RFC 822 (obsoleted by RFC 1327; updates RFC 822, RFC 987, RFC 1026; updated by RFC 1148), December 1989
1137	Mapping between Full RFC 822 and RFC 822 with Restricted Encoding (updates RFC 976), December 1989
1136	Administrative Domains and Routing Domains: A Model for Routing in the Internet, December 1989
1135	Helminthiasis of the Internet, December 1989
1134	Point-to-Point Protocol: A Proposal for Multi-protocol Transmission of Data Grams over Point-to-Point Links (obsoleted by RFC 1171), November 1989
1133	Routing between the NSFNET and the DDN, November 1989
1132	Standard for the Transmission of 802.2 Packets over IPX Networks, November 1989
1131	OSPF Specification (obsoleted by RFC 1247), October 1989
1130	Defense Advanced Research Projects Agency, Internet Activities Board: DARPA IAB IAB Official Protocol Standards (obsoletes RFC 1100; obsoleted by RFC 1360), October 1989
1129	Internet Time Synchronization: The Network Time Protocol, October 1989
1128	Measured Performance of the Network Time Protocol in the Internet System, October 1989
1127	Perspective on the Host Requirements RFCs, October 1989
1126	Goals and Functional Requirements for Inter-autonomous System Routing, October 1989

RFC	Title
1125	Policy Requirements for Inter Administrative Domain Routing, November 1989
1124	Policy Issues in Interconnecting Networks, September 1989
1123	Requirements for Internet Hosts—Application and Support (updated by RFC 1349), October 1989
1122	Requirements for Internet Hosts Communication Layers (updated by RFC 1349), October 1989
1121	Act One—The Poems, September 1989
1120	Internet Activities Board (obsoleted by RFC 1160), September 1989
1119	Network Time Protocol (Version 2) Specification and Implementation (obsoletes RFC 1059, RFC 958; obsoleted by RFC 1305), September 1989
1118	Hitchhikers Guide to the Internet, September 1989
1117	Internet Numbers (obsoletes RFC 1062, RFC 1020, RFC 997; obsoleted by RFC 1166), August 1989
1116	Telnet Linemode Option (obsoleted by RFC 1184), August 1989
1115	Privacy Enhancement for Internet Electronic Mail: Part III—Algorithms, Modes, and Identifiers [draft] (obsoleted by RFC 1423), August 1989
1114	Privacy Enhancement for Internet Electronic Mail: Part II—Certificate-based Key Management [draft] (obsoleted by RFC 1422), August 1989
1113	Privacy Enhancement for Internet Electronic Mail: Part I—Message Encipherment and Authentication Procedures [draft] (obsoletes RFC 989, RFC 1040; obsoleted by RFC 1421), August 1989
1112	Host Extensions for IP Multicasting (obsoletes RFC 988, RVC 1054), August 1989
1111	Request for Comments on Request for Comments: Instructions to RFC Authors (obsoletes RFC 825; obsoleted by RFC 1543), August 1989
1110	Problem with the TCP Big Window Option, August 1989
1109	Report of the Second Ad Hoc Network Management Review Group, August 1989
1108	Security Option for the Internet Protocol (obsoletes RFC 1038), November 1991
1107	Plan for Internet Directory Services, July 1989
1106	TCP Big Window and NAK Options, June 1989
1105	Border Gateway Protocol (BGP) (obsoleted by RFC 1267), June 1989
1104	Models of Policy Based Routing, June 1989

RFC	Title
1103	Proposed Standard for the Transmission of IP Datagrams over FDDI Networks (obsoleted by RFC 1188), June 1989
1102	Policy Routing in Internet Protocols, May 1989
1101	DNS Encoding of Network Names and Other Types (updates RFC 1034, RFC 1035), April 1989
1100	Defense Advanced Research Projects Agency, Internet Activities Board; DARPA IAB IAB Official Protocol Standards (obsoletes RFC 1083; obsoleted by RFC 1360), April 1989
1099	Request for Comments Summary RFC Numbers 1000–1099, December 1991
1098	Simple Network Management Protocol (SNMP) (obsoletes RFC 1067; obsoleted by RFC 1157), April 1989
1097	Telnet Subliminal-message Option, April 1989
1096	Telnet X Display Location Option, March 1989
1095	Common Management information Services and Protocol over TCP/IP (CMOT) (obsoleted by RFC 1189), April 1989
1094	NFS: Network File System Protocol Specification, March 1989
1093	NSFNET Routing Architecture, February 1989
1092	EFP and Policy Based Routing in the New NSFNET Backbone, February 1989
1091	Telnet Terminal-type Option (obsoletes RFC 930), February 1989
1090	SMTP on X.25 SMTP on X 25, February 1989
1089	SNMP over Ethernet, February 1989
1088	Standard for the Transmission of IP Datagrams over NetBIOS Networks, February 1989
1087	Defense Advanced Research Projects Agency, Internet Activities Board; DARPA IAB Ethics and the Internet, January 1989
1086	ISO-TPO Bridge between TCP and X.25, December 1988
1085	ISO Presentation Services on Top of TCP/IP Based Internets, December 1988
1084	BOOTP Vendor Information Extensions (obsoletes RFC 1048; obsoleted by RFC 1395), December 1988
1083	Defense Advanced Research Projects Agency, Internet Activities Board; DARPA IAB IAB Official Protocol Standards (obsoletes RFC 1011; obsoleted by RFC 1360), December 1988

RFC	Title
1082	Post Office Protocol: Version 3: Extended Service Offerings, December 1988
1081	Post Office Protocol: Version 3 (obsoleted by RFC 1225), November 1988
1080	Telnet Remote Flow Control Option (obsoleted by RFC 1372), November 1988
1079	Telnet Terminal Speed Option, December 1988
1078	TCP Port Service Multiplexer (TCPMUX), November 1988
1077	Critical Issues in High Bandwidth Networking, November 1988
1076	HEMS Monitoring and Control Language (obsoletes RFC 1023), November 1988
1075	Distance Vector Multicast Routing Protocol, November 1988
1074	NSFNET Backbone SPF Based Interior Gateway Protocol, October 1988
1073	Telnet Window Size Option, October 1988
1072	TCP Extensions for Long-delay paths (obsoleted by RFC 1323), October 1988
1071	Computing the Internet Checksum (updated by RFC 1141), September 1988
1070	Use of the Internet as a Subnetwork for Experimentation with the OSI Network Layer, February 1989
1069	Guidelines for the Use of Internet-IP Addresses in the ISO Connectionless-Mode Network Protocol (obsoletes RFC 986), February 1989
1068	Background File Transfer Program (BFTP) August 1988
1067	Simple Network Management Protocol (obsoleted by RFC 1098), August 1988
1066	Management Information Base for Network Management of TCP/IP-based Internets (obsoleted by RFC 1156), August 1988
1065	Structure and Identification of Management Information for TCP/IP-based Internets (obsoleted by RFC 1155), August 1988
1064	Interactive Mail Access Protocol: Version 2 (obsoleted by RFC 1176, RFC 1203), July 1988
1063	IP MTU Discovery Options (obsoleted by RFC 1191), July 1988
1062	Internet Numbers (obsoletes RFC 1020; obsoleted by RFC 1117), August 1988
1061	Not yet issued
1060	Assigned numbers (obsoletes RFC 1010; obsoleted by RFC 1340; updated by RFC 1349), March 1990
1059	Network Time Protocol (Version 1) Specification and Implementation (obsoleted by RFC 1305), July 1988

RFC **Title**

1058   Routing Information Protocol (updated by RFC 1388), June 1988

1057   RPC: Remote Procedure Call Protocol Specification: Version 2 (obsoletes RFC 1050), June 1988

1056   PCMAIL: A Distributed Mail System for Personal Computers (obsoletes RFC 993), June 1988

1055   Nonstandard for Transmission of IP Datagrams over Serial Lines: SLIP, June 1988

1054   Host Extensions for IP Multicasting (obsoletes RFC 988; obsoleted by RFC 1112), May 1988

1053   Telnet X.3 PAD Option, May 1988

1052   IAB Recommendation for the Development of Internet Network Management Standards, April 1988

1051   Standard for the Transmission of IP Datagrams and ARP Packets over ARCNET Networks (obsoleted by RFC 1201), March 1988

1050   RPC: Remote Procedure Call Protocol Specification (obsoleted by RFC 1057), April 1988

1049   Content-type Header Field for Internet Messages, April 1988

1048   BOOTP Vendor Information Extensions (obsoleted by RFC 1395), February 1988

1047   Duplicate Messages and SMTP, February 1988

1046   Queuing Algorithm to Provide the Type-of-service for IP Links, February 1988

1045   VMTP: Versatile Message Transaction Protocol: Protocol Specification, February 1988

1044   Internet Protocol on Network System's HYPERchannel: Protocol Specification, February 1988

1043   Telnet Data Entry Terminal Option: DODIIS Implementation (updates RFC 732), February 1988

1042   Standard for the Transmission of IP Datagrams over IEEE 802 Networks (obsoletes RFC 948), February 1988

1041   Telnet 3270 Regime Option, January 1988

1040   Privacy Enhancement for Internet Electronic Mail: Part I: Message Encipherment and Authentication Procedures (obsoletes RFC 989; obsoleted by RFC 1113), January 1988

1039   DoD Statement on Open Systems Interconnection Protocols (obsoletes RFC 945), January 1988

RFC	Title
1038	Draft Revised IP Security Option (obsoleted by RFC 1108), January 1988
1037	NFILE—a File Access Protocol, December 1987
1036	Standard for Interchange of USENET Messages (obsoletes RFC 850), December 1987
1035	Domain Names—Implementation and Specification (obsoletes RFC 973, RFC 882, RFC 883; updated by RFC 1348, RFC 1183, RFC 1101), November 1987
1034	Domain Names—Concepts and Facilities (obsoletes RFC 973, RFC 882, RFC 883; updated by RFC 1348, RFC 1183, RFC 1101), November 1987
1033	Domain Administrators Operations Guide, November 1987
1032	Domain Administrators Guide, November 1987
1031	MILNET Name Domain Transition, November 1987
1030	On Testing the NETBLT Protocol over Divers Networks, November 1987
1029	More Fault Tolerant Approach to Address Resolution for a Multi-LAN System of Ethernets, May 1988
1028	Simple Gateway Monitoring Protocol, November 1987
1027	Using ARP to Implement Transparent Subnet Gateways, October 1987
1026	Addendum to RFC 987 (mapping between X.400 and RFC 822), (obsoleted by RFC 1327; updates RFC 987; updated by RFC 1138, RFC 1148), September 1987
1025	TCP and IP Bake Off, September 1987
1024	HEMS Variable Definitions, October 1987
1023	HEMS Monitoring and Control Language (obsoleted by RFC 1076), October 1987
1022	High-level Entity Management Protocol (HEMP), October 1987
1021	High-level Entity Management System (HEMS), October 1987
1020	Internet Numbers (obsoletes RFC 997; obsoleted by RFC 1062, RFC 1117), November 1987
1019	Report of the Workshop on Environments for Computational Mathematics, September 1987
1018	Some Comments on SQuID, August 1987
1017	Network Requirements for Scientific Research: Internet Task Force on Scientific Computing, August 1987
1016	Something a Host Could Do with Source Quench: The Source Quench Introduced Delay (SQuID), July 1987

RFC	Title
1015	Implementation Plan for Interagency Research Internet, July 1987
1014	XDR: External Data Representation Standard, June 1987
1013	X Window System Protocol, Version !!: Alpha Update, April 1987, June 1987
1012	Bibliography of Request for Comments 1 through 999, June 1987
1011	Official Internet Protocols (obsoletes RFC 997; obsoleted by RFC 1083), May 1987
1010	Assigned Numbers (obsoletes RFC 990; obsoleted by RFC 1340), May 1987
1009	Requirements for Internet Gateways (obsoletes RFC 985), June 1987
1008	Implementation Guide for the ISO Transport Protocol, June 1987
1007	Military Supplement to the ISO Transport Protocol, June 1987
1006	ISO Transport Services on Top of the TCP: Version 3 (obsoletes RFC 983), May 1987
1005	ARPANET AHIP-E Host Access Protocol (Enhanced AHIP), May 1987
1004	Distributed-protocol Authentication Scheme, April 1987
1003	Issues in Defining an Equations Representation Standard, March 1987
1002	Defense Advanced Research Projects Agency, Internet Activities Board, End-to-End Services Task Force, NetBIOS Working Group; DARPA IAB End-to-End Services Task Force NetBIOS Working Group Protocol Standard for a NetBIOS Service on a TCP/UDP Transport: Detailed Specifications, March 1987
1001	Defense Advanced Research Projects Agency, Internet Activities Board, End-to-End Services Task Force, NetBIOS Working Group; DARPA IAB End-to- End Services Task Force NetBIOS Working Group Protocol Standard for a NetBIOS Service on a TCP/UDP Transport: Concepts and Methods, March 1987
1000	The Request for Comments Reference Guide (obsoletes RFC 999), August 1987
999	Request for Comments Summary Notes: 900–999 (obsoleted by RFC 1000), April 1987
998	NETBLT: A Bulk Data Transfer Protocol (obsoletes RFC 969), March 1987
997	Internet Numbers (obsoleted by RFC 1020, RFC 1117; updates RFC 990), March 1987
996	Statistics Server, February 1987
995	International Organization for Standardization; ISO End System to Intermediate System Routing Exchange Protocol for Use in Conjunction with ISO 8473, April 1986

RFC	Title
994	International Organization for Standardization; ISO Final Text of DIS 8473, Protocol for Providing the Connectionless-mode Network Service (obsoletes RFC 926), March 1986
993	PCMAIL: A Distributed Mail System for Personal Computers (obsoletes RFC 984; obsoleted by RFC 1056), December 1986
992	On Communication Support for Fault Tolerant Process Groups, November 1986
991	Official ARPA-Internet Protocols (obsoletes RFC 961; obsoleted by RFC 1011), November 1986
990	Assigned Numbers (obsoletes RFC 960; obsoleted by RFC 1340; updated by RFC 997), November 1986
989	Privacy Enhancement for Internet Electronic Mail: Part I: Message Encipherment and Authentication Procedures (obsoleted by RFC 1040, RFC 1113), February 1987
988	Host Extensions for IP Multicasting (obsoletes RFC 966; obsoleted by RFC 1054, RFC 1112), July 1986
987	Mapping between X.400 and RFC 822 (obsoleted by RFC 1327; updated by RFC 1026, RFC 1138, RFC 1148), June 1986
986	Guidelines for the Use of Internet-IP Addresses in the ISO Connectionless-Mode Network Protocol [working draft] (obsoleted by RFC 1069), June 1986
985	National Science Foundation, Network Technical Advisory Group; NSF NTAG Requirements for Internet Gateways — Draft Requirements for Internet Gateways Draft (obsoleted by RFC 1009), May 1986
984	PSMAI: A Distributed Mail System for Personal Computers (obsoleted by RFC 993), May 1986
983	ISO Transport Arrives on Top of the TCP (obsoleted by RFC 1006), April 1986
982	Guidelines for the Specification of the Structure of the Domain Specific Part (DSP) of the ISO Standard NSAP Address, April 1986
981	Experimental Multiple-path Routing Algorithm, March 1986
980	Protocol Document Order Information, March 1986
979	PSN End-to-End Functional Specification, March 1986
978	Voice File Interchange Protocol (VFIP), February 1986
977	Network News Transfer Protocol, February 1986

RFC	Title
976	UUCP Mail Interchange Format Standard (updated by RFC 1137), February 1986
975	Autonomous Confederations, February 1986
974	Mail Routing and the Domain System, January 1986
973	Domain System Changes and Observations (obsoleted by RFC 1034, RFC 1035; updates RFC 882, RFC 883), January 1986
972	Password Generator Protocol, January 1986
971	Survey of Data Representation Standards, January 1986
970	On Packet Switches with Infinite Storage, December 1985
969	NETBLT: A Bulk Data Transfer Protocol (obsoleted by RFC 998), December 1985
968	Twas the Night before Start-up, December 1985
967	All Victims Together, December 1985
966	Host Groups: A Multicast Extension to the Internet Protocol (obsoleted by RFC 988), December 1985
965	Format for a Graphical Communication Protocol, December 1985
964	Some Problems with the Specification of the Military Standard Transmission Control Protocol, November 1985
963	Some Problems with the Specification of the Military Standard Internet Protocol, November 1985
962	TCP-4 Prime, November 1985
961	Official ARPA-Internet Protocols (obsoletes RFC 944; obsoleted by RFC 991), December 1985
960	Assigned Numbers (obsoletes RFC 943; obsoleted by RFC 1340), December 1985
959	File Transfer Protocol (obsoletes RFC 765 [IEN 149]), October 1985
958	Network Time Protocol (NTP) (obsoleted by RFC 1305), September 1985
957	Experiments in Network Clock Synchronization, September 1985
956	Algorithms for Synchronizing Network Clocks, September 1985
955	Towards a Transport Service for Transaction Processing Applications, September 1985
954	NICNAME/WHOIS (obsoletes RFC 812), October 1985
953	Hostname Server (obsoletes RFC 811), October 1985
952	DoD Internet Host Table Specification (obsoletes RFC 810), October 1985

RFC	Title
951	Bootstrap Protocol (updated by RFC 1497, RFC 1395, RFC 1532, RFC 1542), September 1985
950	Internet Standard Subnetting Procedure (updates RFC 792), August 1985
949	FTP Unique-named Store Command, July 1985
948	Two Methods for the Transmission of IP Datagrams over IEEE 802.3 Networks (obsoleted by RFC 1042), June 1985
947	Multi-network Broadcasting within the Internet, June 1985
946	Telnet Terminal Location Number Option, May 1985
945	DoD Statement on the NRC Report (obsoleted by RFC 1039), May 1985
944	Official ARPA-Internet Protocols (obsoletes RFC 924; obsoleted by RFC 961), April 1985
943	Assigned Numbers (obsoletes RFC 923; obsoleted by RFC 1340), April 1985
942	National Research Council; NRC Transport Protocols for Department of Defense Data Networks, February 1985
941	International Organization for Standardization; ISO Addendum to the Network Service Definition Covering Network Layer Addressing, April 1985
940	Gateway Algorithms and Data Structures Task Force; GADS toward an Internet Standard Scheme for Subnetting, April 1985
939	National Research Council; NRC Executive Summary of the NRC Report on Transport Protocols for Department of Defense Data Networks, February 1985
938	Internet Reliable Transaction Protocol Functional and Interface Specification, February 1985
937	Post Office Protocol: Version 2 (obsoletes RFC 918), February 1985
936	Another Internet Subnet Addressing Scheme, February 1985
935	Reliable Link Layer Protocols, January 1985
934	Proposed Standard for Message Encapsulation, January 1985
933	Output Marking Telnet Option, January 1985
932	Subnetwork Addressing Scheme, January 1985
931	Authentication Server (obsoletes RFC 912; obsoleted by RFC 1413), January 1985
930	Telnet Terminal Type Option (obsoletes RFC 884; obsoleted by RFC 1091), January 1985

RFC	Title
904	Exterior Gateway Protocol Formal Specification (updates RFC 827, RFC 888), April 1984
903	Reverse Address Resolution Protocol, June 1984
902	ARPA Internet Protocol Policy, July 1984
901	Official ARPA—Internet Protocols (obsoletes RFC 880; obsoleted by RFC 924), June 1984
900	Assigned Numbers (obsoletes RFC 870; obsoleted by RFC 1340), June 1984
899	Requests for Comments Summary Notes: 800–899, May 1984
898	Gateway Special Interest Group Meeting Notes, April 1984
897	Domain Name System Implementation Schedule (updates RFC 881; updated by RFC 921), February 1984
896	Congestion Control in IP/TCP Internetworks, January 1984
895	Standard for the Transmission of IP Datagrams over Experimental Ethernet Networks, April 1984
894	Standard for the Transmission of IP Datagrams over Ethernet Networks, April 1984
893	Trailer Encapsulations, April 1984
892	International Organization for Standardization; ISO Transport Protocol Specification [draft] (obsoleted by RFC 905), December 1983
891	DCN Local-network Protocols, December 1983
890	Exterior Gateway Protocol Implementation Schedule, February 1984
889	Internet Delay Experiments, December 1983
888	"STUB" Exterior Gateway Protocol (updated by RFC 904), January 1984
887	Resource Location Protocol, December 1983
886	Proposed Standard for Message Header Managing, December 1983
885	Telnet End of Record Option, December 1983
884	Telnet Terminal Type Option (obsoleted by RFC 930), December 1983
883	Domain Names: Implementation Specification (obsoleted by RFC 1034, RFC 1035; updated by RFC 973), November 1983
882	Domain Names: Concepts and Facilities (obsoleted by RFC 1034, RFC 1035; updated by RFC 973), November 1983
881	Domain Names Plan and Schedule (updated by RFC 897), November 1983

RFC	Title
880	Official Protocols (obsoletes RFC 840; obsoleted by RFC 901), October 1983
879	TCP Maximum Segment Size and Related Topics, November 1983
878	ARPANET 1822L Host Access Protocol (obsoletes RFC 851), December 1983
877	Standard for the Transmission of IP Datagrams over Public Data Networks (obsoleted by RFC 1356), September 1983
876	Survey of SMTP Implementations, September 1983
875	Gateways, Architectures, and Heffalumps, September 1982
874	A Critique of X.25, September 1982
873	Illusion of Vendor Support, September 1982
872	TCP-on-a-LAN, September 1982
871	Perspective on the ARPANET Reference Model, September 1982
870	Assigned Numbers (obsoletes RFC 820; obsoleted by RFC 1340), October 1983
869	Host Monitoring Protocol, December 1983
868	Time Protocol, May 1983
867	Daytime Protocol, May 1983
866	Active Users, May 1983
865	Quote of the Day Protocol, May 1983
864	Character Generator Protocol, May 1983
863	Discard Protocol, May 1983
862	Echo Protocol, May 1983
861	Telnet Extended Options: List Option (obsoletes NIC 16239), May 1983
860	Telnet Timing Mark Option (obsoletes NIC 16238), May 1983
859	Telnet Status Option (obsoletes RFC 651), May 1983
858	Telnet Suppress Go Ahead Option (obsoletes NIC 15392), May 1983
857	Telnet Echo Option (obsoletes NIC 15390), May 1983
856	Telnet Binary Transmission (obsoletes NIC 15389), May 1983
855	Telnet Option Specifications (obsoletes NIC 18640), May 1983
854	Telnet Protocol Specification (obsoletes RFC 765, NIC 18639), May 1983
853	Not issued
852	ARPANET Short Blocking Feature, April 1983

RFC	Title
851	ARPANET 1822L Host Access Protocol (obsoletes RFC 802; obsoleted by RFC 878), April 1983
850	Standard for Interchange of USENET Messages (obsoleted by RFC 1036), June 1983
849	Suggestions for Improved Host Table Distribution, May 1983
848	Who Provides the "Little" TCP Services? March 1983
847	Summary of Smallberg Surveys (obsoletes RFC 846), February 1983
846	Who Talks TCP? Survey of 22 February 1983 (obsoletes RFC 845; obsoleted by RFC 847), February 1983
845	Who Talks TCP? Survey of 15 February 1983 (obsoletes RFC 843; obsoleted by RFC 846), February 1983
844	Who Talks ICMP, Too? Survey of 18 February 1983 (updates RFC 843), February 1983
843	Who Talks TCP? Survey of 8 February 1983 (obsoletes RFC 842; obsoleted by RFC 845; updated by RFC 844), February 1983
842	Who Talks TCP? Survey of 1 February 1983 (obsoletes RFC 839; obsoleted by RFC 843), February 1983
841	National Bureau of Standards; NBS Specification for Message Format for Computer Based Message Systems, January 1983
840	Official Protocols (obsoleted by RFC 880), April 1983
839	Who Talks TCP? (obsoletes RFC 838; obsoleted by RFC 842), January 1983
838	Who Talks TCP? (obsoletes RFC 837; obsoleted by RFC 839), January 1983
837	Who Talks TCP? (obsoletes RFC 836; obsoleted by RFC 838), January 1983
836	Who Talks TCP? (obsoletes RFC 835; obsoleted by RFC 837), January 1983
835	Who Talks TCP? (obsoletes RFC 834; obsoleted by RFC 836), December 1982
834	Who Talks TCP? (obsoletes RFC 833; obsoleted by RFC 835), December 1982
833	Who Talks TCP? (obsoletes RFC 832; obsoleted by RFC 834), December 1982
832	Who Talks TCP? (obsoleted by RFC 833), December 1982
831	Backup Access to the European Side of SATNET, December 1982
830	Distributed System for Internet Name Service, October 1982
829	Packet Satellite Technology Reference Sources, November 1982

RFC	Title
828	Data Communications: IFIP's International "Network" of Experts, August 1982
827	Exterior Gateway Protocol (EGP) (updated by RFC 904), October 1982
826	Ethernet Address Resolution Protocol: or Converting Network Protocol Addresses to 48-bit Ethernet Address for Transmission on Ethernet Hardware, November 1982
825	Request for Comments on Requests for Comments (obsoleted by RFC 1111), November 1982
824	CRONUS Virtual Local Network, August 1982
823	DARPA Internet Gateway (updates IEN 109, IEN 30), September 1982
822	Standard for the Format of ARPA Internet Text Messages (obsoletes RFC 733; updated by RFC 1327, RFC 1148, RFC 1138), August 1982
821	Simple Mail Transfer Protocol (obsoletes RFC 788), August 1982
820	Assigned Numbers (obsoletes RFC 790; obsoleted by RFC 1340), August 1982
819	Domain Naming Convention for Internet User Applications, August 1982
818	Remote User Telnet Service, November 1982
817	Modularity and Efficiency in Protocol Implementation, July 1982
816	Fault Isolation and Recovery, July 1982
815	IP Datagram Reassembly Algorithms, July 1982
814	Name, Addresses, Ports, and Routes, July 1982
813	Window and Acknowledgment Strategy in TCP, July 1982
812	NICNAME/WHOIS (obsoleted by RFC 954), March 1982
811	Hostnames Server (obsoleted by RFC 953), March 1982
810	DoD Internet Host Table Specification (obsoletes RFC 608; obsoleted by RFC 852), March 1982
809	UCL Facsimile System, February 1982
808	Summary of Computer Mail Services Meeting Held at BBN on 10 January 1979, March 1982
807	Multimedia Mail Meeting Notes, February 1982
806	National Bureau of Standards; NBS Proposed Federal Information Processing Stand: Specification for Message Format for Computer Based Message Systems (obsoleted by RFC 841), September 1981

RFC	Title
805	Computer Mail Meeting Notes, February 1982
804	International Telecommunication Union, International Telegraph and Telephone Consultative Committee; ITU CCITT CCITT Draft Recommendation T.4 [Standardization of Group 3 Facsimile Apparatus for Document Transmission], 1981
803	Dacom 450/500 Facsimile Data Transcoding, November 1981
802	ARPANET 1822L Host Access Protocol (obsoleted by RFC 851), November 1981
801	NCP/TCP Transition Plan, November 1981
800	Requests for Comments Summary Notes 700–799, November 1981
799	Internet Name Domains, September 1981
798	Decoding Facsimile Data from the Rapicom 450, September 1981
797	Format for Bitmap Files, September 1981
796	Address Mappings (obsoletes IEN 115), September 1981
795	Service Mappings, September 1981
794	Pre-emption (updates IEN 125), September 1981
793	Transmission Control Protocol, September 1981
792	Internet Control Message Protocol (obsoletes RFC 777; updated by RFC 950), September 1981
791	Internet Protocol (obsoletes RFC 760; updated by RFC 1349), September 1981
790	Assigned Numbers (obsoletes RFC 776; obsoleted by RFC 1340), September 1981
789	Vulnerabilities of Network Control Protocols: An Example, July 1981
788	Simple Mail Transfer Protocol (obsoletes RFC 780; obsoleted by RFC 821), November 1981
787	Connectionless Data Transmission Survey/Tutorial, July 1981
786	Mail Transfer Protocol: ISI TOPS20 MTP-NIMAIL Interface, July 1981
785	Mail Transfer Protocol: ISI TOPS20 File Definitions, July 1981
784	Mail Transfer Protocol: ISI TOPS20 Implementation, July 1981
783	TFTP Protocol (revision 2) (obsoletes IEN 133; obsoleted by RFC 1350), June 1981
782	Virtual Terminal Management Model, 1981
781	Specification of the Internet Protocol (IP) Timestamp Option, May 1981
780	Mail Transfer Protocol (obsoletes RFC 772; obsoleted by RFC 788), May 1981

RFC	Title
779	Telnet Send-location Option, April 1981
778	DCNET Internet Clock Service, April 1981
777	Internet Control Message Protocol (obsoletes RFC 760; obsoleted by RFC 792), April 1981
776	Assigned Numbers (obsoletes RFC 770; obsoleted by RFC 1340), January 1981
775	Directory Oriented FTP Commands, December 1980
774	Internet Protocol Handbook (obsoletes RFC 766), October 1980
773	Comments on NCP/TCP Mail Service Transition Strategy, October 1980
772	Mail Transfer Protocol (obsoleted by RFC 780), September 1980
771	Mail Transition Plan, September 1980
770	Assigned Numbers (obsoletes RFC 762; obsoleted by RFC 1340), September 1980
769	Rapicom 450 Facsimile File Format, September 1980
768	User Datagram Protocol, August 1980
767	Structured Format for Transmission of Multi-media Documents, August 1980
766	Internet Protocol Handbook: Table of Contents (obsoleted by RFC 774), July 1980
765	File Transfer Protocol Specification (obsoletes RFC 542; obsoleted by RFC 959), June 1980
764	Telnet Protocol Specification (obsoleted by RFC 854), June 1980
763	Role Mailboxes, May 1980
762	Assigned Numbers (obsoletes RFC 758; obsoleted by RFC 1340), January 1980
761	DoD Standard Transmission Control Protocol, January 1980
760	DoD Standard Internet Protocol (obsoletes IEN 123; obsoleted by RFC 791, RFC 777), January 1980
759	Internet Message Protocol, August 1980
758	Assigned Numbers (obsoletes RFC 755; obsoleted by RFC 1340), August 1979
757	Suggested Solution to the Naming, Addressing, and Delivery Problem for ARPANET Message Systems, September 1979
756	NIC Name Server—A Datagram-based Information Utility, July 1979
755	Assigned Numbers (obsoletes RFC 750; obsoleted by RFC 1340), May 1979
754	Out-of-net Host Addresses for Mail, April 1979

RFC	Title
753	Internet Message Protocol, May 1979
752	Universal Host Table, January 1979
751	Survey of FTP Mail and MLFL, December 1978
750	Assigned Numbers (obsoletes RFC 739; obsoleted by RFC 1340), September 1978
749	Telnet SUPDUP-Output Option, September 1978
748	Telnet Randomly-lose Option, April 1978
747	Recent Extensions to the SUPDUP Protocol, March 1978
746	SUPDUP Graphics Extension, March 1978
745	JANUS Interface Specifications, March 1978
744	A Message Archiving & Retrieval Service, January 1978
743	FTP Extension: XRSQ/XRCP, December 1977
742	NAME/FINGER Protocol (obsoleted by RFC 1288), December 1977
741	Specifications for the Network Voice Protocol (NVP), November 1977
740	NETRJS Protocol (obsoletes RFC 599), November 1977
739	Assigned Numbers (obsoletes RFC 604, RFC 503; obsoleted by RFC 1340), November 1977
738	Time Server, October 1977
737	FTP Extension: XSEN, October 1977
736	Telnet SUPDUP Option, October 1977
735	Revised Telnet Byte Macro Option (obsoletes RFC 729), November 1977
734	SUPDUP Protocol, October 1977
733	Standard for the Format of ARPA Network Text Messages (obsoletes RFC 724; obsoleted by RFC 822), November 1977
732	Telnet Data Entry Terminal Option (obsoletes RFC 731; updated by RFC 1043), September 1977
731	Telnet Data Entry Terminal Option (obsoleted by RFC 732), June 1977
730	Extensible Field Addressing, May 1977
729	Telnet Byte Macro Option (obsoleted by RFC 735), May 1977
728	Minor Pitfall in the Telnet Protocol, April 1977
727	Telnet Logout Option, April 1977

RFC	Title
697	CWD Command of FTP (Not Online), July 1975
696	Comments on the IMP/Host and Host/IMP Protocol Changes (Not Online), July 1975
695	Official Change in Host-Host Protocol, July 1975
694	Protocol Information (Not Online), June 1975
693	Not issued
692	Comments on IMP/Host Protocol Changes (RFCs 687 and 690), June 1975
691	One More Try on the FTP, May 1975
690	Comments on the Proposed Host/IMP Protocol Changes (Not Online) (updates RFC 687; updated by RFC 692), June 1975
689	Tenex NCP Finite State Machine for Corrections, May 1975
688	Tentative Schedule for the New Telnet Implementation for the TIP (Not Online), June 1975
687	IMP/Host and Host/IMP Protocol Changes (obsoleted by RFC 704; updated by RFC 690), June 1975
686	Leaving Well Enough Alone (Not Online), May 1975
685	Response Time in Cross Network Debugging, April 1975
684	Commentary on Procedure Calling as a Network Protocol, April 1975
683	FTPSRV—Tenex Extension for Paged Files, April 1975
682	Not issued
681	Network UNIX, March 1975
680	Message Transmission Protocol (Not Online), April 1975
679	February, 1975 Survey of New-Protocol Telnet Servers (Not Online), February 1975
678	Standard File Formats, December 1974
677	Maintenance of Duplicate Databases (Not Online), January 1975
676	Not issued
675	Specification on Internet Transmission Control Program (Not Online), December 1974
674	Procedure Call Documents: Version 2, December 1974
673	Not issued

RFC	Title
672	Multi-site Data Collection Facility, December 1974
671	Note on Reconnection Protocol (Not Online), December 1974
670	Not issued
669	November, 1974 Survey of New-Protocol Telnet Servers (Not Online), December 1974
668	Not issued
667	BBN Host Ports (Not Online), December 1974
666	Specification of the Unified User-Level Protocol (Not Online), November 1974
665	Not issued
664	Not issued
663	Lost Message Detection and Recovery Protocol, November 1974
662	Performance Improvement in ARPANET File Transfers from Multics, November 1974
661	Protocol Information (Not Online), November 1974
660	Some Changes to the IMP and the IMP/Host Interface, October 1974
659	Announcing Additional Telnet Options (Not Online), October 1974
658	Telnet Output Linefeed Disposition, October 1974
657	Telnet Output Vertical Tab Disposition Option, October 1974
656	Telnet Output Vertical Tabstops Option, October 1974
655	Telnet Output Formfeed Disposition Option, October 1974
654	Telnet Output Horizontal Tab Disposition Option, October 1974
653	Telnet Output Horizontal Tabstops Option, October 1974
652	Telnet Output Carriage-return Disposition Option, October 1974
651	Revised Telnet Status Option (obsoleted by RFC 859), October 1974
650	Not issued
649	Not issued
648	Not issued
647	Proposed Protocol for Connecting Host Computers to ARPA-like Networks via Front End Processors (Not Online), November 1974
646	Not issued

RFC	Title
645	Network Standard Data Specification Syntax (Not Online), June 1974
644	On the Problem of Signature Authentication for Network Mail, July 1974
643	Network Debugging Protocol, July 1974
642	Ready Line Philosophy and Implementation (Not Online), July 1974
641	Not issued
640	Revised FTP Reply Codes, June 1974
639	Not issued
638	IMP/TIP Preventive Maintenance Schedule (Not Online), April 1974
637	Change of Network Address for SU-DSL (Not Online), April 1974
636	TIP/Tenex Reliability Improvements, June 1974
635	Assessment of ARPANET Protocols (Not Online), April 1974
634	Change in Network Address for Haskins Lab (Not Online), April 1974
633	IMP/TIP Preventive Maintenance Schedule (Not Online), April 1974
632	Throughput Degradations for Single Packet Messages (Not Online), May 1974
631	International Meeting on Minicomputers and Data Communication: Call for Papers (Not Online), April 1974
630	FTP Error Code Usage for More Reliable Mail Service (Not Online), April 1974
629	Scenario for Using the Network Journal (Not Online), March 1974
628	Status of RFC Numbers and a Note on Preassigned Journal Numbers (Not Online), March 1974
627	ASCII Text File of Hostnames (Not Online), March 1974
626	On a Possible Lockup Condition in IMP Subnet Due to Message Sequencing, March 1974
625	On-line Hostnames Service (Not Online), March 1974
624	Comments on the File Transfer Protocol (obsoletes RFC 607), February 1974
623	Comments on On-line Host Name Service (Not Online), February 1974
622	Scheduling IMP/TIP Down Time (Not Online), February 1974
621	NIC User Directories at SRI ARC (Not Online), March 1974
620	Request for Monitor Host Table Updates, March 1974
619	Mean Round-trip Times in the ARPANET (Not Online), March 1974

RFC	Title
618	Few Observations on NCP Statistics, February 1974
617	Note on Socket Member Assignment, February 1974
616	Latest Network Maps, February 1973
615	Proposed Network Standard Data Pathname Syntax, March 1974
614	Response to RFC 607: "Comments on the File Transfer Protocol" (updates RFC 607), January 1974
613	Network Connectivity: A Response to RFC 603 (Not Online) (updates RFC 603), January 1974
612	Traffic Statistics (December 1973) (Not Online), January 1974
611	Two Changes to the IMP/Host Protocol to Improve User/Network Communications (Not Online), February 1974
610	Further Datalanguage Design Concepts (Not Online), December 1973
609	Statement of Upcoming Move on NIC/NLS Service (Not Online), January 1974
608	Host Names On-line (Not Online) (obsoleted by RFC 810), January 1974
607	Comments on the File Transfer Protocol (obsoleted by RFC 624; updated by RFC 614), January 1974
606	Host Names On-line, December 1973
605	Not issued
604	Assigned Link Numbers (Not Online) (obsoletes RFC 317; obsoleted by RFC 1340), December 1973
603	Response to RFC 597: Host Status (Not Online) (updates RFC 597; updated by RFC 613), December 1973
602	"The stockings were hung by the chimney with care," December 1973
601	Traffic Statistics (November 1973) (Not Online), December 1973
600	Interfacing an Illinois Plasma Terminal to the ARPANET (Not Online), November 1973
599	Update on NetRJS (obsoletes RFC 189; obsoleted by RFC 740), December 1973
598	Network Information Center; SRI NIC RFC Index—December 5, 1973 (Not Online), December 1973
597	Host Status (updated by RFC 603), December 1973
596	Second Thoughts on Telnet Go-Ahead (Not Online), December 1973

RFC	Title
595	Second Thoughts in Defense on the Telnet Go-Ahead (Not Online), December 1973
594	Speedup of Host-IMP Interface, December 1973
593	Telnet and FTP Implementation Schedule Change (Not Online), November 1973
592	Some Thoughts on System Design to Facilitate Resource Sharing, November 1973
591	Addition to the Very Distant Host Specifications (Not Online), November 1973
590	MULTICS Address Change, November 1973
589	CCN NETRJS Server Messages to Remote User, November 1973
588	London Node Is Now Up, October 1973
587	Announcing New Telnet Options, October 1973
586	Traffic Statistics (October 1973), November 1973
585	ARPANET Users Interest Working Group Meeting (Not Online), November 1973
584	Charter for ARPANET Users Interest Working Group (Not Online), November 1973
583	Not issued
582	Comments on RFC 580: Machine Readable Protocols (Not Online) (Updates RFC 580), November 1973
581	Corrections to RFC 560: Remote Controlled Transmission and Echoing Telnet Option, November 1973
580	Note to Protocol Designers and Implementers (updated by RFC 582), October 1973
579	Traffic Statistics (September 1973), November 1973
578	Using MIT-Mathlab MACSYMA from MIT-DMS Muddle, October 1973
577	Mail Priority (Not Online), October 1973
576	Proposal for Modifying Linking (Not Online), September 1973
575	Not issued
574	Announcement of a Mail Facility at UCSB, September 1973
573	Data and File Transfer: Some Measurement Results, September 1973
572	Not issued
571	Tenex FTP Problem, November 1973
570	Experimental Input Mapping between NVT ASCII and UCSB On Line System (Not Online), October 1973

RFC	Title
569	NETED: A Common Editor for the ARPA Network, October 1973
568	Response to RFC 567—Cross Country Network Bandwidth (Not Online) (updated by RFC 568), September 1973
567	Cross Country Network Bandwidth (updated by RFC 568), September 1973
566	Traffic Statistics (August 1973), September 1973
565	Storing Network Survey Data at the Datacomputer, August 1973
564	Not issued
563	Comments on the RCTE Telnet Option, August 1973
562	Modifications to the Telnet Specification (Not Online), August 1973
561	Standardizing Network Mail Headers (updated by RFC 680), September 1973
560	Remote Controlled Transmission and Echoing Telnet Option, August 1973
559	Comments on the New Telnet Protocol and Its Implementation, August 1973
558	Not issued
557	Revelations in Network Host Measurements (Not Online), August 1973
556	Traffic Statistics (July 1973), August 1973
555	Responses to Critiques of the Proposed Mail Protocol (Not Online), July 1973
554	Not issued
553	Draft Design for a Text/Graphics Protocol, July 1973
552	Single Access to Standard Protocols (Not Online), July 1973
551	[Letter from Feinroth re: NYU, ANL, and LBL entering the net, and FTP protocol] (Not Online), August 1973
550	NIC NCP Experiment, August 1973
549	Minutes of Network Graphics Group Meeting, July 15–17, 1973
548	Hosts Using the IMP Going Down Message, August 1973
547	Change to the Very Distant Host Specification, August 1973
546	Tenex Load Averages for July 1973, August 1973
545	Of What Quality Be the UCSB Resources Evaluators? July 1973
544	Locating On-line Documentation at SRI-ARC (Not Online), July 1973
543	Network Journal Submission and Delivery (Not Online), July 1973
542	File Transfer Protocol (obsoletes RFC 354; obsoleted by RFC 765), July 1973

RFC	Title
514	Network Make-work, June 1973
513	Comments on the New Telnet Specifications, May 1973
512	More on Lost Message Detection, May 1973
511	Enterprise Phone Service to NIC from ARPANET Sites, May 1973
510	Request for Network Mailbox Addresses, May 1973
509	Traffic Statistics (April 1973), May 1973
508	Real-time Data Transmission on the ARPANET, May 1973
507	Not issued
506	FTP Command Naming Problem, June 1973
505	Two Solutions to a File Transfer Access Problem, June 1973
504	Distributed Resources Workshop, April 1973
503	Socket Number List (Not Online) (obsoletes RFC 433; obsoleted by RFC 1340), April 1973
502	Not issued
501	Un-muddling "Free File Transfer," May 1973
500	Integration of Data Management Systems on a Computer Network, April 1973
499	Harvard's Network RJE, April 1973
498	On Mail Service to CCN, April 1973
497	Traffic Statistics (March 1973) (Not Online), April 1973
496	TNLS Quick Reference Card Is Available (Not Online), April 1973
495	Telnet Protocol Specifications (obsoletes RFC 158), May 1973
494	Availability of MIX and MIXAL in the Network, April 1973
493	Graphics Protocol, April 1973
492	Response to RFC 467 (updates RFC 467), April 1973
491	What Is "Free"? April 1973
490	Surrogate RJS for UCLA-CCN, March 1973
489	Comment on Resynchronization of Connection Status Proposal, March 1973
488	NLS Classes at Network Sites, March 1973
487	Free File Transfer, April 1973
486	Data Transfer Revisited, March 1973

RFC	Title
485	MIX and MIXAL at UCSB, March 1973
484	Not issued
483	Cancellation of the Resource Notebook Framework Meeting, March 1973
482	Traffic Statistics (February 1973), March 1973
481	Not issued
480	Host-dependent FTP Parameters, March 1973
479	Use of FTP by the NIC Journal, March 1973
478	FTP Server-Server Interaction — II, March 1973
477	Remote Job Service at UCSB, May 1973
476	IMP/TIP Memory Retrofit Schedule R.2 (obsoletes RFC 447), March 1973
475	FTP and Network Mail System, March 1973
474	Announcement of NGWG Meeting: Call for Papers, March 1973
473	MIX and MIXAL? February 1973
472	Illinois' Reply to Maxwell's Request for Graphics Information (NIC 14925) (Not Online), March 1973
471	Workshop on Multi-site Executive Programs, March 1973
470	Change in Socket for TIP News Facility, March 1973
469	Network Mail Meeting Summary, March 1973
468	FTP data, March 1973
467	Proposed Change to Host-Host Protocol: Resynchronization of Connection Status (Not Online) (updated by RFC 492), February 1973
466	Telnet Logger/Server for Host LL-67, February 1973
465	Not issued
464	Resource Notebook Framework, February 1973
463	FTP Comments and Response to RFC 430, February 1973
462	Responding to User Needs, February 1973
461	Telnet Protocol Meeting Announcement, February 1973
460	NCP Survey, February 1973
459	Network Questionnaires, February 1973
458	Mail Retrieval via FTP, February 1973

RFC	Title
457	TIPUG, February 1973
456	Memorandum: Date Change of Mail Meeting (Not Online), February 1973
455	Traffic Statistics (January 1973) (Not Online), February 1973
454	File Transfer Protocol — Meeting Announcement and a New Proposed Document, February 1973
453	Meeting Announcement to Discuss a Network Mail System, February 1973
452	Not issued
451	Tentative Proposal for a Unified User Level Protocol, February 1973
450	MULTICS Sampling Timeout Change, February 1973
449	Current Flow-control Scheme for IMPSYS (updates RFC 442), January 1973
448	Print Files in FTP, February 1973
447	IMP/TIP Memory Retrofit Schedule (obsoletes RFC 434; obsoleted by RFC 476), January 1973
446	Proposal to Consider a Network Program Resource Notebook, January 1973
445	IMP/TIP Preventive Maintenance Schedule, January 1973
444	Not issued
443	Traffic Statistics (December 1972), January 1973
442	Current Flow-control Scheme for IMPSYS (updated by RFC 449), January 1973
441	Inter-Entity Communication — An Experiment, January 1973
440	Scheduled Network Software Maintenance (Not Online), January 1973
439	PARRY Encounters the DOCTOR, January 1973
438	FTP Server-server Interaction, January 1973
437	Data Reconfiguration Service at UCSB, January 1973
436	Announcement of RJS at UCSB, January 1973
435	Telnet Issues (updates RFC 318), January 1973
434	IMP/TIP Memory Retrofit Schedule, January 1973
433	Socket Number List (obsoletes RFC 349; obsoleted by RFC 1340), December 1972
432	Network Logical Map, December 1972
431	Update on SMFS Login and Logout (obsoletes RFC 399), December 1972
430	Comments on File Transfer Protocol, February 1973

RFC	Title
429	Character Generator Process, December 1972
428	Not issued
427	Not issued
426	Reconnection Protocol, January 1973
425	But My NCP Costs $500 a day…, December 1972
424	Not issued
423	UCLA Campus Computing Network Liaison Staff for ARPANET (obsoletes RFC 389), December 1972
422	Traffic Statistics (November 1972), December 1972
421	Software Consulting Service for Network Users, November 1972
420	CCA ICCC Weather Demo, January 1973
419	To: Network Liaisons and Station Agents, December 1972
418	Server File Transfer under TSS/360 at NASA Ames, November 1972
417	Link Usage Violation, December 1972
416	ARC System Will Be Unavailable for Use during Thanksgiving Week, November 1972
415	Tenex Bandwidth, November 1972
414	File Transfer Protocol (FTP) Status and Further Comments (updates RFC 385), December 1972
413	Traffic Statistics (October 1972) (Not Online), November 1972
412	User FTP Documentation, November 1972
411	New MULTICS Network Software Features, November 1972
410	Removal of the 30-Second Delay When Hosts Come Up, November 1972
409	Tenex Interface to UCSB's Simple-Minded File System, December 1972
408	NETBANK, 1972
407	Remote Job Entry Protocol (obsoletes RFC 360), October 1972
406	Scheduled IMP Software Releases, October 1972
405	Correction to RFC 404 (obsoletes RFC 404), October 1972
404	Host Address Changes Involving Rand and ISI (obsoleted by RFC 405), October 1972

RFC	Title
403	Desirability of a Network 1108 Service, January 1973
402	ARPA Network Mailing Lists (obsoletes RFC 363), October 1972
401	Conversion of NGP-O Coordinates to Device Specific Coordinates, October 1972
400	Traffic Statistics (September 1972), October 1972
399	SMFS Login and Logout (obsoleted by RFC 431; updates RFC 122), September 1972
398	ICP Sockets, September 1972
397	Not issued
396	Network Graphics Working Group Meeting—Second Iteration, November 1972
395	Switch Settings on IMPs and TIPs, October 1972
394	Two Proposed Changes to the IMP-Host Protocol, September 1972
393	Comments on Telnet Protocol Changes, October 1972
392	Measurement of Host Costs for Transmitting Network Data, September 1972
391	Traffic Statistics (August 1972) (obsoletes RFC 378), September 1972
390	TSO Scenario, September 1972
389	UCLA Campus Computing Network Liaison Staff for ARPA Network (obsoleted by RFC 423), August 1972
388	NCP Statistics (Not Online) (updates RFC 323), August 1972
387	Some Experiences in Implementing Network Graphics Protocol Level 0, August 1972
386	Letter to TIP Users-2, August 1972
385	Comments on the File Transfer Protocol (updates RFC 354; updated by RFC 414), August 1972
384	Official Site Idents for Organizations in the ARPA Network (obsoletes RFC 289), August 1972
383	Not issued
382	Mathematical Software on the ARPA Network, August 1972
381	Three Aids to Improved Network Operation, July 1972
380	Not issued
379	Using TSO at CCN, August 1972
378	Traffic Statistics (July 1972) (obsoleted by RFC 391), August 1972

RFC	Title
351	Graphics Information Form for the ARPANET Graphics Resources Notebook, June 1972
350	User Accounts for UCSB On-Line System, May 1972
349	Proposed Standard Socket Numbers (obsoleted by RFC 1340), May 1972
348	Discard Process, May 1972
347	Echo Process, May 1972
346	Satellite Considerations, May 1972
345	Interest in Mixed Integer Programming (MPSX on NIC 360/91 at CCN), May 1972
344	Network Host Status (obsoletes RFC 342; obsoleted by RFC 353), May 1972
343	IMP System Change Notification (obsoletes RFC 331; obsoleted by RFC 359), May 1972
342	Network Host Status (obsoletes RFC 332; obsoleted by RFC 344), May 1972
341	Not issued
340	Proposed Telnet Changes, May 1972
339	MLTNET: A "Multi Telnet" Subsystem for Tenex, May 1972
338	EBCDIC/ASCII Mapping for Network RJE, May 1972
337	Not issued
336	Level 0 Graphic Input Protocol, May 1972
335	New Interface, IMP/360, May 1972
334	Network Use on May 8, 1972, May 1972
333	Proposed Experiment with a Message Switching Protocol, May 1972
332	Network Host Status (obsoletes RFC 330; obsoleted by RFC 342), April 1972
331	IMP System Change Notification (obsoleted by RFC 343), April 1972
330	Network Host Status (obsoletes RFC 326; obsoleted by RFC 332), April 1972
329	Stanford Research Inst., Network Information Center; SRI NIC ARPA Network Mailing Lists (obsoletes RFC 303; obsoleted by RFC 363), May 1972
328	Suggested Telnet Protocol Changes (Not Online), April 1972
327	Data and File Transfer Workshop Notes (Not Online), April 1972
326	Network Host Status (obsoletes RFC 319; obsoleted by RFC 330), April 1972

RFC	Title
299	Information Management System, February 1972
298	Network Host Status (obsoletes RFC 293; obsoleted by RFC 306), February 1972
297	TIP Message Buffers, January 1972
296	DS-1 Display System, January 1972
295	Report of the Protocol Workshop, January 1972
294	On the Use of "Set Data Type" Transaction in File Transfer Protocol (updates RFC 265), January 1972
293	Network Host Status (obsoletes RFC 288; obsoleted by RFC 298), January 1972
292	Graphics Protocol: Level 0 Only, January 1972
291	Data Management Meeting Announcement, January 1972
290	Computer Networks and Data Sharing: A Bibliography (obsoletes RFC 243), January 1972
289	What We Hope Is an Official List of Host Names (obsoleted by RFC 384), December 1971
288	Network Host Status (obsoletes RFC 287; obsoleted by RFC 293), January 1972
287	"Status of Network Hosts" (obsoletes RFC 267; obsoleted by RFC 288), December 1971
286	Network Library Information System (Not Online), December 1971
285	Network Graphics, December 1971
284	Not issued
283	NETRJT: Remote Job Service Protocol for TIPS (updates RFC 189), December 1971
282	Graphics Meeting Report, December 1971
281	Suggested Addition to File Transfer Protocol, December 1971
280	Draft of Host Names, November 1971
279	Not issued
278	Revision of the Mail Box Protocol (obsoletes RFC 221), November 1971
277	Not issued
276	NIC Course, November 1971
275	Not issued
274	Establishing a Local Guide for Network Usage, November 1971

RFC	Title
273	"More on Standard Host Names" (obsoletes RFC 237), October 1971
272	Not issued
271	IMP System Change Notifications, January 1972
270	Correction to BBN Report No. 1822 (NIC NO 7958) (updates NIC 7959), January 1972
269	Some Experience with File Transfer (updates RFC 122, RFC 238), December 1971
268	Graphics Facilities Information, November 1971
267	Network Host Status (obsoletes RFC 266; obsoleted by RFC 287), November 1971
266	"Network Host Status" (obsoletes RFC 255; obsoleted by RFC 267), November 1971
265	File Transfer Protocol (obsoletes RFC 172; obsoleted by RFC 354; updated by RFC 294), November 1971
264	Data Transfer Protocol (obsoletes RFC 171; obsoleted by RFC 354), December 1971
263	"Very Distant" Host Interface, December 1971
262	Not issued
261	Not issued
260	Not issued
259	Not issued
258	Not issued
257	Not issued
256	IMPSYS Change Notification, November 1971
255	"Status of Network Hosts" (obsoletes RFC 252; obsoleted by RFC 266), October 1971
254	Scenarios for Using ARPANET Computers (Not Online), October 1971
253	Second Network Graphics Meeting Details, October 1971
252	Network Host Status (obsoletes RFC 240; obsoleted by RFC 255), October 1971
251	Weather Data, October 1971
250	Some Thoughts on File Transfer, October 1971
249	Coordination of Equipment and Supplies Purchase, October 1971
248	Not issued

RFC	Title

221 Mail Box Protocol: Version 2 (obsoletes RFC 196; obsoleted by RFC 278), August 1971

220 Not issued

219 User's View of the Datacomputer, September 1971

218 Changing the IMP Status Reporting Facility, September 1971

217 Specifications Changes for OLS, RJE/RJOR, and SMFS (updates RFC 74, RFC 105, RFC 122), September 1971

216 Telnet Access to UCSB's On-line System, September 1971

215 NCP, ICP, and Telnet: The Terminal IMP Implementation, August 1971

214 "Network Checkpoint" (obsoletes RFC 198), August 1971

213 IMP System Change Notification, August 1971

212 University of Southern California, Information Sciences Inst.; USC ISI NWG Meeting on Network Usage (obsoletes RFC 207; updated by RFC 222), August 1971

211 ARPA Network Mailing Lists (obsoletes RFC 168; obsoleted by RFC 300), August 1971

210 Improvement of Flow Control, August 1971

209 Host/IMP Interface Documentation, August 1971

208 Address Tables, August 1971

207 "September Network Working Group Meeting" (obsoleted by RFC 212), August 1971

206 User Telnet—Description of an Initial Implementation, August 1971

205 NETCRT—A Character Display Protocol, August 1971

204 Sockets in Use (updated by RFC 234), August 1971

203 Achieving Reliable Communication, August 1971

202 Possible Deadlock in ICP, July 1971

201 Not issued

200 RFC List by Number (obsoletes RFC 170, RFC 160; obsoleted by MIC 7724), August 1971

199 Suggestions for a Network Data-tablet Graphics Protocol, July 1971

198 Site Certification—Lincoln Labs 360/67 (obsoletes RFC 193; obsoleted by RFC 214), July 1971

RFC	Title
171	Data Transfer Protocol (obsoleted by RFC 264; updates RFC 114; updated by RFC 238), June 1971
170	Stanford Research Inst., Network Information Center; SRI NIC RFC List by Number (obsoleted by RFC 200), June 1971
169	Computer Networks, May 1971
168	ARPA Network Mailing Lists (obsoletes RFC 155; obsoleted by RFC 211), May 1971
167	Socket Conventions Reconsidered, May 1971
166	Data Reconfiguration Service: An Implementation Specification, May 1971
165	Preferred Official Initial Connection Protocol (obsoletes RFC 145, RFC 143, RFC 123; updated by NIC 7101), May 1971
164	Minutes of Network Working Group Meeting, 5/16 through 5/19/71, May 1971
163	Data Transfer Protocols, May 1971
162	NETBUGGERS3, May 1971
161	Solution to the Race Condition in the ICP (Not Online), May 1971
160	Stanford Research Inst., Network Information Center; SRI NIC RFC Brief (obsoleted by RFC 200; updates NIC 6716), May 1971
159	Not issued
158	Telnet Protocol: A Proposed Document (obsoleted by RFC 495; updates RFC 139; updated by RFC 318), May 1971
157	Invitation to the Second Symposium on Problems in the Optimization of Data Communications Systems, May 1971
156	Status of the Illinois Site: Response to RFC 116 (updates RFC 116), April 1971
155	ARPA Network Mailing Lists (obsoletes RFC 95; obsoleted by RFC 168), May 1971
154	Exposition Style, May 1971
153	SRI ARC-NIC Status, May 1971
152	SRI Artificial Intelligence Status Report, May 1971
151	Comments on a Proffered Official ICP: RFCs 123, 127 (updates RFC 127), May 1971
150	Use of IPC Facilities: A Working Paper (Not Online), May 1971

RFC	Title
149	Best Laid Plans (updates RFC 140), May 1971
148	Comments on RFC 123 (updates RFC 123), May 1971
147	"Definition of a Socket" (updates RFC 129), May 1971
146	Views on Issues Relevant to Data Sharing on Computer Networks, May 1971
145	Initial Connection Protocol Control Commands (obsoletes RFC 127; obsoleted by RFC 165), May 1971
144	Data Sharing on Computer Networks, April 1971
143	Regarding Proffered Official ICP (obsoleted by RFC 165), May 1971
142	Time-out Mechanism in the Host-Host Protocol (Not Online), May 1971
141	Comments on RFC 114: A File Transfer Protocol (updates RFC 114), April 1971
140	Agenda for the May NWG Meeting (updated by RFC 149), May 1971
139	Discussion of Telnet Protocol (updates RFC 137; updated by RFC 158), May 1971
138	Status Report on Proposed Data Reconfiguration Service, April 1971
137	Telnet Protocol—A Proposed Document (updated by RFC 139), April 1971
136	Host Accounting and Administrative Procedures (Not Online), April 1971
135	Response to NWG/RFC 110 (updates RFC 110), April 1971
134	Network Graphics Meeting, April 1971
133	File Transfer and Recovery, April 1971
132	"Typographical Error in REC 107" (obsoleted by RFC 154; updates RFC 107), April 1971
131	Response to RFC 116: May NWG Meeting (updates RFC 116), April 1971
130	Response to RFC 111: Pressure from the Chairman (updates RFC 111), April 1971
129	Request for Comments on Socket Name Structure (updated by RFC 147), April 1971
128	Bytes, April 1971
127	Comments on RFC 123 (obsoleted by RFC 145; updates RFC 123; updated by RFC 151), April 1971
126	Graphics Facilities at Ames Research Center, April 1971
125	Response to RFC 86: Proposal for Network Standard Format for a Graphics Data Stream (updates RFC 86; updated by RFC 177), April 1971
124	"Typographical Error in RFC 107" (updates RFC 107), April 1971

RFC	Title
123	Proffered Official ICP (obsoletes RFC 66, RFC 80; obsoleted by RFC 165; updates RFC 98, RFC 101, updated by RFC 127, RFC 148), April 1971
122	Network Specifications for UCSB's Simple-Minded File System (updated by RFC 217, RFC 269, RFC 399), April 1971
121	Network On-line Operators, April 1971
120	Network PL1 Subprograms, April 1971
119	Network Fortran Subprograms, April 1971
118	Recommendations for Facility Documentation, April 1971
117	Some Comments on the Official Protocol, April 1971
116	"Structure of the May NWG Meeting" (updates RFC 99; updated by RFC 131, RFC 156), April 1971
115	Some Network Information Center Policies on Handling Documents, April 1971
114	File transfer Protocol (updated by RFC 141, RFC 172, RFC 171), April 1971
113	Network Activity Report: UCSB Rand (updated by RFC 227), April 1971
112	User/Server Site Protocol: Network Host Questionnaire Responses, April 1971
111	Pressure from the Chairman (updates RFC 107; updated by RFC 130), March 1971
110	Conventions for Using an IBM 2741 Terminal as a User Console for Access to Network Server Hosts (updated by RFC 135), March 1971
109	Level III Server Protocol for the Lincoln Laboratory NIC 360/67 Host, March 1971
108	Attendance List at the Urbana NWG Meeting, February 17–19, 1971 (updates RFC 101), March 1971
107	Output of the Host-Host Protocol Glitch Cleaning Committee (updates RFC 102; updated by RFC 179, RFC 132, RFC 124, RFC 111, NIC 7147), March 1971
106	User/Server Site Protocol Network Host Questionnaire, March 1971
105	Network Specifications for Remote Job Entry and Remote Job Output Retrieval at UCSB (updated by RFC 217), March 1971
104	Link 191, February 1971
103	Implementation of Interrupt Keys, February 1971
102	Output of the Host-Host Protocol Glitch Cleaning Committee (updated by RFC 107), February 1971
101	Notes on the Network Working Group Meeting, Urbana, Illinois, February 17, 1971 (updated by RFC 108, RFC 123), February 1971

RFC	Title
100	Categorization and Guide to NWG/RFCs, February 1971
99	Network Meeting (updated by RFC 116), February 1971
98	Logger Protocol Proposal (updated by RFC 123), February 1971
97	First Cut at a Proposed Telnet Protocol, February 1971
96	Interactive Network Experiment to Study Modes of Access to the Network Information Center, February 1971
95	Distribution of NWG/RFC's through the NIC (obsoleted by RFC 155), February 1971
94	Some Thoughts on Network Graphics, February 1971
93	Initial Connection Protocol, January 1971
92	Not issued
91	Proposed User-User Protocol, December 1970
90	CCN as a Network Service Center, January 1971
89	Some Historic Moments in Networking, January 1971
88	NETRJS: A Third Level Protocol for Remote Job Entry (obsoleted by RFC 189), January 1971
87	Topic for Discussion at the Next Network Working Group Meeting, January 1971
86	Proposal for a Network Standard Format for a Data Stream to Control Graphics Display (updated by RFC 125), January 1971
85	Network Working Group Meeting, December 1970
84	List of NWG/RFC's 1-80, December 1970
83	Language-machine for Data Reconfiguration, December 1970
82	Network Meeting Notes, December 1970
81	Request for Reference Information, December 1970
80	Protocols and Data Formats (obsoleted by RFC 123), December 1970
79	Logger Protocol Error, November 1970
78	NCP Status Report: USCB/Rand, October 1970
77	Network Meeting Report, November 1970
76	Connection by Name: User-Oriented Protocol, October 1970
76A	Syntax and Semantics for the Terminal User Control Language for the Proposed PDP-11-ARPA Network Terminal System, October 1970

RFC	Title
75	Network Meeting, October 1970
74	Specifications for Network Use of the UCSB On-Line System (updated by RFC 217, RFC 225), October 1970
73	Response to NWG/RFC 67, September 1970
72	Proposed Moratorium on Changes to Network Protocol, September 1970
71	Reallocation in Case of Input Error, September 1970
70	"Note on Padding" (updated by RFC 228), October 1970
69	"Distribution List Change for MIT" (updates RFC 52), September 1970
68	Comments on Memory Allocation Control Commands: CEASE, ALL, GVB, RET, and RFNM, August 1970
67	Proposed Change to Host/IMP Spec to Eliminate Marking, 1970
66	NIC—Third Level Ideas and Other Noise (obsoleted by RFC 123), August 1970
65	Comments on Host/Host Protocol Document #1 (Not Online), August 1970
64	Getting Rid of Marking, July 1970
63	Belated Network Meeting Report, July 1970
62	Systems for Interprocess Communication in a Resource Sharing Computer Network (obsoletes RFC 61), August 1970
61	Note on Interprocess Communication in a Resource Sharing Computer Network (obsoleted by RFC 62), July 1970
60	Simplified NCP Protocol, July 1970
59	Flow Control—Fixed versus Demand Allocation, June 1970
58	Logical Message Synchronization, June 1970
57	Thoughts and Reflections on NWG/RFC 54 (updates RFC 54), June 1970
56	Third Level Protocol: Logger Protocol (Not Online), June 1970
55	Prototypical Implementation of the NCP (Not Online), June 1970
54	Official Protocol Proffering (Not Online) (updated by RFC 57), June 1970
53	Official Protocol Mechanism, June 1970
52	Updated Distribution List (updated by RFC 69), July 1970
51	Proposal for a Network Interchange Language, May 1970
50	Comments on the Meyer Proposal, April 1970

RFC	**Title**

RFC	Title
23	Transmission of Multiple Control Messages, October 1969
22	Host-Host Control Message Formats, October 1969
21	Network Meeting, October 1969
20	ASCII Format for Network Interchange, October 1969
19	Two Protocol Suggestions to Reduce Congestion at Swap Bound Nodes, October 1969
18	[Link Assignments], September 1969
17	Some Questions re: Host-IMP Protocol, August 1969
16	M.I.T. (obsoletes RFC 10; obsoleted by RFC 24), September 1969
15	Network Subsystem for Time Sharing Hosts (Not Online), September 1969
14	Not issued
13	[Referring to NWG/RFC 11], August 1969
12	IMP-Host Interface Flow Diagrams, August 1969
11	Implementation of the Host-Host Software Procedures in GORDO (obsoleted by RFC 33), August 1969
10	Documentation Conventions (obsoletes RFC 3; obsoleted by RFC 16), July 1969
9	Host Software, May 1969
8	Functional Specifications for the ARPA Network, May 1969
7	Host-IMP Interface, May 1969
6	Conversation with Bob Kahn, April 1969
5	Decode Encode Language, June 1969
4	Network Timetable, March 1969
3	Documentation Conventions (obsoleted by RFC 10), April 1969
2	Host Software, April 1969
1	Host Software, April 1969

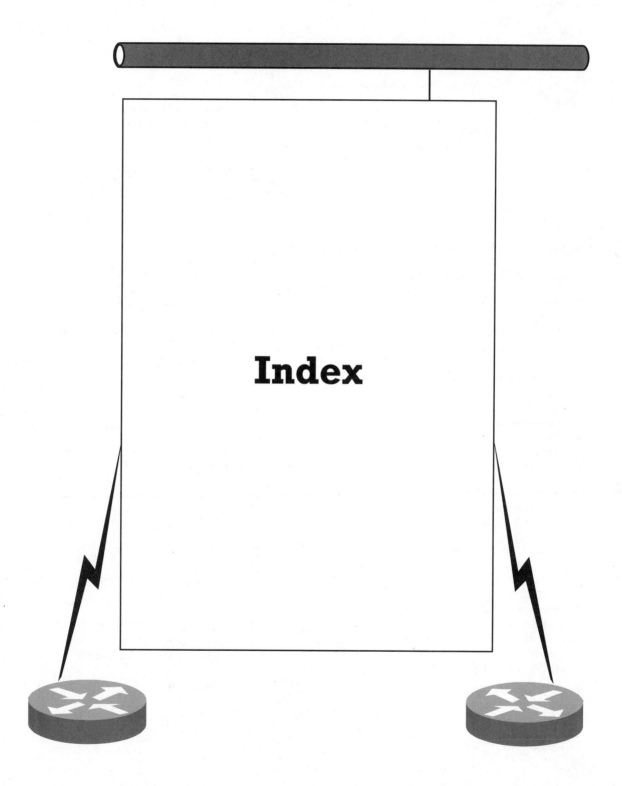

Index

Note: Boldface numbers indicate illustrations.

W

Z

About the Authors

Louis D. Rossi, CCSI, provides Novell and Cisco training to thousands of network professionals across the country. He obtained his Novell CNE certification and Certified Novell Instructor certification in 1993, his Master CNE in 1994, and his CCSI certification in 1996.

Louis R. Rossi, CCSI, formed his own consulting firm, Andrews Rossi, Inc., and has conducted hundreds of Cisco router, Catalyst Switch, and Novell Operating System classes throughout the U.S. He has obtained many certifications, including the Novell CNE-4, CNI, MCNE, and CCIE and has designed, implemented, and trouble-shot networks for Citicorp, Chase Manhattan, and many other clients.

Thomas Rossi, CCSI, has his own consulting company, Capernaum. He completed his MCSE in 1996 and obtained his CCSI in 1997.

The Latest in Cisco Preparation Materials

Let CCprep.com help you put together the pieces for your Cisco Certification Goals!!

℧ **At least 60 Sample Questions from the CCNA, CCDA, CCNP, CCDP, and CCIE written Exams**

℧ **Sample Lab Objectives similar to the ones that will be seen on the CCIE Practical Exam.**

℧ **Expert online answer board.**

℧ **News on the latest in Cisco Certifications.**

℧ **Recommended Readings**

℧ **CCNA Bootcamps and Certified Cisco Training from GeoTrain, a Cisco Traing Partner Distingushed.**

℧ **Online Employment Section to help find the right position for you.**

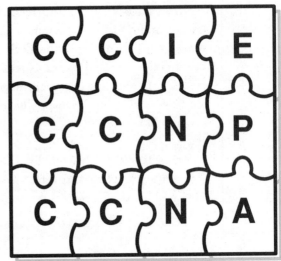

Check us out at

CCprep.com

or call us at

1-877-CCIE-123

CCPrep.com is in no way endorsed by or affiliated with Cisco Systems Inc.